Parallel Lives of Jesus

Parallel Lives of Jesus

A Guide to the Four Gospels

Edward Adams

WESTMINSTER
JOHN KNOX PRESS
LOUISVILLE · KENTUCKY

Published in the United States of America in 2011 by
Westminster John Knox Press
100 Witherspoon Street
Louisville, KY 40202

Published in Great Britain in 2011 by
Society for Promoting Christian Knowledge
36 Causton Street
London SW1P 4ST

11 12 13 14 15 16 17 18 19 20—10 9 8 7 6 5 4 3 2 1

Except as otherwise indicated, Scripture quotations and versification are from the New Revised Standard Version of the Bible, copyright © 1989 by the Division of Christian Education of the National Council of the Churches of Christ in the U.S.A., and used by permission.

Book design by Sharon Adams
Cover design by Night & Day Design
Cover illustration: Angel © Marc Fischer/istockphoto.com; Ox © Tsung-Heng Chen/istockphoto.com;
Eagle © Massimo Merlini/istockphoto.com; Lion © Lappa85/istockphoto.com.

Library of Congress Cataloging-in-Publication Data

Adams, Edward.
    Parallel lives of Jesus : a guide to the four gospels / Edward Adams.
        p. cm.
    Includes bibliographical references (p.   ).
    ISBN 978-0-664-23331-0 (alk. paper)
    1. Bible. N.T. Gospels—Introductions.   I. Title.
    BS2555.52.A34   2011
    226'.061—dc23
                                                         2011033183

∞ The paper used in this publication meets the minimum requirements
of the American National Standard for Information Sciences—Permanence
of Paper for Printed Library Materials, ANSI Z39.48-1992.

Most Westminster John Knox Press books are available at special quantity discounts when purchased in bulk by corporations, organizations, and special-interest groups. For more information, please e-mail SpecialSales@wjkbooks.com.

I dedicate this book to my father, Edward Adams,
who first taught me to read the Gospels as four yet one.

Contents

Acknowledgments

I must thank a number of people who helped in the production of this book. I am especially indebted to Richard Burridge, my colleague at King's College London. His writings on the Gospels have deeply influenced the present work. My take on the Gospels as "parallel lives" of Jesus rests on his research on the genre of the Gospels. Richard's suggestion, made in his *Four Gospels, One Jesus?* that the four Gospels can be read as "four versions of the one story of Jesus" inspired the model I adopted here for approaching the unity and individuality of the Gospels. I am grateful to Richard for reading an earlier manuscript of this work and making important suggestions for improvement, and also for his encouragement throughout the period I have been writing the book. I thank Philip Law of SPCK with whom I first discussed this project and who also read and reacted to an earlier draft.

My doctoral research was in Pauline studies, but as a lecturer, the bulk of my teaching over the years has been in the area of Gospels. For several years, I was teaching assistant to Graham Stanton at King's, a role I look back on as a tremendous privilege. Graham was a great enthusiast for reading the Gospels comparatively, using a synopsis, and one of my responsibilities under him was to lead a first-year undergraduate seminar in which students engaged with parallel Gospel passages (something I had also done at Glasgow University as a teaching assistant to Joel Marcus, in the year before coming to King's). I soon developed my own enthusiasm for "parallel analysis," which features heavily in the present book. I am grateful to students who bore with me in my early years at King's, and subsequently, as I wrestled with and formed opinions on a wide range of issues in Gospel scholarship. This book is to a significant extent the fruit of teaching and learning from them.

I am grateful to the Kensington Episcopal Area Licensed Lay Ministers for allowing me to try out on them the approach to the oneness and plurality of the Gospels I develop in this book and for their encouraging response.

I thank Bridget Gilfillan Upton of Heythrop College for introducing me to the film *Rashomon* when she gave a paper titled "Japanese Classical Cinema and the Four Gospel Tradition: A Marriage Made in Heaven?" at the Biblical Studies Research Seminar, King's College London in 2001.

Thanks go to the staff at WJK for all their hard work in bringing this book to print. In particular I want to thank Marianne Blickenstaff for her generous and insightful feedback. With her combination of specialist subject knowledge, teaching experience, and editorial skill, she has contributed much to the final form of this book. I also thank S. David Garber for his meticulous copyediting, which saved me from many a faux pas.

Thanks are due to my father who read over and commented on the manuscript. Finally, I thank my wife, Ruth, for her understanding especially during a time of intensive work on this book, and my boys, Jacob and Caleb, for providing such wonderful, light relief.

Introduction

In their New Testament setting, the four Gospels stand under the singular heading "The Gospel" and are individuated, "According to Matthew," and so on. The Gospel titles are almost certainly not original, but they are ancient. No other titles are known for the Gospels. The titles were adopted into the canon and signal that the books to which they are attached exhibit commonality and individuality.

This is a guide to the four Gospels, or the Fourfold Gospel, that seeks to enable readers to engage with these texts in terms of their oneness and plurality. Although the canon draws attention to the commonality and individuality of the Gospels, it does not provide a method for negotiating these dimensions; finding and applying such a method belongs to the task of interpretation. Here I offer a model drawn from narratology (the study of narrative). Comparing them with multiple-narrative novels and films, I suggest that the four Gospels can profitably be read as four distinct yet overlapping narrative renditions of a shared story.

The main title of the book reflects the current scholarly consensus that the New Testament Gospels are a form of ancient biography; hence, in generic terms, they are "lives" of Jesus. Insofar as they are parallel accounts of Jesus' ministry, death, and resurrection, telling the same core story about the biographical subject, they may be called "parallel lives" of Jesus (to borrow the name given to the series of biographies written by Plutarch).

READING THE GOSPELS IN PARALLEL

The nature of the four canonical Gospels as parallel narratives of Jesus' life allows them to be read in close comparison. The layout of the Gospels in standard versions of the Bible is not conducive to a comparative reading of them, but a resource called a "synopsis" has been devised for this purpose. A synopsis sets out parallel Gospel passages side by side so that they can be "viewed together" (*syn* = with; *opsis* = view). The first three Gospels are especially amenable to this arrangement because they have so many passages in common; hence they are known as the "Synoptic Gospels." Many Gospel synopses have appeared since the first synopsis (produced by J. J. Griesbach) was published in 1776. Most concentrate on the Synoptic Gospels, but some, such as Kurt Aland's *Synopsis of the Four Gospels*, one of the best synopses currently available, include passages from John's Gospel as well.

Examining parallel Gospel passages with the aid of a synopsis is a core feature of formal Gospel study in universities, colleges, and seminaries. It is a great way of exploring the commonality and individuality of the Gospels. One can quickly spot similarities across matching passages and see where they differ. In the third part of this book, we look in close detail at selected parallel episodes found in three or all four Gospels. The parallel passages are laid out in parallel columns as in a synopsis. The shared story is delineated, and then we examine each Gospel version of that story by using a narrative-critical scheme of analysis. This narrative-critical approach to parallel analysis differs from the more common redaction-critical way of dealing with parallel Gospel passages (on redaction criticism, see chap. 1), which focuses on the editorial changes made by Gospel writers (usually Matthew and Luke) to their source text (usually Mark). Redaction criticism remains an indispensible tool for Gospel study, but the narrative-critical approach allows for comparison across a broader range of literary features.

THE STRUCTURE OF THE BOOK

The book is divided into three parts. Part 1 is titled "Approaching the Four Gospels." Part 2 considers "The Individual Gospels and Their Narrative Features." Part 3 examines "Selected Parallel Episodes." The structure of the book reflects a progressive narrowing of the subject matter: from the Gospels generally, to the Gospels individually, to specific Gospel passages. The book is designed to be read from start to finish (though not in one sitting!), but readers can also use it as a book to dip into.

FOR FURTHER READING

The Fourfold Gospel

Burridge, Richard A. *Four Gospels, One Jesus?* 2nd ed. London: SPCK, 2005.

Childs, Brevard S. *The New Testament as Canon*. London: SMC Press, 1984.

Hengel, Martin. *The Four Gospels and the One Gospel of Jesus Christ*. London: SCM Press, 2000.

Hill, Charles E. *Who Chose the Gospels? Probing the Great Gospel Conspiracy*. Oxford: Oxford University Press, 2010.

Stanton, Graham N. *Jesus and Gospel*. Cambridge: Cambridge University Press, 2004.

Strauss, Mark L. *Four Portraits, One Jesus: An Introduction to Jesus and the Gospels*. Grand Rapids: Zondervan, 2007.

Watson, Francis. "The Fourfold Gospel." In *The Cambridge Companion to the Gospels*, edited by S. C. Barton, 34–52. Cambridge: Cambridge University Press, 2006.

Gospel Synopses

Aland, Kurt, ed. *Synopsis of the Four Gospels*. New York: American Bible Society, 1982.

Throckmorton, Burton H., Jr., ed. *Gospel Parallels: A Comparison of the Synoptic Gospels*. 5th ed. Nashville: Thomas Nelson, 1992.

PART I

Approaching the Four Gospels

This first section provides introductory information about the Gospels and explains our model for reading them as four yet one. Chapter 1, "Grappling with the Gospels," first takes an initial look at the unity and individuality of the Gospels. We begin with the commonality, observing the common shape of the Gospels and the similar features of the Synoptic Gospels. Then we look at some of the differences, first between the Synoptic Gospels and John, and then between Matthew, Mark, and Luke. We discover that although the four Gospels exhibit shared characteristics, each asserts its individuality in particular ways. Attention then turns to introductory issues. How did the Gospels come to be written? Who wrote them? For whom were they written and for what purposes? Particular emphasis falls on the question, What are the Gospels? The reasons for viewing the Gospels as "lives" are specified, and we consider the interpretive implications of this generic classification.

Chapter 2, "Four Narratives, One Story," explains the distinction between "story" and "narrative" and shows its relevance to the unity and plurality of the Fourfold Gospel. The central story that the four Gospels manifest is set out and common narrative features are identified.

1

Grappling with the Gospels

The four Gospels look very alike.[1] All four are narratives of the life and teachings of Jesus of Nazareth, the central figure of the Christian faith. All four concentrate on a particular phase of his life: the period of his public ministry culminating in his arrest, trial, death, and subsequent resurrection. Two of the four, Matthew's and Luke's Gospels, have birth stories, and Luke recounts an incident involving Jesus as a twelve-year-old boy; but the main narrative development in all four begins with his baptism by John the Baptist (though Jesus' baptism is alluded to rather than narrated in John's Gospel). All four report his miracles (especially his healings), his gathering of disciples, his attraction of public attention, his teaching, and his conflicts with the religious authorities; in each Gospel a disproportionate amount of attention is given to his last days. The four narratives parallel each other to a significant degree. They relate the same broad sweep of events and have numerous particular episodes in common (the feeding of the five thousand, the triumphal entry into Jerusalem, the betrayal by Judas, the arrest of Jesus, Peter's denial, and so forth). The common shape of the four Gospels distinguishes them from other surviving "Gospels" from the early centuries of the Christian era.[2]

---

1. On the common characteristics of the four Gospels, see Loveday Alexander, "What Is a Gospel?" in *The Cambridge Companion to the Gospels*, ed. Stephen C. Barton (Cambridge: Cambridge University Press, 2006), 13–33, here 14–17; Larry W. Hurtado, *Lord Jesus Christ: Devotion to Jesus in Earliest Christianity* (Grand Rapids: Wm. B. Eerdmans Publishing Co., 2003), 262–70.

2. It is possible that some apocryphal Gospels that are known only by name, or are extant in fragments, or are known only through quotations of them (such as the so-called Jewish Christian Gospels—the *Gospel of the Hebrews*, the *Gospel of the Nazarenes*, and the *Gospel of the Ebionites*) might have resembled the canonical Gospels more closely. But none of the extant works, stemming from the early centuries of the church, that are designated "gospels" either by themselves or by others, corresponds in literary shape to the four canonical Gospels.

THE SIMILARITY OF THE SYNOPTIC GOSPELS

The similarity of Synoptic Gospels—Matthew, Mark, and Luke—is especially striking. These Gospels follow the same general narrative progression: preliminaries to Jesus' mission; ministry in Galilee; journey to Jerusalem; arrest, trial, crucifixion, and resurrection. They share many specific episodes. Shared textual units or "pericopae" (the singular is "pericope"; from *peri* + *coptō*, meaning "cut around") include the following:

> John the Baptist's ministry
> Jesus' baptism
> The temptation of Jesus
> The healing of Peter's mother-in-law
> The healing of a paralyzed man
> The call of Matthew/Levi
> The healing of a man with a withered hand
> The parable of the Sower and its interpretation
> The feeding of the five thousand
> Peter's confession
> The first prediction of the passion
> The transfiguration
> The healing of an epileptic boy
> Jesus' encounter with the rich, young ruler
> The triumphal entry into Jerusalem
> The cleansing of the temple
> The prediction of the temple's destruction
> The "eschatological" discourse
> The preparation for the Passover
> The Lord's Supper
> Jesus' prayer in Gethsemane
> The arrest of Jesus
> Peter's denial of Jesus
> Jesus' appearance before Pilate

All these pericopae occur in exactly this order in all three Gospel narratives, though with varying intervening material. The wording used in parallel passages is often very close, as can be seen from the call of Levi/Matthew, set out in parallel (synoptically, viewed together), below.

Matthew 9:9	Mark 2:14	Luke 5:27–28
As Jesus was walking along,	As he was walking along,	After this he went out
he saw a man called Matthew sitting at the tax booth;	he saw Levi son of Alphaeus sitting at the tax booth,	and saw a tax collector named Levi, sitting at the tax booth;
and he said to him, "Follow me." And he got up	and he said to him, "Follow me." And he got up	and he said to him, "Follow me." And he got up, left everything,
and followed him.	and followed him.	and followed him.

The Gospel writers, or "evangelists" (from the Greek [Gk.] *euangelion* = *eu* + *angelion*, "good news," often translated as "gospel"), narrate this incident in similar terms, with only slight verbal differences. Additionally, the Synoptic Gospels give the same broad account of Jesus' activities: proclaiming the kingdom of God, teaching the disciples, speaking in parables, sharing in table, fellowship with "tax collectors and sinners," healing the sick, casting out demons.

The similarity of the Synoptic Gospels, especially the agreements in order and wording, points to a literary relationship. The most widely accepted account of that relationship is that Mark's Gospel served as the main source for the other two. This is the theory of Markan Priority, which is the bedrock of modern scholarly study of the Synoptic Gospels.[3] The theory of Markan Priority relates to the "triple tradition," which is material common to all three Synoptic Gospels.[4]

There is another body of parallel material called the "double tradition": pericopae common to Matthew and Luke but absent from Mark, which consist mainly of teachings of Jesus. On the majority view, the double tradition is a source used independently by Matthew and Luke.[5] The alleged shared

---

3. On the arguments for Markan priority, see Mark Goodacre, *The Synoptic Problem: A Way through the Maze* (London: T&T Clark International, 2001), 56–83; Robert H. Stein, *The Synoptic Problem: An Introduction* (Grand Rapids: Baker Book House, 1987), 45–88. A minority of scholars hold to the priority of Matthew. Delbert Royce Burkett (*Rethinking the Gospel Sources: From Proto-Mark to Mark* [New York and London: T&T Clark International, 2004]) has recently argued for a more complex solution to the Synoptic Problem involving an early version of Mark that was known in different forms.

4. There are also passages shared between Mark and *one* of the other two, which many scholars include within the triple tradition. Goodacre (*Synoptic Problem*, 48–50) treats this material separately as "Not Quite Triple Tradition."

5. Stein, *Synoptic Problem*, 89–112.

source is normally regarded as written, though some conjecture that it is a collection of oral traditions or a mixture of oral traditions and written material. The hypothetical source has come to be known as Q (an abbreviation of the German word *Quelle*, "source").

Markan Priority and Q together form the two-source hypothesis, the most popular solution to the Synoptic Problem (the problem of how the Synoptic Gospels relate to each other). In recent years, an alternative to the two-source hypothesis has been growing in strength and accepts the priority of Mark but explains the double tradition in terms of Luke's direct use of Matthew.[6]

THE DISTINCTIVENESS OF JOHN'S GOSPEL

The likeness of the Synoptic Gospels to each other distinguishes them from the Gospel of John. The Synoptics describe a ministry conducted chiefly in Galilee, followed by a single, fatal visit to Jerusalem around the time of the festival of Passover.[7] In the Fourth Gospel, Jesus' ministry is set for the most part in Judea; he makes several trips to Jerusalem at festival times (2:13; 5:1; 7:10; 10:22; 12:12).

While John's narrative broadly parallels the Synoptic narratives, many specific events reported in the Synoptic Gospels are absent. Of the twenty-four pericopae listed above, John includes seven: ministry of John the Baptist, feeding of the five thousand, triumphal entry, cleansing of the temple, arrest, Peter's denial, appearance before Pilate. He alludes to Jesus' baptism but does not directly describe it, mentioning only the descent of the Spirit that accompanies it (see further chap. 5). Also, he narrates a cleansing of the temple at the beginning of Jesus' ministry rather than at the end, where it occurs in the Synoptics. John's version of common episodes is often quite different from the Synoptic accounts. For example, John gives a more extensive report of Jesus' trial before Pilate (John 18:28–19:16), which includes a dialogue between the two characters.

In John's Gospel the nonappearance of so many events that are integral to the Synoptic narration of Jesus' ministry is surprising. The absence of the Lord's Supper is especially noteworthy. Like the Synoptists, John narrates

---

6. This is known as the "Farrer theory," named after Austin Farrer, who first proposed it. See Austin Farrer, "On Dispensing with Q," in *Studies in the Gospels: Essays in Memory of R. H. Lightfoot*, ed. D. E. Nineham (Oxford: Basil Blackwell, 1955), 55–88. The Farrer view is championed in current scholarship by Mark Goodacre. For a critique of Q and a corresponding interpretation of the double tradition in terms of Luke's use of Matthew, see Goodacre, *Synoptic Problem*, 122–61.

7. In Luke, Jesus attends the Passover festival in Jerusalem as a boy (2:41–42), and in Matthew 4:5 and Luke 4:9, the devil takes Jesus to Jerusalem during the temptation.

Jesus' final meal with his disciples, at which Jesus predicts Judas's betrayal and Peter's denial, but there is no reference to words of institution said over the bread and wine. Instead, he describes Jesus' washing the disciples' feet (an incident exclusive to this Gospel).

Conversely, John includes in his narrative numerous well-known incidents that are entirely unique to this Gospel, including these:

> The miracle of changing water into wine (2:1–11)
> The conversation with Nicodemus (3:1–21)
> The meeting with the Samaritan woman (4:1–42)
> The healing of a lame man at the pool of Bethesda (5:1–15)
> The healing of the man born blind (chap. 9)
> The raising of Lazarus (11:1–44)
> Jesus' washing the disciples' feet (13:1–17)
> The Farewell Discourses (chaps. 14–16)
> The high-priestly prayer (chap. 17)
> Jesus' special resurrection appearance to Mary Magdalene (20:11–18)
> Jesus' appearance to Thomas (20:24–29)

The contours of Jesus' ministry in John's Gospel are broadly the same as in the Synoptics, but curiously, there are no exorcisms (i.e., expulsions of demons from individuals). Also, Jesus doesn't speak much about the kingdom of God (the actual phrase occurs only twice in the Gospel). Instead, he talks a lot about "eternal life." Moreover, he doesn't teach in parables, as is his custom in the Synoptics. Rather, he employs symbolism: "I am the bread of life," and so forth.

The differences between John and the Synoptics raise the question of how this Gospel relates to them. Does John write with knowledge of any of the Synoptics, or in complete independence of them? Until the twentieth century, it was generally accepted that John wrote to supplement the other three Gospels. Around the middle of the twentieth century, scholarly opinion changed, leading to the dominant view that John wrote independently of the Synoptics.[8] On this theory, pericopae that John shares with the Synoptics stem from mutual reliance on common oral traditions. In more recent years, the view has been gaining ground that John knew, but was not literally dependent on, at least one of the Synoptics: the Gospel of Mark.[9] This view seems to make best sense of the evidence. On the one

8. Influential was the work of Percival Gardner-Smith in *Saint John and the Synoptic Gospels* (Cambridge: Cambridge University Press, 1938).

9. See Richard Bauckham, "John for Readers of Mark," in *The Gospels for All Christians: Rethinking the Gospel Audiences*, ed. Richard Bauckham (Grand Rapids: Wm. B. Eerdmans Publishing Co., 1998), 147–71.

hand, it is clear that John has not "copied" from Mark in the way that Matthew and Luke seem to have done. On the other hand, structural similarities and occasional small but striking verbal coincidences between John and Mark in parallel passages (e.g., the unusual Gk. *pistikos*, "pure" or "genuine," in John 12:3 and Mark 14:3)[10] suggest that the former was familiar with the latter.

DISTINGUISHING FEATURES
OF THE SYNOPTIC GOSPELS

Despite their close similarity, the Synoptic Gospels are by no means identical. Although the basic narrative pattern is the same, there are obvious differences between them, especially at the beginning and end of the Gospels.

Beginnings: Matthew begins with a genealogy, tracing Jesus' ancestry back to Abraham through King David. Luke also opens with a birth narrative, but it differs markedly from Matthew's. Matthew's birth narrative is focused on Joseph. Luke's version concentrates on Mary. In contrast to both Matthew and Luke, Mark has no birth narrative. Mark's starting point is the ministry of John the Baptist. He gives no account of Jesus' origins. Jesus makes his first appearance in this Gospel at the scene of his baptism.

Endings: Mark's Gospel ends rather oddly, with the women's fleeing from the empty tomb and saying nothing to anyone (16:8).[11] Jesus makes no postresurrection appearances. Both Matthew and Luke narrate appearances of the risen Jesus, but their appearance stories differ. Matthew narrates a manifestation of Jesus to the women who visit the tomb (28:8–10) and then to the disciples on a mountain in Galilee, where Jesus gives the Great Commission (28:16–20). Luke tells of Jesus' appearance to two disciples on the road to Emmaus (24:13–35) and then to the disciples in Jerusalem (24:36–49). The disciples witness Jesus' ascent into heaven from the vicinity of Bethany and joyously return to Jerusalem (24:50–53).

Although the Synoptics have many individual pericopae in common, each one has unique material. About three hundred verses of Matthew have no parallel in either Mark or Luke. Matthew's unique contents, often labeled M, include the following pericopae:

---

10. Noted by Judith Lieu, "How John Writes," in *The Written Gospel*, ed. Marcus Bockmuehl and Donald A. Hagner (Cambridge: Cambridge University Press, 2005), 182 n. 20.

11. The oldest and most reliable written copies of the Gospel of Mark end at 16:8. Later manuscripts provide two alternate endings, which describe Jesus' postresurrection appearances, but most scholars do not think this extra material is original to the Gospel. The ending of Mark will be discussed in chap. 3 below.

The annunciation to Joseph (1:18–25)
The visit of the Magi (2:1–12)
The flight to Egypt (2:13–15)
The slaughter of the innocents (2:16–18)
The parable of the Wheat and the Tares (13:24–30, 36–43)
The parable of the Pearl of Great Price (13:45–46)
The coin in the fish's mouth (17:24–27)
The parable of the Laborers in the Vineyard (20:1–16)
The parable of the Wise and Foolish Maidens (25:1–13)
The parable of the Sheep and the Goats (25:31–46)
Judas's remorse and suicide (27:3–10)
Pilate's wife's dream (27:19)
The bribing of the guards (28:11–15)
The Great Commission (28:16–20)

It is only in Matthew's Gospel that we find the Sermon on the Mount (chaps. 5–7), probably the most well-known teaching of Jesus. However, many of the sayings that contribute to this discourse can also be found in Luke's Gospel (especially in Luke's so-called Sermon on the Plain, Luke 6:20–49) and so belong to the double tradition.

Mark's Gospel has relatively little unique material because nearly all of its contents are paralleled in Matthew or Luke, and frequently both (the substance of 606 out of the 661 verses of Mark is reproduced in Matthew, and some 380 of the 661 verses of Mark reappear in Luke). Mark's distinctive material includes the following pericopae:

Jesus thought to be out of his mind (3:20–21)
The healing of the deaf and mute man (7:32–37)
The healing of the blind man near Bethsaida (8:22–26)
The young man who flees after Jesus' arrest (14:51–52)

These passages are peculiar in both senses of the word: they belong exclusively to this Gospel, and they have somewhat unusual features. In 3:20–21, Jesus is regarded as mad, and his own family tries to seize him. In 7:32–37, Jesus' method of healing involves an unusual degree of physical contact (he puts his fingers into the man's ears, spits, and touches his tongue). In 8:22–26, Jesus heals in two stages. At the first touch, the blind man's sight is partially restored; after the second touch, he sees everything clearly. In 14:51–52, a naked young man makes a cameo appearance. The nature of Mark's exclusive content fits with Markan priority (over against the view that Mark was dependent on Matthew and Luke): one can more readily imagine Matthew and Luke dropping these potentially embarrassing passages than Mark deliberately including them while discarding material such as the Sermon on the Mount.

The material exclusive to Luke, sometimes labeled L, comprises about one-third of the Gospel's entire contents and accounts for some of its most distinctive features. Some of the most memorable stories from the Gospels belong to Luke's special material, including these:

> The annunciation to Mary (1:26–38)
> The story of the shepherds (2:8–20)
> Jesus as a boy in the temple (2:41–52)
> The raising of the widow's son at Nain (7:11–17)
> The parable of the Good Samaritan (10:30–37)
> The parable of the Rich Fool (12:13–21)
> The parable of the Lost Coin (15:8–10)
> The parable of the Prodigal Son and the Elder Brother (15:11–32)
> The parable of the Unjust Steward (16:1–13)
> The parable of the Rich Man and Lazarus (16:19–31)
> The cleansing of ten lepers (17:11–19)
> The story of Zacchaeus (19:1–10)
> Jesus' postresurrection appearance to two disciples on the way to Emmaus (24:13–35)
> The ascension of Jesus into heaven (24:50–53)

Although the order in which shared stories are narrated is often the same across the Synoptics, there are some differences in the placement of episodes. Jesus' rejection at Nazareth, for example, comes at a much earlier point in Luke's Gospel (4:16–30) than in Matthew (13:53–58) and Mark (6:1–6a). Also, the question about fasting comes later in Matthew (9:14–17) than in Mark (2:18–22) and Luke (5:33–39).

Parallel passages are hardly ever 100 percent identical, and the variations are often significant. In the example given earlier (Matt. 9:9; Mark 2:14; Luke 5:27–28), the three accounts differ on the name of the individual called: "Matthew" in Matthew's Gospel, but "Levi" in Mark and Luke. This is clearly a significant difference! The traditional explanation is that this person had two names and that Matthew gives one name, while Mark and Luke give the other.[12] The fact that only Matthew names this individual "Matthew" is taken by some as support for the view that the apostle Matthew wrote this Gospel. Luke alone comments that Levi "left everything" to follow Jesus. A similar remark is made in Luke 5:11, in connection with the call of Peter, James, and John. Luke places particular emphasis on renunciation of possessions as a condition of discipleship (cf. 14:33, a saying found only in Luke's Gospel). Also, Luke specifies that Levi was a tax collector (a specification we find later in Matthew's Gospel: 10:3).

---

12. This explanation is not widely accepted in critical scholarship. For a recent discussion of the issue, see Richard Bauckham, *Jesus and the Eyewitnesses: The Gospels as Eyewitness Testimony* (Grand Rapids: Wm. B. Eerdmans Publishing Co., 2006), 108–12.

This coheres with Luke's particular interest in Jesus' sympathy for tax collectors (Luke 18:9–14; 19:1–10). On the assumption that Matthew and Luke use Mark as a literary resource, scholars usually see their variations from Mark's text in parallel pericopae as intentional changes to it (see on redaction criticism below).

Although the Synoptists agree in the range of activities that characterize Jesus' ministry, they differ in the emphasis they place on these activities. Matthew gives structural prominence to Jesus' teaching. Mark emphasizes Jesus' miracles. Luke gives particular attention to Jesus' practice of eating and drinking with tax collectors and sinners.

The Synoptic Gospels, then, do not simply repeat each other; at every level they display interesting and important differences.

FOUR INDIVIDUAL GOSPELS

To sum up so far: The Gospels exhibit a significant degree of commonality. Yet each Gospel has particularities that set it apart from the others. John's Gospel is the most distinct, but each of the four distinguishes itself from the others in certain ways.

Matthew's Gospel is the most *Jewish* of the four and the one that is most clearly oriented toward the Old Testament. Matthew portrays Jesus as "Son of David" and indicates that Jesus has come to fulfill the Law and the Prophets. Matthew exhibits a particular awareness of traditional Jewish practices: almsgiving (Matt. 6:1–4), tithing (23:23), fasting (6:16–18), and the wearing of phylacteries (23:5). He not only shows more interest in the Jewish law than do the other Gospel writers; in the Sermon on the Mount he also records sayings of Jesus that add extra rigor to the Law (Matt. 5–7). Although the language of fulfillment is common to all, this Gospel contains more Old Testament quotations than any of the others. Matthew has about sixty direct citations of the Old Testament and countless allusions and references to it. Matthew's Gospel forms a bridge between the two Testaments, expressing continuity and newness. It is appropriate, then, that it is the first in the canonical order. This Gospel is also the most *organized* of the four, with Jesus' teaching concentrated into five main blocks (chaps. 5–7; 10; 13; 18; 24–25), like the five books of the Torah. Matthew's Gospel was the most popular Gospel in the early Christian centuries. It was cited more frequently than any of the others. At the end of the fourth century, commentaries written on this Gospel far outnumbered those on the other three Gospels.[13]

---

13. David C. Sim, "The Rise and Fall of the Gospel of Matthew," *Expository Times* 120 (July 2009): 478–85, here 479.

Mark's Gospel is the most *action packed* of the four Gospels, with much more space given to the deeds of Jesus than to his words. This Gospel has proportionally more miracles than any of the other Gospels: Mark records eighteen specific miracles performed by Jesus. Mark's is the Gospel that most readily lends itself to dramatic performance (all the Gospels were probably originally designed to be read aloud in gatherings for worship since most people were illiterate). The Gospel of Mark can be read aloud or told in about two hours. Those who have witnessed theatrical recitations of Mark (sometimes involving only one actor) can testify to its dramatic impact. It is also the *shortest* of the four Gospels, at around 11,242 words (Matthew is around 18,305 words; Luke, 19,428; John, 15,416).[14]

Luke's Gospel is the most *socially oriented* of the four, laying special emphasis on Jesus' concern for the poor, the disadvantaged, and those on the edges of society. Luke's Gospel contains a significant amount of material on poverty and wealth. Luke gives particular attention to Jesus' contacts with women and highlights, as no other Gospel writer does, the role that women play in Jesus' ministry. Women figure more prominently in this Gospel than in any of the others (especially in Luke 1–2). On one estimate, Luke refers to thirteen women not mentioned in the other two Gospels.[15] The social orientation of Luke's Gospel makes it particularly attractive to modern readers. Luke's Gospel is the basis for the most widely viewed movie depiction of the life of Jesus. Released in 1979, the film *Jesus* has been seen by several billion people worldwide and has been translated into over a thousand languages.[16] Luke's Gospel is also the only one of the four to have a sequel in the New Testament: the book of Acts. Luke is the *longest* of the four Gospels, nearly twice the length of Mark. Luke's Gospel and the book of Acts are the two lengthiest writings in the entire New Testament and together account for nearly one-quarter of it.

John's Gospel is simultaneously the *simplest* and *most profound* Gospel. It has been described as "a stream in which children can wade and elephants swim."[17] Its plainness and clarity make it accessible to new readers, and its depth continually challenges and stimulates those who know it well. It is the most *evangelistic* of the four Gospels (even if it was not written with evangelistic intent), with statements such the well-known saying in John 3:16: "For God so loved the world that he gave his only Son, so that everyone who

---

14. Robert Morgenthaler, *Statistik des neutestamentlichen Wortschatzes* (Zurich and Frankfurt: Gotthelf-Verlag, 1958), 164; cf. Richard A. Burridge, *What Are the Gospels? A Comparison with Graeco-Roman Biography* (Cambridge: Cambridge University Press, 1992), 199, 225. An exact word count cannot be given because of variations among the manuscripts.

15. Mark L. Strauss, *Four Portraits, One Jesus: An Introduction to Jesus and the Gospels* (Grand Rapids: Zondervan, 2007), 287.

16. See http://www.jesusfilm.org.

17. Graham N. Stanton, *The Gospels and Jesus* (Oxford: Oxford University Press, 1989), 102.

believes in him may not perish but may have eternal life." And it is the most *theologically rich* of the four, with its deeper exploration of certain subjects such as the relationship between Jesus and God the Father. Although Matthew's Gospel was the most favored Gospel in the ancient church, John's Gospel has been the most popular and most studied Gospel for most of the church's history. A preference for it has been expressed by some of the church's greatest theologians, including Augustine and Martin Luther.[18]

The four Gospels have traditionally been symbolized by different creaturely images: Matthew as a human being; Mark as a lion; Luke as an ox; John as an eagle.[19] These images appear in paintings, church architecture, and illuminated Gospels, such as the Lindisfarne Gospels and the Book of Kells.[20] The application of these symbols (drawn from Ezek. 1 and Rev. 1) to the four Gospels acknowledges the individuality of each one.

THE FORMATION OF THE GOSPELS

How did the Gospels come to be written? According to the standard scholarly reconstruction, the process of formation ran as follows. At first some sayings of Jesus and stories about him were transmitted orally. Then this material began to be put into written form. Finally, the evangelists took the oral and written sources at their disposal and produced their Gospels. The final phase, the actual writing of the Gospels, is generally dated to the period 65–100 CE. Early church tradition dates Mark's Gospel soon after Peter's death in Rome, assumed to be around 65 CE. Modern scholars tend to place it around 70 CE, either just before or just after the destruction of Jerusalem.[21] Matthew and Luke's Gospels tend to be dated in the 80s and John's Gospel around 95 CE.

The three-stage scheme is hypothetical; yet in his Gospel prologue (1:1–4), Luke seems to acknowledge such a process when he refers to "eyewitnesses and servants of the word" who "handed on" Jesus material (oral transmission), the "many" attempts to commit the gospel events to writing (the formation of written sources), and his own efforts in "investigating everything carefully" so as to produce his own "orderly account" (the composition of the Gospels).

18. Cf. Francis Watson, "The Fourfold Gospel," in *The Cambridge Companion to the Gospels*, ed. Stephen C. Barton (Cambridge: Cambridge University Press, 2006), 34–52, here 39.

19. Irenaeus, the first church father to employ these images, applies the lion to John and the eagle to Mark (*Against Heresies* 3.11.8–9). The traditional allocation of the symbols stems from Jerome. See further Richard A. Burridge, *Four Gospels, One Jesus?* (London: SPCK, 1994), 23–27.

20. Burridge, *Four Gospels*, 29–31.

21. Recently, though, a date as early as the mid-40s has been proposed: see James G. Crossley, *The Date of Mark's Gospel: Insights from the Law in Earliest Christianity*, JSNTSup 266 (London: T&T Clark International, 2005).

The three main historical methods of Gospel criticism—form, source, and redaction criticism—investigate each stage in the process of formation.[22] *Form criticism* is concerned with the oral stage; it isolates the individual pericopae of the (mainly Synoptic) Gospels and analyzes them by their *forms* (miracle stories, pronouncement stories, parables, et al.), assigning each form to a distinct life setting in the early church (miracle stories to apologetic contexts, pronouncement stories to popular preaching, parables to storytelling scenarios, et al.). *Source criticism* tries to delineate the literary sources used by the evangelists in the production of their Gospels. As we have seen, the majority view of Synoptic sources is that Matthew and Luke independently used Mark and the hypothetical Q. *Redaction criticism* ("redaction" refers to the process of editing for publication) looks at how the evangelists edited the written and oral sources available to them to produce the Gospels as we have them. Attention is given to the changes the evangelists make to their sources (especially additions, omissions, and alterations). Analysis of these changes is used to determine the Gospel writers' particular theological tendencies.

The three stages through which it is posited that the Gospels came to be— the oral phase, the period of written sources, the composition of the Gospels themselves—most likely overlapped. This second and third stages would certainly have coincided in the case of Mark's Gospel if, as most agree, it was used as a literary source by Matthew and Luke. It is also likely that some written material was in circulation during the oral period. Indeed, it is quite possible, as Graham Stanton has argued, that disciples of Jesus recorded in writing some of his words and deeds during the period of his ministry.[23]

AUTHORSHIP, AUDIENCES, AND AIMS

Authorship

Who wrote the Gospels? The four Gospels are traditionally assigned to Matthew, the tax collector and disciple (Matt. 9:9); Mark, the travel companion of Paul (Col. 4:10; 2 Tim. 4:11) and associate of Peter (1 Pet. 5:13); Luke, physician and coworker with Paul (Col. 4:14; 2 Tim. 4:11); and John, the son of Zebedee (Mark 1:29; 3:17). However, none of the Gospels names its actual author. As we have noted, the Gospel titles with their attributions of authorship were almost certainly added later.[24] Strictly speaking, the Gospels are anonymous!

22. Cf. Strauss, *Four Portraits*, 46.
23. Graham N. Stanton, *Jesus and Gospel* (Cambridge: Cambridge University Press, 2004), 188–89.
24. Martin Hengel (*The Four Gospels and the One Gospel of Jesus Christ* [Harrisburg, PA: Trinity Press International, 2000]), however, has recently argued that the titles are early and reliable.

Critical scholarship has generally doubted the traditional attributions. Even so, there are many good scholars who cautiously accept them—on the basis of strong external testimony in the case of the first three Gospels (the early church fathers are totally unanimous in assigning the first three Gospels to Matthew, Mark, and Luke; one might have expected some variation in patristic opinion if the attributions were educated guesses),[25] and on a mixture of external and internal evidence in the case of the Fourth Gospel.[26] The internal evidence for John the apostle's authorship of the Fourth Gospel relates to the beloved disciple ("the disciple whom Jesus loved"; 21:20), who is apparently set forth as the author in 21:24 ("This is the disciple who is testifying to these things and has written them"). It is argued that John the son of Zebedee best fits the profile of this anonymous figure. However, the evidence relating to the beloved disciple is by no means straightforward. Other identifications have been proposed (e.g., Lazarus, Thomas), and it is not clear that John 21:24 is saying that the beloved disciple is the actual writer of the Gospel. Assuming that the phrase "these things" refers to the Gospel as a whole (rather than just to chap. 21), "has written them" could be interpreted to mean that the Gospel derives from the beloved disciple's oral or written testimony (taking the underlying Gk. in the sense of "has *caused* them to be written"; cf. 19:22) rather than his composition; another/others could have taken this testimony and from it composed the Gospel.[27] Many scholars think that the Gospel of John, at least in its final form, was the product not of a single writer but of a group.[28] This view receives some support from the "we" of 21:24 ("We know that his [the beloved disciple's] testimony is true").

In terms of the interpretation of the Gospels, little depends on knowing the exact identity of their authors. This book follows the established practice in Gospel scholarship of referring to the Gospel authors by their traditional names.

Audiences

For whom were the Gospels written? It is generally accepted that all four Gospels were originally written for Christians rather than nonbelievers. In

25. These three, it is pointed out, are marginal figures in the NT, none of them an obvious choice as an authoritative witness, and one of them, Mark, with a less than stellar record (cf. Acts 15:38–39).

26. The external evidence is less clear-cut in the case of the Fourth Gospel. The early church father Papias (ca. 130 CE), in a quotation preserved by Eusebius (*Ecclesiastical History* 3.39.3–4), mentions "the elder John." Some scholars have concluded that the Gospel should be assigned to this figure (most recently, Bauckham, *Jesus and the Eyewitnesses*, 412–37). But it is debated whether John the elder is to be distinguished from or identified with John the apostle.

27. But see the arguments against this in Bauckham, *Jesus and the Eyewitnesses*, 358–62.

28. On this view, the Gospel was written in stages.

the second half of the twentieth century, the prevailing view was that the Gospels were written for specific Christian communities, fairly narrowly conceived. Hence, scholars would speak of "the Matthean community," "the Markan community," and so forth, and various attempts were made to give definition to these communities.[29] Richard Bauckham challenged the consensus in an important essay published in 1998, arguing that from the outset the Gospels were meant to circulate widely in the early church.[30] Some have endorsed Bauckham's thesis; others have reacted strongly against it. Margaret Mitchell, for example, points out that Bauckham's claim runs counter to early church traditions associating each Gospel with a particular Mediterranean locale: Mark with Rome and/or Alexandria, Matthew with Judea, Luke with Achaia, John with Ephesus and/or Patmos.[31] The debate is ongoing; a mediating view suggests that the Gospels were written both for specific believing audiences and with a view to circulation within a wide Christian readership.

Aims

Why were the Gospels written? The impetus to write down Jesus' sayings and activities, as noted above, was likely present from an early stage. The production of written Gospels was probably not, therefore, a big-bang moment in the early church but the extension of a process perhaps already under way during Jesus' ministry (though the turn to the biographical genre, on which see below, was a distinctly new development in the process).

In the writing of the Gospels, an important factor was probably the desire to preserve the memory of Jesus. On the conventional dating, the penning of the Gospels coincides with the passing away of the first Christian generation. It is just at this point, as Jesus was fast receding from living memory, that a permanent record of his activities and teachings would have become necessary.[32]

Beyond this general motivation, the evangelists had their own individual reasons for writing. The Gospel writers' individual purposes may be partly deduced from the specific contents of their books and their particular theological emphases. Thus Matthew probably wrote at least in part to show that Jesus is the fulfillment of Old Testament and Jewish expectations. Luke and John

29. See Raymond E. Brown, *The Community of the Beloved Disciple* (New York: Paulist Press, 1979).

30. Richard Bauckham, "For Whom Were Gospels Written?" in *The Gospels for All Christians: Rethinking the Gospel Audiences*, ed. Richard Bauckham (Grand Rapids: Eerdmans, 1998), 9–48.

31. Margaret M. Mitchell, "Patristic Counter-Evidence to the Claim That 'The Gospels Were Written for All Christians,'" *New Testament Studies* 51 (2005): 36–79.

32. Cf. Arthur G. Patzia, *The Making of the New Testament: Origin, Collection, Text and Canon* (Leicester: Apollos, 1995), 47.

offer explicit statements of purpose. In the final clause of his preface (Luke 1:1–4, addressed to a certain Theophilus), Luke declares that he has decided to write the Gospel "so that you may know the truth concerning the things about which you have been instructed." John appears to supply an evangelistic motive for the writing of his Gospel: "These are written so that you *may come to believe* that Jesus is the Messiah, the Son of God" (20:31; italics mine). But as the NRSV notes indicate, other manuscripts read *"may continue to believe."* It is probably better to interpret the purpose statement of 20:31 in terms of sustaining and enhancing *existing* faith rather than creating new faith, since the Gospel as a whole seems to presume a believing audience. One may still recognize the evangelistic appeal of the Gospel (as indicated above).

WHAT ARE THE GOSPELS?

We have not yet addressed the question, What kind of texts are the Gospels? To what genre do they belong? A genre is a specific category or type of literature, such as romance, science fiction, or detective story. Knowing the genre of a piece of literature can make a difference in the way we interpret and react to it. We will respond rather differently to the report of some heinous crime when we read it in a detective novel than when we read it in a newspaper.

The Gospels as Gospels

The four narrative texts with which we are concerned are universally called "Gospels." The four are also often referred to collectively as "the Fourfold Gospel." However, "Gospel" was not a preexisting literary type, a ready-made mold into which the evangelists could pour their material. There are no examples of earlier works, either Jewish or Greco-Roman, called "Gospels." Moreover, none of the four Gospels explicitly calls itself a "Gospel." As we have noted, it is virtually certain that the traditional titles, "The Gospel according to Matthew," and so forth, were applied to the Gospels after they were written.[33] Mark uses the word "gospel," *euangelion* (lit., "good news"), in his opening verse. The precise meaning of this line is debated, but it is commonly agreed that *euangelion* is not being used as a genre indicator. Very quickly, though, the classification "Gospel" became established. Certainly in the second half of the second century, the four were being called "Gospels." Justin, in his *First Apology*, written around 160 CE, speaks of the memoirs of

---

33. Some manuscripts simply have "According to Matthew," etc., i.e., without a preceding "The Gospel."

the apostles, "which are called Gospels" (66.3).[34] The word "Gospel" also is applied to writings other than the four canonical Gospels (e.g., the *Gospel of the Hebrews*, *Gospel of the Nazarenes*, *Gospel of the Ebionites*, et al.).

The word *euangelion* is used throughout the New Testament for the oral preaching of "good news." The apostle Paul, whose writings are the earliest in the New Testament, uses the word for the proclamation of salvation, focusing on the death and resurrection of Jesus (e.g., Rom. 1:1, 9, 16; 10:16). Beyond the opening sentence of his composition, Mark uses the term *euangelion* for the good news proclaimed by Jesus—that the kingdom of God has drawn near (Mark 1:14–15)—and for the good news preached subsequently by Jesus' followers (13:10; 14:9). Matthew qualifies the gospel announced by Jesus and others as "good news of the kingdom" (Matt. 4:23; 9:35; 24:14). In the book of Acts, the term is used of the apostles' preaching (Acts 15:7; 20:24).

The New Testament use of the word *euangelion* for the oral proclamation of salvation was probably influenced by the use of the related verb *euange-lizomai*, meaning to "bring good news," in the Septuagint (the Gk. translation of the Old Testament, the standard abbreviation for which is LXX).[35] In Isaiah 52:7, the prophet states, "How beautiful upon the mountains are the feet of the messenger who announces peace, who brings good news, who announces salvation. . . ." In Isaiah 61:1, the speaker proclaims, "The spirit of the Lord GOD is upon me, because the LORD has anointed me; he has sent me to bring good news to the oppressed." In Luke 4:16–21, Jesus is depicted as reading this Scripture and applying it to himself (see further in chap. 5). The verb is used by Paul (e.g., Rom. 1:15; 10:15; 15:20), and it occurs with some frequency in Luke's Gospel and the book of Acts (e.g., Luke 1:19; 2:10; 3:18; Acts 5:42; 8:4).

The word *euangelion* figured in Roman imperial propaganda, though it is almost always used in the plural, whereas in the New Testament, it always occurs in the singular. The famous Priene Inscription heralds the birthday of Augustus as "the beginning of good news for the world."[36] The formulation is a striking parallel to Mark 1:1: "The beginning of the good news of Jesus Christ." Some scholars think that Mark may be deliberately contrasting the gospel of Jesus Christ with the good tidings associated with Augustus and his successors.[37]

Mark's opening sentence was probably the catalyst for the subsequent application of the term "Gospel" to his own work and other written narratives

34. This is the first example of the plural *euangelia* being used for written Gospels. Ignatius, ca. 110 CE, refers several times to "the Gospel" (e.g., *Smyrn.* 5.1; 7.2) in a way suggesting that a written work, most likely Matthew's Gospel, is in view. See further Stanton, *Jesus and Gospel*, 53–55.

35. The singular noun *euangelion* is absent from the Septuagint.

36. Stanton, *Jesus and Gospel*, 32.

37. See, e.g., Adam Winn, *The Purpose of Mark's Gospel: An Early Christian Response to Roman Imperial Propaganda* (Tübingen: Mohr Siebeck, 2008), 98.

about Jesus. Although Mark does not use the term as a literary classification, he makes it possible for such a move to be made. The nomenclature is appropriate to the four canonical Gospels since, as we will see in the next chapter, the core story embodied in them corresponds to what was probably a common pattern of early "gospel" preaching.

The Gospels as Lives of Jesus

If the evangelists did not knowingly write "Gospels," what kind of works did they think they were writing? In the nineteenth century, it was common to view the Gospels as biographies. During this period many writers used the Gospels as resources for penning their own "lives of Jesus," in which they endeavored to trace Jesus' psychological development. However, in the 1920s opinion began to shift under the influence of scholars like Karl Ludwig Schmidt and Rudolf Bultmann, who argued that the Gospels are low-grade collections of stories and sayings passed on orally over a period of time. In terms of genre, the Gospels were regarded as sui generis, unlike any other type of writing in ancient literature, totally without antecedent. But new forms of literature generally do not materialize "out of nothing"; rather, they emerge as adaptations of existing literary types. Even if the evangelists were creating a new kind of writing, common literary practice would dictate that they would have looked to existing models to guide them in their composition. In more recent years, there has been a revival of the view that the Gospels belong to the ancient biographical genre. The research of Richard Burridge has been pivotal in this respect, helping to create what amounts to a new consensus within scholarship on the Gospels.

Clearly the Gospels are not biographies in the modern sense. Far too much of the life of Jesus is missing for modern appetites, and too many personal details are left out, such as his likes and dislikes, what he looked like, his early life and experiences, his personality, and so forth. Matthew and Luke have birth and infancy narratives, but the main story really begins with Jesus' embarkation on his public ministry, which according to Luke (3:23) occurred when Jesus was "about thirty years old." Many celebrities (actors, models, sports stars) have already penned their "life story" by the age of thirty! The evangelists do not try to explore Jesus' inner development, nor do they give attention to the social and circumstantial factors that influenced and shaped him. But if the Gospels of the New Testament do not conform to expectations for modern biographies, they do compare well, as Burridge has shown, with ancient biographies, such as Tacitus's *Agricola* and Plutarch's *Parallel Lives of Greeks and Romans*.[38]

---

38. Burridge, *What Are the Gospels?* 154–90.

First, they are of similar length to Greco-Roman biographies. Ancient biographies, or "lives"(Gk. *bioi*), are medium-length works, "about 5,000 to 25,000 words at the very extremes."[39] Plutarch's *Parallel Lives* average around 10,000 or 11,000 words, about the size of Mark's Gospel. Plutarch's longest works in this series are about 19,000 to 20,000 words, about the size of Matthew or Luke, the two largest Gospels.

Second, the canonical Gospels are similar to ancient "lives" in form and content. Ancient biographies do not cover the whole life of the subject but tend to concentrate on the individual's public career.[40] They often begin with the subject's family background, his birth, and a few stories illustrating his upbringing, but then move quickly to his public debut. When the subject is a philosopher or teacher, more attention is given to his teachings. A feature of a number of biographies is the disproportionate amount of attention given to the subject's death.

Third, the Gospels share with biographies a singular focus on one individual. This is the hallmark of all biographical writing. In ancient biographies, as in the Gospels, the narrative subject is also the grammatical subject of a high percentage of the verbs.[41]

There are respects in which the Gospels differ from biographies of Greek and Roman antiquity, but the distinctiveness of the Gospels as a collection arises more from the unique features of the life of their subject and the extraordinary claims the evangelists make about him than from their formal literary characteristics.

What does the identification of the Gospels as ancient "lives" of Jesus mean for the interpretation of these texts? It means, first, that they should be read as books about *Jesus*.[42] This seems to state the obvious, but for a good part of the twentieth century, as a result of the influence of Schmidt, Bultmann, and others, the Gospels were viewed as reflecting primarily the situations, needs, and beliefs of the early church. A biography is a narrative focused to an exceptionally high degree on one individual. The Gospels are intensely focused on Jesus of Nazareth. He is at the center of the story and appears in almost every narrative episode, usually dominating the scene. Whatever other motives the evangelists had in writing the Gospels, their main general aim was to give an account of the words and deeds of Jesus and to convey the truth, as they saw it, about his identity and significance.

---

39. Ibid., 169.
40. Ibid., 178–80.
41. Ibid., 162–63.
42. Ibid., 256–58.

The identification of the Gospels as ancient biographies also means that they should be read in accordance with the biographical conventions of the period. Therefore, one should not look for a precise chronological arrangement of Jesus' activities. Ancient biographers were not fastidious about chronology or the exact order in which things happened. The Synoptic Gospels, as we have seen, agree to a remarkable extent on the order of Jesus' deeds, but there are some variations. Clearly Matthew and Luke felt free to alter the order of Mark (on the assumption of their dependence on Mark) for their own narrative purposes. Nor should one expect to find, as a rule, the "very words" (*ipsissima verba*) of Jesus, who would have spoken primarily in Aramaic rather than Greek, the language in which the Gospels were written (though occasionally the Aramaic is preserved, especially in Mark). Ancient biographers often paraphrased, abridged, and interpreted the words of their subjects; it seems clear that the evangelists, to varying degrees, did the same. Whatever theory of inspiration one brings to the Gospels, one should not require a level of exactitude in the narration of Jesus' actions and words beyond what the Gospel writers were aiming to achieve. An appreciation of the biographical genre of the Gospels enables present-day readers to align their expectations of these works with the intentions of the biographer-evangelists.

One of the best-known examples of Greco-Roman biographical writing is Plutarch's *Parallel Lives of Greek and Romans*. In this set of works, Plutarch's strategy is to pair a famous Greek figure of the past with a corresponding Roman personage, to describe the career and character of each one, and then to offer a formal comparison of the two. Thus he matches Theseus and Romulus, Alexander the Great and Julius Caesar, and Demosthenes and Cicero. Twenty-three pairs of "lives" survive, nineteen of which have a formal comparison of the two individuals.[43] Four single "lives" are also extant. If the four canonical Gospels are to be regarded as "lives" of Jesus, it seems fitting to call them "parallel lives" of Jesus, not because they follow the pattern of Plutarch's *Parallel Lives*, but because they are parallel, overlapping biographies of the same individual. Written within a short time of each other (mid-60s to mid-90s CE), "the Gospels are almost unique" among the literature of the Roman imperial era, "as multiple, contemporary accounts of a single life."[44] Calling them "parallel lives" of Jesus calls attention to their biographical character, their overlapping nature, and the individual on whom they focus.

---

43. M. C. Howatson and Ian Chilvers, *The Concise Oxford Companion to Classical Literature* (Oxford and New York: Oxford University Press, 1993), 434–36, here 435.

44. Simon Swain, "Biography and Biographic in the Literature of the Roman Empire," in *Portraits: Biographical Representation in the Greek and Latin Literature of the Roman Empire*, ed. Mark J. Edwards and Simon Swain (Oxford: Clarendon Press, 1997), 1–38, here 33.

CONCLUSION

We have covered a lot of ground in this opening chapter. We have seen that the four Gospels have a common shape and that the first three Gospels are very similar. Yet each Gospel has distinguishing qualities that set it apart from the rest. We have considered questions relating to the composition of Gospels, paying special attention to the issue of genre. We have seen how Gospel scholars have come round to viewing the Gospels as a subtype of ancient biography. Given this generic identification, and given that the four Gospels are parallel accounts of Jesus' ministry, the four can aptly be called "parallel lives" of Jesus. In the next chapter, we directly address the question of how to read the Gospels as four yet one.

FOR FURTHER READING

Apocryphal Gospels

Ehrman, Bart, and Zlatko Plese. *The Apocryphal Gospels: Texts and Translations*. Oxford: Oxford University Press, 2011.

Elliott, James Keith, ed. *The Apocryphal New Testament: A Collection of Apocryphal Christian Literature in an English Translation*. Oxford: Oxford University Press, 2005.

Foster, Paul. *The Apocryphal Gospels: A Very Short Introduction*. Oxford: Oxford University Press, 2009.

Klauck, Hans-Josef. *Apocryphal Gospels: An Introduction*. Translated by Brian McNeil. London: T&T Clark International, 2003.

Schneemelcher, Wilhelm, and R. McL. Wilson. *New Testament Apocrypha*. Vol. 1, *Gospels and Related Writings*. Rev. ed. Louisville, KY: Westminster John Knox Press, 2006.

The Synoptic Problem

Burkett, Delbert Royce. *Rethinking the Gospel Sources*. Vol. 1, *From Proto-Mark to Mark*. New York: T&T Clark International, 2004.

———. *Rethinking the Gospel Sources*. Vol. 2, *The Unity and Plurality of Q*. Society of Biblical Literature: Early Christianity and Its Literature 1. Atlanta: Society of Biblical Literature, 2009.

Farmer, William R. *The Gospel of Jesus: The Pastoral Relevance of the Synoptic Problem*. Louisville, KY: Westminster John Knox Press, 1994.

Goodacre, Mark. *The Synoptic Problem: A Way through the Maze*. London: T&T Clark International, 2001.

Kloppenborg, John S. *Q, the Earliest Gospel: An Introduction to the Original Stories and Sayings of Jesus*. Louisville, KY: Westminster John Knox Press, 2008.

Stein, Robert H. *Studying the Synoptic Gospels: Origin and Interpretation*. Louisville, KY: Westminster John Knox Press, 2001.

———. *The Synoptic Problem: An Introduction*. Grand Rapids: Baker Books, 1987.

Gospel Traditions, Form and Redaction Criticism

Anderson, Janice Capel, and Stephen D. Moore, eds. *Mark and Method: New Approaches to Biblical Studies*. Minneapolis: Fortress Press, 1992.

Bauckham, Richard. *Jesus and the Eyewitnesses: The Gospels as Eyewitness Testimony*. Grand Rapids: Wm. B. Eerdmans Publishing Co., 2006.

Bultmann, Rudolf, *The History of the Synoptic Tradition*. Oxford: Basil Blackwell.

Byrskorg, Samuel, *Story as History—History as Story: The Gospel Tradition in the Context of Ancient Oral History* WUNT 123; Tübingen: Mohr Siebeck, 2000.

Fee, Gordon D. *New Testament Exegesis*. 3rd ed. Louisville, KY: Westminster John Knox Press, 2002.

Hayes, John H., and Carl R. Holladay. *Biblical Exegesis: A Beginner's Handbook*. 3rd ed. Louisville, KY: Westminster John Knox Press, 2007.

McKnight, Edgar V. *What Is Form Criticism?* Philadelphia: Fortress Press, 1969.

Perrin, Norman. *What Is Redaction Criticism?* Philadelphia: Fortress Press, 1969.

Gospel Genre and Introductions

Aune, David E. *The New Testament in Its Literary Environment*. Library of Early Christianity 8. Louisville, KY: Westminster John Knox Press, 1987.

Barton, Stephen C., ed. *The Cambridge Companion to the Gospels*. Cambridge: Cambridge University Press, 2006.

Blomberg, Craig L. *Jesus and the Gospels: An Introduction and Survey*. Nashville: Broadman & Holman Academic, 1997.

Burridge, Richard A. *What Are the Gospels? A Comparison with Graeco-Roman Biography*. Cambridge: Cambridge University Press, 1992.

Cousar, Charles B. *An Introduction to the New Testament: Witnesses to God's New Work*. Louisville, KY: Westminster John Knox Press, 2006.

Ehrman, Bart D. *A Brief Introduction to the New Testament*. Oxford: Oxford University Press, 2008.

Griffith-Jones, Robin. *The Four Witnesses: The Rebel, the Rabbi, the Chronicler, and the Mystic*. New York: HarperOne, 2004.

Nickle, Keith F. *The Synoptic Gospels: An Introduction*. Louisville, KY: Westminster John Knox Press, 2001.

Stanton, Graham N. *The Gospels and Jesus*. 2d ed. Oxford: Oxford University Press, 2002.

2

Four Narratives, One Story

A frequently invoked analogy to the Fourfold Gospel is that of four different pictures or portraits of the same individual.[1] Richard Burridge uses the illustration of four selected pictures of Winston Churchill, hanging on the walls of Chartwell, Churchill's country home.[2] One picture shows Churchill in conference with President Roosevelt; another, a painting by Churchill himself, shows him at family tea; a third presents him in military uniform, giving his characteristic wartime "V for victory" salute; in a fourth, he is on holiday and relaxing with his painting. Each picture brings out a different aspect of his life and persona: the statesman, the family man, the man of war, and the quiet artist. Each presents a different image, yet all are recognizably portraits of the same man. In a similar way, Burridge suggests, the Gospels present different images of the one Jesus Christ. These differing images, Burridge warns, must not be harmonized into one single snapshot.

The picture analogy is helpful for the purpose of explaining the commonality and individuality of the Gospels, and it does justice to the fact that the Gospels are narratives sharply focused on one individual. Yet, the comparison is drawn from the realm of portraiture, and the Gospels are narrative texts, not paintings or photographs. Another way of thinking about the unity and individualism of the Gospels draws on a distinction made by narrative theorists (which is also used in film studies) and views the Gospels as four

1. See, e.g., William Temple, *Readings in Saint John's Gospel*, First Series, *Chapters I–XII* (London: Macmillan, 1940), xvi; Richard A. Burridge, *Four Gospels, One Jesus?* (London: SPCK, 1994), 1–2; Mark L. Strauss, *Four Portraits, One Jesus: An Introduction to Jesus and the Gospels* (Grand Rapids: Zondervan, 2007), 24.
2. Burridge, *Four Gospels*, 1–2.

"narrative" versions of a single "story."[3] This story/narrative distinction has the advantage of providing a framework for exploring and analyzing the Gospels' commonality and individuality, both at the whole-text level and across parallel narrative passages.

NARRATIVE CRITICISM IN THE STUDY OF THE GOSPELS

The application of narrative theory to the Gospels is a relatively recent but now well-established development in New Testament studies.[4] "Narrative criticism," as it is has come to be known, arose partly as a corrective to the tendency of historical criticism to concentrate on the process of formation rather than the Gospel texts in their finished form. Whereas form and source criticism focus on individual units of tradition and separate literary sources underlying a Gospel, and redaction criticism is interested in the points in the text where the evangelist's editorial activity is most apparent, narrative criticism deals with the Gospels as whole texts.

A narrative-critical approach to the Gospel involves the utilization of categories borrowed from the study of modern novels. Narrative readings of the Gospels thus give attention to narrative voice, narrative viewpoint, plot, and so forth. This is not to treat the Gospels as works of fiction, since "narrative" embraces both fictional and fact-based narratives. The Gospels are responsive to this kind of study because they are a form of narrative (ancient biography). Certain adjustments have to be made in view of the fact that the Gospels are ancient texts, not modern ones, but the basic categories of analysis apply.

Critics of the methodology object that the interpretation of the Gospels in narrative terms divorces the Gospels from their historical authors and the historical contexts within which the texts emerged. It is true that some narrative critics apply the methodology ahistorically, focusing on the text and its impact on present-day readers rather than on the author and his intentions, and on the inner "world" of the text rather than the context out of which it arose. However, it is possible to take a narrative approach to the Gospels while retaining a robust view of the texts as authored, seeing their "narrative artistry" as deriving from the evangelists themselves as narrative artists (without necessarily attributing every narrative feature of their texts to authorial intention), and maintaining a keen interest in the historical realities and processes behind the texts. Narrative criticism is not, therefore, in conflict

---

3. Ibid., 166.
4. An important pioneering study is by David Rhoads and Donald Michie, *Mark as Story: An Introduction to the Narrative of a Gospel* (Philadelphia: Fortress Press, 1982).

with historical criticism. Narrative analysis can complement historical-critical approaches and traditional exegesis.

STORY AND NARRATIVE

Fundamental to narratology is a distinction between *what* is narrated and *how* it is narrated.[5] The former is designated "story"; there is variation among narratologists in the name given to the latter,[6] but for the sake of convenience we will call it "narrative."[7] Story encompasses the basic, unadulterated elements of a tale, while narrative is the presentation and elaboration of these elements in a given text. Story is the raw material; narrative is the creative working on it to produce the manufactured article: the narrative text.[8]

Story exists only at the theoretical level. What readers actually encounter is the narrative expression of the story in the form of a text (which need not be a literary text, but a film, a play, etc.). The underlying story is reconstructed or, perhaps better, "constructed" from a narrative text by analytical means.

The distinction between story and narrative implies that a given story might be narrated in countless ways, and that each telling would be different from the others.[9] Any narrative of the life of Julius Caesar (drawing on the ancient sources available) would recount the same essential story, describing his rise through the political ranks, his governorship of Spain, his conquest of Gaul, his crossing the Rubicon thus launching the civil war, his defeat of Pompey at Pharsalus, his dictatorship and political reforms, and the conspiracy against him led by Cassius and Brutus, resulting in his murder by stabbing in the senate house in 44 BCE. Narrative presentations of Caesar's life, though, could take many different forms. The order could be manipulated in numerous ways. One version might proceed chronologically through Caesar's life; another might begin with his fatal stabbing and tell the story of his life in retrospect; a different account might pass over his earlier life relatively quickly and concentrate on his role in the civil war and his reign as dictator. The basic story could be embellished in a myriad of ways and inflated by the inclusion of other incidents, whether real or fictitious. Different aspects of

5. Seymour B. Chatman, *Story and Discourse: Narrative Structure in Fiction and Film* (Ithaca, NY, and London: Cornell University Press, 1978), 19. The Russian formalists used the terms *fabula* and *sjuzhet* (or *zyughet*) to express the distinction.

6. Chatman calls it "discourse" (ibid.).

7. Following, e.g., Joel B. Green, "Hermeneutical Approaches to the New Testament Tradition," in *Eerdmans Commentary on the Bible*, ed. James D. G. Dunn and John W. Rogerson (Grand Rapids and Cambridge: Wm. B. Eerdmans Publishing Co., 2003), 972–88, here 979–81.

8. Michael J. Toolan, *Narrative: A Critical Linguistic Introduction* (London: Routledge, 1988), 10.

9. Cf. Green, "Hermeneutical Approaches," 979–80.

Caesar might come to the fore: Caesar the solider and general, Caesar the politician, Caesar the private man. And different evaluations could be made of his character and actions.

The idea that the same story can be told in different ways has been exploited in literature and cinema. The most famous cinematic use of the so-called multiple-narrative technique is the 1950 Japanese film *Rashomon*, directed by Akira Kurosawa. The film is about the murder of a samurai and the violation of his wife. The story is told by four witnesses: a woodcutter, a bandit, the murdered samurai (through a medium), and his wife. Each witness relates a different version of events. A more recent movie that employs the device is *Vantage Point*. An example of the multiple-narrative technique in contemporary literature is Iain Pears's 1998 novel *An Instance of the Fingerpost*, a murder mystery set in Oxford in the 1660s. The story is narrated four times by four different characters, two of whom are fictionalized historical personages (the mathematician John Wallis and the historian Anthony Wood). Each narrator gives his own account or perception of what happened. They all relate the core events of the story, but each one has a distinct angle of telling, and each interprets, embellishes, and elaborates on the central chain of occurrences in different ways.

The Fourfold Gospel is not a deliberately planned multiple narrative like these examples. The four Gospels were written by different individuals, none of whom realized at the time of writing that he would be contributing to a four-Gospel collection. But the four Gospels in their canonical form nonetheless exhibit the phenomenon of one basic story multiply rendered. Indeed, the Fourfold Gospel is arguably the best example of this phenomenon in literature.

THE ELEMENTS OF STORY

There is more to be said about the difference between story and narrative. Stories, analyzed within narratology, have three main elements: events, characters, and setting.[10]

Events: The things that happen. The events that make up a story may be fictional or nonfictional or a combination of both. Narratologists sometimes distinguish between two types of events: "actions," which characters make happen; and "happenings," which take place without the intervention of characters (e.g., a tree falls in a storm).[11] The events of a story must be connected

---

10. Toolan, *Narrative*, 12. For Chatman (*Story and Discourse*, 19), stories consist of two main elements, events and existents, but he subdivides the latter into characters and settings.

11. Chatman, *Story and Discourse*, 19.

in a nonrandom way.[12] A succession of occurrences does not in itself make a story: relationships between the events must be identifiable.

Characters: The participants in the series of events. Characters tend to fulfill certain stereotypical roles, such as hero (or protagonist) and opponent (or antagonist). The hero is the central character around whom the events of the story revolve. The opponent is the hero's principal adversary. Characters are usually individuals, but they can also be collective entities (clan, tribe, mob, and so forth).

Setting: The when *and* where *of a story.* The "when" is the "temporal" setting; the "where" is the "spatial" setting. Story settings in time and space can be quite vague or entirely imaginary, as in fairy tales and fantasies, or highly specific and real, as in historical narrative and historical fiction. A story can also be loosely connected to the setting given to it, to the extent that dates and places could change and the story would be largely unaffected.

In addition to these three main components, stories can also be said to exhibit a *basic structure*: in terms first articulated by Aristotle (*Poetics* 7.3), a story has a beginning, middle, and end. Many narratologists see this structural pattern as belonging to "plot" (see below) rather than story, but the "natural" beginning, middle, and end of a story can often be manipulated in the course of emplotment. It is appropriate, therefore, to distinguish between the natural or logical progression of the events of a story from start to finish, and the order in which events may unfold in narration.

ASPECTS OF NARRATIVE

As stated above, narrative is the creative working on the story elements to make a narrative text. Narratologists delineate various aspects of narrative, of which the following might be regarded as especially important:[13]

Narrative voice and viewpoint relate to the narrator and the viewing position assumed by the narrator.[14] "Narrative voice" refers to whether the narrator uses first or third person. The "viewpoint" refers to whether the narrator's telling of the story is limited or omniscient.

The narrator (distinguishable from the author) may be a character in the story, speaking in the first person. For example, in J. D. Salinger's *The Catcher*

---

12. Toolan, *Narrative*, 7.

13. The list that follows in the main text is adopted and adapted from various sources, including Ian Boxall, *New Testament Interpretation* (Norwich: SCM Press, 2007), 115–18; Green, "Hermeneutical Approaches," 980–81; Roads and Michie, *Mark as Story*, passim; Strauss, *Four Portraits*, 69–78.

14. Rhoads and Michie, *Mark as Story*, 35.

in the Rye, the story is narrated by Holden Caulfield, a teenage boy who has just been expelled from school. The author writes in the guise of a troubled teenager, using his diction and conveying his moods, feelings, and attitudes. Alternatively, the narrator may be outside the story, writing in the third person. Third-person narration is the most common narrative mode.

The narrator may adopt an omniscient or limited viewpoint.[15] An omniscient narrator has access to all characters' thoughts, feelings, and motives. A limited narrator operates within the constraints of the perceptions and knowledge of a single character (usually, but not always, the hero) or a few characters, or writes without any insight into any character's inner being. First-person narrators are usually limited in their viewpoint. The first-person, limited viewpoint is often used in detective novels (such as the Philip Marlowe mysteries) so that readers, along with the narrator, discover the culprit's identity. Sometimes (but more rarely), first-person narrators can be omniscient, as in the case of Mary Alice Young, the narrator in the TV series *Desperate Housewives*.

Third-person narrators can be limited or omniscient. The third-person, omniscient perspective is the most frequently used narrative viewpoint. It carries the greatest sense of authority and reliability.

Textual structure refers to how the narrative text is organized and divided up. Narratives in the form of full-length books are usually formally divided into chapters. Literary narratives can also be structured in other ways, such as a series of letters (the "epistolary novel," of which C. S. Lewis's *The Screwtape Letters* is a good example) or diary entries.

Plot is the way in which the events that make up the story are presented and connected. At the level of story, events take place in a chronological sequence, but at the level of plot, events may be presented out of their natural order. In Homer's *Odyssey*, the plot begins toward the conclusion of the total sequence of events; preceding events are narrated via flashback (see below). The film *Citizen Kane* begins with the death of the main character. The story unfolds through interviews and flashbacks as a newspaper journalist tries to resolve the mystery of Kane's decease.[16]

A distinction is sometimes drawn between tightly plotted narratives, such as detective novels, in which the main events are causally connected, and episodic narratives, such as Chaucer's *The Canterbury Tales*, in which the plot is more or less a series of loosely connected episodes.[17] The stages in the development of a plot often relate to the divisions of the narrative text.

Style means the way in which the narrative is written. In analyzing style, attention is paid to grammatical and syntactical preferences, the range of

15. Ibid., 35–36.
16. Robert Kernan, *Building Better Plots* (Cincinnati: Writers Digest Books, 1999), 198.
17. On episodic plots, see ibid., 196–97.

vocabulary employed, frequently occurring words and phrases, the expressive manner (laconic, verbose), and so forth.

Narrative technique refers to the literary and rhetorical devices employed in the narration of the plot. Some commonly used devices may be highlighted.

- *Flashback* is a switch back in time to reveal an event that happened earlier.
- *Flash-forward* is a shift forward in time to a scene that takes place later in the chronological sequence.
- *Foreshadowing* is an anticipation of something that happens later.
- *Inclusio*, or framing, is the use of the same scene or narrative element at the beginning and end of a narrative (a device often used in films; *Chariots of Fire*, for example, begins and ends with the main characters running along a beach).
- *Intercalation* means inserting one story into another (as in Homer's *Odyssey*).
- *Irony* involves some level of mismatch between appearance and reality, or between expectation and actuality. Three types of literary irony are often distinguished:[18] In (1) *verbal irony* a character says one thing but means the opposite. In (2) *dramatic irony* a character is wholly or partially ignorant about something integral to the story that is known by readers or viewers (as in the movie *Toy Story* when Buzz Lightyear does not realize that he is a toy; or in the movie *The Truman Show* where everyone knows that Truman is the star of a reality TV show except Truman himself). In (3) *situational irony* there is a discrepancy between intention and result.
- *Intertextuality* (a term coined by Julia Kristeva)[19] involves referencing other texts. References to other or earlier texts can be direct, as when a literary work is explicitly mentioned or cited by a character; or indirect, as when an event or scene recalls an antecedent in an earlier work (via allusion). As well as being an aspect of narrative, intertextuality can exist at the story level: for example, when the raw story narrated is deliberately based on an older story (as in the case of the movie *O Brother, Where Art Thou?* set in the American South during the 1930s; the film loosely parallels Homer's *Odyssey*).

Narrative time means the way in which story time is handled at the narrative level. Thus narrative time embraces temporal movement within the narrative (whether strictly linear, or shifting back and forth along the story time line as, for example, in the movie *I Am Legend*), the explicit marking of time, and the duration of one event in relation to another in the course of narration. An event or episode can be narrated at some length or relayed in a sentence or two. Narrative time is seldom constant. Some narratives (especially crime

18. Rhoads and Michie, *Mark as Story*, 59–60; Roger Fowler (ed.), *A Dictionary of Modern Critical Terms*, rev. ed. (London: Routledge & Kegan Paul, 1987), 128–29; en.wikipedia.org/wiki/Irony.

19. Julia Kristeva, *Desire in Language: A Semiotic Approach to Literature and Art* (New York: Columbia University Press, 1980), 15.

thrillers) begin slowly and progressively "speed up." Some narratives try to replicate "real time" (e.g., the movie Western *High Noon*; the TV series *24*).

Narrative space refers to the way in which spatiality is manifested and handled. Analyzing narrative space goes beyond the mere identification of settings. It considers patterns of movement within the narrative.[20] Many stories involve the hero's undertaking of a journey, as in Homer's *Odyssey* and in Tolkien's *The Lord of the Rings* (Frodo's journey to Mordor). The journey motif is intrinsic to "road movies." In Steven Saylor's book *Roma*, there is spatial progression through time (1,000 years), as Rome develops from pastoral site to world-city. In examining narrative space, attention is also given to prominent or frequently occurring settings in a narrative and to the evaluation of spaces (neutral, bad, dangerous, paradisiacal, etc.).

Characterization is accomplished by how characters are portrayed in the narrative.[21] Character traits emerge through the descriptive comments of the narrator, through their assessment by other (reliable) characters in the narratives, and by their actions and interactions. Narratologists make a distinction between "round" characters, who are complex and who change and develop in the course of the narrative, and "flat" characters, who have fewer traits and who are more consistent.[22]

Themes are issues and ideas presented or dealt with in the narrative. Ideas typically explored in narratives include love, loyalty, honor, wealth, poverty, and personal transformation.

THE SHARED STORY IN THE FOUR GOSPELS

Using the elements of story listed above, we can identify a core story embodied in all four Gospels. There is a common series of *events*: the appearance and ministry of John the Baptist, the descent of the Spirit upon Jesus, the call of the first disciples, and so forth. These events are actions; they do not just happen.

There are common *characters*: Jesus; John the Baptist; the twelve disciples, of whom Peter and Judas stand out; Jesus' mother; Mary Magdalene; and others. Jesus is the hero: the whole story revolves around him. The Jewish religious authorities collectively occupy the role of opponent (all four Gospels also show demonic, as well as human, opposition to Jesus).

There is a common spatiotemporal *setting*: first-century Palestine. Actions mainly take place in the regions of Galilee and Judea. Specific locations mentioned in all four Gospels include Nazareth, the river Jordan, the Sea of (or

20. Rhoads and Michie, *Mark as Story*, 68–72.
21. Ibid., 101–3.
22. Ibid., 102–3.

Lake) Galilee, Capernaum, and Jerusalem. The setting reflects the political situation in Palestine after the death of Herod the Great, with Roman rule in Judea being exercised through governors. Jesus is tried and condemned to death by Pontius Pilate, who was governor of Judea from 26/27 to 36/37. Jesus' execution takes place on the day before the Sabbath, and the empty tomb is discovered on the first day of the week.

The common story shows a *basic structure* of beginning, middle, and end. Indeed, the story exhibits the classic three-act structure,[23] still commonly used in drama and in films. The first act introduces the hero and contains the inciting incident, which calls the hero to action or sets the hero on the journey.[24] The second act is marked by rising action as the hero deals with the confronting forces of opposition. A crisis point is reached at the end of this act, a point of no return. The third act contains the climax, the dramatic high point of the story, the event or sequence of events to which the whole story has been leading. The shared story of the four Gospels may be summarized as follows:

Beginning: John the Baptist and Jesus

John the Baptist appears as "a voice of one crying out in the wilderness," in fulfillment of Isaiah's prophecy. His role is that of forerunner, and he proclaims the coming of the Messiah. Jesus makes his public debut in the context of John's ministry. The descent of the Spirit on him, inaugurating his ministry, is the inciting incident that sets Jesus on the course of his mission.

Middle: The Ministry of Jesus

Jesus calls and gathers a close circle of followers: twelve men, whom he nurtures and instructs so that they participate in his public ministry. He preaches to the crowds and performs miraculous deeds, curing people of their infirmities, resuscitating the dead, and manipulating nature (by multiplying loaves and fishes in order to feed five thousand). The people wonder about his identity; the disciples know that he is the Messiah. He achieves fame but also provokes opposition from the Jewish religious leaders, who accuse him of serious religious error. For example, he appears to disregard the Sabbath command by healing on the Sabbath. Jesus in turn is critical of the religious leaders. The mounting conflict reaches its peak in the conspiracy to have Jesus arrested and executed.

23. Kernen, *Building Better Plots*, 14–27.
24. Ibid., 38–45.

Climax: Jerusalem, Passion, and Resurrection

Jesus enters Jerusalem in a manner imbued with kingly and probably messianic symbolism. He has a final meal with his disciples, at which he announces that he will be betrayed. Peter protests his loyalty, but Jesus prophesies that Peter will deny him. Jesus is betrayed by Judas, arrested, and hauled before the Jerusalem authorities. Just as predicted, Peter denies him three times. Jesus is brought before Pilate, the Roman governor, who knows that Jesus is innocent and tries to release him. Eventually Pilate condemns him to crucifixion. Jesus is mocked and crucified as a would-be king of the Jews. He dies on the cross and is quickly buried. On the first day of the week, however, his tomb is discovered empty. Jesus is no longer dead but has risen.

Each Gospel, of course, has its own raw story—with events, characters, and settings—which is much larger than what we have just described. Each of these larger stories differs from and overlaps with the others to varying degrees (Mark and Matthew overlap substantially). But this is the basic story that they are unified in telling.

The shared story is an abstraction from the four canonical Gospels (and carries no canonical authority), but it seems to bear some relation to early Christian preaching.[25] The evangelistic message of the early church centered on the death and resurrection of Jesus Christ. Paul's summary of the "gospel" in 1 Corinthians 15:1–11 makes this clear: the message he passed on to the Corinthians and which they received involved the truths that Christ died, was buried, was raised on the third day, in accord with the Scriptures, and that he was seen alive. But as Stanton has argued, the missionary proclamation of Christ's death and resurrection must also have included a sketch of the life of Jesus; the preaching of "Christ crucified" (1 Cor. 1:23) would hardly have made sense without it, especially in a Gentile context.[26]

In Acts 10:36–43, Peter's evangelistic message to the Gentile Cornelius and the company he has gathered together is summarized as follows:

> You know the message he sent to the people of Israel. . . . That message spread throughout Judea, beginning in Galilee after the baptism that John announced: how God anointed Jesus of Nazareth with the Holy Spirit and with power; how he went about doing good and healing all who were oppressed by the devil, for God was with him. We are witnesses to all that he did both in Judea and in Jerusalem. They put him

25. Larry Hurtado (*Lord Jesus Christ: Devotion to Jesus in Earliest Christianity* [Grand Rapids: Wm. B. Eerdmans Publishing Co., 2003], 270) contends that "the canonical Gospels are heavily conditioned and shaped by the basic pattern of proclamation that characterized known Christian circles from the earliest decades of the young religious movement. . . ."

26. Graham N. Stanton, *Jesus and Gospel* (Cambridge: Cambridge University Press, 2004), 53.

to death by hanging him on a tree; but God raised him on the third
day and allowed him to appear, not to all the people but to us who were
chosen by God as witnesses, and who ate and drank with him after he
rose from the dead. He commanded us to preach to the people and to
testify that he is the one ordained by God as judge of the living and the
dead. All the prophets testify about him that everyone who believes in
him receives forgiveness of sins through his name.

This is the fullest summary of the gospel given in the book of Acts. The
extent to which the summary corresponds to the shared story of the canonical
Gospels is striking. The gospel story begins with John's baptism and Jesus'
anointing by the Spirit (i.e., the Spirit's descent upon him, initiating his mission), moves to his ministry of "doing good and healing," which is the middle
section of the story, and concludes with the death-resurrection complex. The
words, "beginning in Galilee," to be sure, fit the Synoptic outline better than
John. Also, certain details, such as the interpretation of Jesus' baptism as his
"anointing," and the theme of eating and drinking with the risen Jesus, reflect
Lukan emphases, though the latter is also found in John's Gospel. But the core
story of all the canonical Gospels is more or less articulated here. C. H. Dodd
famously argued that Acts 10:36–43 reflects the common pattern of preaching in the early church.[27] We cannot be certain of this (Acts itself implies that
preaching patterns were varied), but the summary does appear to be "traditional" and may at least reflect one influential strand of proclamation.

SHARED NARRATIVE FEATURES

Using the categories of narrative analysis, we can see how the same story
recounted in all four Gospels is developed and presented in different ways. In
the next four chapters, we will look at the individual narrative renditions of
the shared story. It is important, though, to recognize that the Gospels also
exhibit shared narrative characteristics.[28]

Narrative voice and viewpoint. All four Gospels are written in third-person
narrative mode. The narrator is outside the events of the story. This applies
even to John's Gospel, despite the revelation regarding the beloved disciple
at the end (21:24). Even if the narrator is now identifying himself with the
beloved disciple (as we saw in chap. 1, this is not certain), right up to this point
he has assumed the viewing position of an external storyteller, referring to
the beloved disciple in the third person. In all four Gospels the third-person

27. C. H. Dodd, "The Framework of the Gospel Narrative," *Expository Times* 43 (1932):
396–400.
28. Compare Strauss, *Four Portraits*, 69–78.

narrator is to an extent omniscient, with a level of access into the conscious-
ness of characters, including the main character Jesus. The third-person
omniscient perspective, as noted above, evokes reliability and authority.

Textual structure. In all four Gospels, textual structure is indicated by discourse or textual markers rather than by formal divisions in the text. The
chapter-and-verse divisions of the Gospels, and the Bible as a whole, were
added later and do not necessarily reflect structuring patterns within a text.

Plot. In all four Gospels, the story unfolds in a broadly linear fashion. The
ministry of Jesus is described episodically. Jesus is almost always the link
between the various incidents. The account of the passion, though, is more
tightly plotted and is a continuous and consecutive narrative.

Style. All four Gospels are written in Koine (*koinē*, common) Greek, the
popular form of ancient Greek used throughout the Mediterranean world.
They also betray "Semitic" influence (the influence of Hebrew, Aramaic, or
the LXX). The four display a certain degree of lexical overlap, as might be
expected, given their common subject matter. The Synoptic Gospels certainly
exhibit extensive verbal agreement. All four evangelists generally write with
an economy of words. The crucifixion of Jesus is narrated in a remarkably
restrained manner, without lurid detail.

Narrative technique. In all four Gospels, Jesus' death is foreshadowed by
an earlier attempt or plot to kill him (by Herod in Matthew; by the Pharisees
and Herodians in Mark; by the lynch-mob in Nazareth in Luke; by the Jewish
leaders in Jerusalem in John). In all four Gospels, there is verbal irony in the
inscription "King of the Jews." There is dramatic irony, too, in the mockery
and crucifixion of Jesus as a would-be king. His opponents do not realize, but
readers know, that Jesus is indeed the true messianic king. All four evangelists
extensively reference earlier texts (thus exemplifying intertextuality) in the
form of the Jewish Scriptures. For example, all four Gospel writers cite Isaiah
40:3 in connection with the ministry of John the Baptist (Matt. 3:3; Mark 1:3;
Luke 3:4; John 1:23). Old Testament passages, themes, events, and figures are
used to convey the significance of Jesus' actions, words, and person. Through
the constant referencing of the Old Testament, the shared story is shown to
stand in continuity with Israel's history.

Narrative time. In all four Gospels, time generally travels in a forward-
moving direction. In all four, time slows down considerably after the triumphal entry into Jerusalem.

Narrative space. In the four Gospels, Jerusalem is the final destination of
Jesus' movements (a journey in the Synoptics; to and fro between Galilee and
Jerusalem in John). In all four, the holy city is threatening and dangerous space.

Characterization. In all four Gospels, Jesus is a round character insofar as
he has a range of traits and qualities, but relatively static insofar as he does not

really develop or change. Yet his "character" is progressively revealed in the course of the narrative. In the four Gospels, crucial to the characterization of Jesus is his identification. The identity of Jesus is revealed especially in the titles applied to him. The four evangelists agree in the most significant titles used for Jesus: "Christ," or "Messiah"; "Son of God"; "Lord"; and "Son of Man."[29]

The twelve disciples are portrayed with conflicting traits; in this respect they are more rounded than Jesus. The religious authorities are relatively one-dimensional, though Luke's portrait of the Pharisees (see chap. 5) is more nuanced.

Themes. In all four Gospels are similar subsidiary themes: discipleship, love, eschatology (i.e., the last things), and so forth. In all four, Jesus speaks about God's kingdom. In the Synoptic Gospels, the kingdom of God is the central theme of Jesus' preaching; in John's Gospel, it is a marginal interest.

CONCLUSION

The narratological distinction between story and narrative offers a neat approach to the unity and individuality of the four Gospels. We can find a core unity in the central story that the four Gospels share and individuality in the differing narrative renderings of it. This is not to say that unity across the four Gospels is *only* to be found in the shared story; as we have just seen, among the Gospels is a significant amount of unity at the narrative level. Unity at the level of narrative is even more pronounced in the Synoptic Gospels. The common story can nevertheless be taken as a fixed point of orientation for reading the Gospels in terms of their unity, and the categories of narrative analysis are extremely convenient for bringing out the individuality and traits of each Gospel.[30]

Having set out the shared story, then, we now look in turn at each of the four renditions of it.

FOR FURTHER READING

Narratology

Bal, Mieke. *Narratology: Introduction to the Theory of Narrative.* Toronto: University of Toronto Press, 1985. 3rd ed., 2009.

29. On the background to these and other christological titles, see the helpful and accessible treatment in Christopher M. Tuckett, *Christology and the New Testament: Jesus and His Earliest Followers* (Edinburgh: Edinburgh University Press, 2000), 1–37.

30. This has already been demonstrated by Burridge (*Four Gospels*) and especially by Strauss (*Four Portraits*, 171–343).

Burridge, Richard A. *Four Gospels, One Jesus?* London: SPCK, 1994.

Chatman, Seymour B. *Story and Discourse: Narrative Structure in Fiction and Film.* Ithaca, NY, and London: Cornell University Press, 1978.

Toolan, Michael J. *Narrative: A Critical Linguistic Introduction.* London: Routledge, 1988.

Narrative Approaches to the Gospels

Burridge, Richard A. *Four Gospels, One Jesus?* 2nd ed. London: SPCK, 2005.

Carter, Warren. *John: Storyteller, Interpreter, Evangelist.* Peabody, MA: Hendrickson Publishers, 2006.

———. *Matthew: Storyteller, Interpreter, Evangelist.* Peabody, MA: Hendrickson Publishers, 2004.

Culpepper, R. Alan. *Anatomy of the Fourth Gospel: A Study in Literary Design.* Philadelphia: Fortress Press, 1983.

Rhoads, David, and Donald Michie. *Mark as Story: An Introduction to the Narrative of a Gospel.* Philadelphia: Fortress Press, 1982.

Smith, Stephen H. *A Lion with Wings: A Narrative-Critical Approach to Mark's Gospel.* Sheffield: Sheffield Academic, 1996.

Stibbe, Mark W. G. *John as Storyteller: Narrative Criticism and the Fourth Gospel.* Cambridge: Cambridge University Press, 1994.

Strauss, Mark L. *Four Portraits, One Jesus: An Introduction to Jesus and the Gospels.* Grand Rapids: Zondervan, 2007.

Tannehill, Robert C. *The Narrative Unity of Luke–Acts: A Literary Interpretation.* Vol. 1, *The Gospel according to Luke.* Philadelphia: Fortress Press, 1986.

PART II

The Individual Gospels
and Their Narrative Features

The four Gospels tell the same story, but each one bears its own distinct narrative stamp. In this section we look at the narrative aspects of each individual Gospel: structure, plot, style, narrative time, narrative space, characterization, and themes. With regard to characterization, we focus naturally on Jesus, the biographical subject and the hero of the shared story. In discussing the characterization of Jesus, we deal first with the titles used of him (esp. "Messiah," "Son of God," "Lord," and "Son of Man"), and then we look at particular emphases in the way he is presented. We also consider how the disciples and the religious authorities are characterized.

The aim of this section is twofold: (1) to give an overall account of each Gospel and its contents, as befitting a guidebook; and (2) to draw attention to the more individuating aspects of each Gospel narrative, in line with the particular burden of this guidebook. We begin with the Gospel of Mark, which is generally taken to be the earliest of the four Gospels.

3

The Gospel according to Mark

Of the four New Testament Gospels, Mark is the one that most obviously manifests the shared story we have identified. It is also the Gospel that most closely corresponds to the outline of the gospel message given in Acts 10:36–43:[1] Mark's Gospel begins with "the baptism that John announced," to which Jesus submitted (cf. Mark 1:1–11); it then describes Jesus' ministry in Galilee, "how he went about doing good and healing" (from 1:14); it moves with Jesus to Judea (10:1) and Jerusalem (from 11:1) and ends with his death and resurrection (chaps. 14–16). Yet the evangelist has taken what was probably a familiar summary of Jesus' life and ministry used in early Christian preaching and shaped it into his own distinctive biographical narrative.

Like the other evangelists, Mark's characterization of Jesus underscores his identity as Messiah, Son of God, Lord, and Son of Man. Of these titles, "Son of God" carries for Mark the highest christological significance. In the first half of the Gospel, Jesus is portrayed as a dynamic wonder-worker, with godlike abilities. In the second half, he cuts a more subdued figure, and Jesus' suffering is emphasized. Mark shows that Jesus' style of messiahship does not conform to traditional expectation; Jesus' role as the Messiah is shaped to a large extent by his role as suffering Son of Man.

---

1. As observed by C. H. Dodd, "The Framework of the Gospel Narrative," *Expository Times* 43 (1932): 396–400.

TEXTUAL STRUCTURE

Peter's confession at Caesarea Philippi (8:27–30), located almost precisely at midpoint in the Gospel, is regarded by many scholars as the pivot on which Mark's narrative turns. To Jesus' question, addressed to his disciples, "Who do you say that I am?" Peter replies, "You are the Messiah." After Peter's christological affirmation and for the first time in the Gospel, Jesus speaks of his coming suffering and death. From this point onward, events move in the direction of the cross.

Taking Peter's confession and the first passion prediction as a narrative divider, the Gospel falls neatly into two halves. The first half tells of Jesus' Galilean ministry and gives particular attention to his mighty works. In the second half, the narrative proceeds from Galilee to Jerusalem, and the emphasis falls on Jesus' suffering. The saying of Jesus in 10:45 seems to encapsulate the bipartite design of the Gospel:

> For the Son of Man came
> > not to be served but to serve, (1:16–8:30)
> > and to give his life a ransom for many. (8:31–15:47)

Within the first half, many scholars see narrative transitions at 3:7 and 6:6b; at both points we are given a summary of Jesus' activity (3:7–12; 6:6b). In each case, the immediately preceding pericope is a story of rejection (by the Pharisees, 3:1–6; by Jesus' own townspeople, 6:1–6a), and what follows is a story about the disciples (the appointment of the Twelve, 3:13–19a; the sending out of the Twelve, 6:7–13). In the second half of the narrative, the transitions are easier to spot. There is a clear transition at 11:1, with the narration of Jesus' arrival at Jerusalem. The section included between 8:31 and 10:52 forms a coherent structure around the three passion predictions of 8:31; 9:31; and 10:32–34. At 14:1, Mark begins his account of the passion. The death of Jesus, eliciting the definitive christological confession of the Gospel, constitutes the climax of the narrative. The story of the empty tomb functions for Mark as an epilogue. The structure of Mark's Gospel can thus be understood as follows:[2]

1:1–15	Prologue
1:16–8:30	Ministry in Galilee (in three sections: 1:16–3:6; 3:7–6:6a; 6:6b–8:30)
8:31–15:47	From Galilee to Jerusalem, and the Passion (in three sections: 8:31–10:52; 11:1–13:37; 14:1–15:47)
16:1–8	Epilogue

2. Adapting Craig L. Blomberg, *Jesus and the Gospels: An Introduction and Survey* (Leicester: Apollos, 1997), 116–17.

PLOT

The development of Mark's plot aligns with the structure of his narrative text.

Prologue (1:1–15)

After the introductory statement (1:1), announcing "the beginning of the good news of Jesus Christ," a quotation (1:2–3) combines Isaiah 40:3 and Malachi 3:1. The citation introduces the figure of John the Baptist, who is a voice in the wilderness, the messenger sent to "prepare the way of the Lord." The coming, baptism, and preaching of John are narrated (1:4–8). Then Jesus makes his first appearance in the Gospel: he freely submits himself to John's baptism. The baptismal episode, in which Jesus is identified as God's Son, is immediately followed by the temptation in the wilderness, which Mark describes only briefly (1:12–13). Jesus emerges from the wilderness and his skirmish with Satan to proclaim "the good news of God," announcing that "the time is fulfilled, and the kingdom of God has come near" (1:14–15).

Ministry in Galilee (1:16–8:26)

Following the summary statement of Jesus' proclamation, Mark narrates the calling of the first disciples (1:16–20). Jesus calls Simon, Andrew, James, and John, who stop what they are doing and follow him (1:16–20). In Capernaum, Jesus preaches and conducts an exorcism in the synagogue (1:21–28), heals Simon Peter's mother-in-law (1:29–31), and cures many others in the town (1:32–34). From Capernaum, Jesus' ministry progresses to other towns in Galilee (1:35–39). The story of the cleansing of a leper (1:40–45) underlines the growing fame of Jesus (cf. 1:28, 37). Such is his success and expanding reputation that from this point onward, he can "no longer go into a town openly" (1:45). But conflict soon emerges. Mark narrates five stories that involve controversy with the Jewish religious leaders: the healing of a paralyzed man (2:1–12), Jesus' meal with tax collectors and sinners in Levi's house (2:15–17), the dispute about the disciples' failure to fast (2:18–22), the controversy aroused by the disciples' plucking grain on the Sabbath (2:23–28), the Sabbath-day healing of a man with a withered hand (3:1–6). The series of conflicts reaches its climax in the resolution of the Pharisees and the Herodians to destroy Jesus (3:6), anticipating the plot to kill Jesus, of which we read in 14:1–2.

The mention of Jesus' opponents' intent to kill him marks a minor peak in the narrative (foreshadowing what will happen later). Mark next gives a summary of Jesus' activity (3:7–12) and reports the appointment of the twelve disciples

(3:13–19). There follow two intertwined stories of opposition: Jesus' own family tries to restrain him, and certain scribes from Jerusalem accuse him of being in league with Beelzebul (3:20–35). Mark has twice noted that people were amazed at Jesus' teaching ability and the authority with which he spoke (1:21, 27); we are now given a sampling of the content of Jesus' teaching. Recorded are three parables: the Sower (4:1–20), the Seed Growing Secretly (4:26–29), and the Mustard Seed (4:30–32). Jesus explains privately to the Twelve that while they have been given "the secret of the kingdom of God," to "those outside" he speaks in parables (4:11–12). Mark then narrates four dramatic miracles (the stilling of the storm, 4:35–41; the healing of the Gerasene demoniac, 5:1–20; the raising of Jairus's daughter and the healing of the woman with a hemorrhage, 5:21–43) before telling of Jesus' rejection at Nazareth, his hometown (6:1–6a), which seems to constitute another peak point in the narrative.

A flashback report of John the Baptist's execution by Herod (6:17–29) separates the sending out of the Twelve and their return (6:7–13, 30–31). Following the feeding of the five thousand (6:30–45), the walking on the water (6:46–52), and an epitome of Jesus' activity (6:53–56), Mark gives an extended account of a purity dispute between Jesus and some Pharisees and scribes (7:1–23). One incident involving purity is followed by another. The exorcism of the daughter of the Syro-Phoenician woman (7:24–30) shows Jesus' agreeing to help a Gentile woman. The next story, the healing of the deaf-mute (7:31–37), continues the Gentile connection: it takes place in the region of the Decapolis, predominantly Gentile territory. A second feeding miracle follows, this time involving four thousand (8:1–10). Mark then narrates a brief incident in which Jesus refuses the Pharisees' demand for a sign from heaven (8:11–12). A discussion about bread leads to a warning about the leaven of the Pharisees and the leaven of Herod (8:13–21). The healing of a blind man (8:22–26), which is unique to this Gospel, paves the way for Peter's confession of Jesus at Caesarea Philippi. There is a structural similarity between the two episodes, with the blind man's partial vision of people looking like trees corresponding to the popular view of Jesus as a prophetic figure, and the blind man's fully restored sight corresponding to Peter's articulation of the conviction that Jesus is the Messiah. Peter's confession (8:27–30) is the turning point of the whole narrative. Upon Peter's acknowledgment of him as the Christ, Jesus speaks of his coming suffering and death, challenging Peter's expectations regarding Jesus' messianic role.

From Galilee to Jerusalem and the Passion (8:31–15:47)

With Jesus' prediction of the passion (8:31–33), the tone of the Gospel abruptly changes. The suffering of Jesus is now the dominant emphasis; it is foretold three times within a relatively short space (8:31; 9:31; 10:32–34). Peter reproaches Jesus for speaking in terms of suffering and rejection (8:32–33), and Jesus responds with a sharp rebuke: "Get behind me, Satan!" Jesus then teaches his disciples about the cost of following him (8:34–9:1). He warns that those who are ashamed of him now will be shamed when the Son of Man comes in glory.

The voice from the cloud at the transfiguration (9:2–8) singles out Jesus as God's beloved Son, echoing the divine declaration at the baptism. The descent from the mount of transfiguration is the occasion for a conversation about the returning Elijah, prophesied in Malachi 4:5, whom Jesus implicitly identifies with John the Baptist (9:9–13). The story of a demon-possessed boy (9:14–29) is followed by the second passion prediction (9:30–32) and a dispute among the disciples as to which of them is the greatest, which leads Jesus to stress the need for servant-like behavior (9:33–37). The curious story about the strange exorcist (9:38–40) segues into another series of sayings on discipleship (9:41–50). Then Jesus begins his journey toward Jerusalem (10:1; cf. 10:17, 46, 52). In response to a question put to him by some Pharisees, Jesus gives teaching on marriage and divorce (10:2–12). Teaching about children follows (10:13–16). The story of the rich young ruler (10:17–22) leads into further instructions about discipleship (10:23–31, specifically on riches and rewards). The third passion prediction (10:32–34) is followed by the misguided request of James and John for positions of power, which triggers yet more teaching on discipleship (10:35–45). Then we have the story of the healing of blind Bartimaeus (10:46–52), which takes place at Jericho, just fifteen miles away from Jerusalem.

Jesus' arrival in Jerusalem, where he is destined to die, is a key moment in Mark's narrative. Jesus' triumphal entry (11:1–11), with its kingly symbolism, paves the way for confrontation with the religious establishment in the city. The confrontation in Jerusalem begins with the cleansing of the temple (11:15–19), which provokes murderous intentions against Jesus. This episode is sandwiched between the cursing of the fig tree and its subsequent wilting (11:12–14, 20–25). The fig-tree incident presages coming judgment and also provides a lesson about faith. Mark then narrates a series of exchanges between Jesus and the religious authorities. In the first (11:27–33), the Jewish leaders ask Jesus about the source of his authority. In the second (12:1–12), Jesus tells the provocative parable of the Vineyard, after which the authorities try to arrest him. Jesus is then asked three challenging questions: about paying tax to Caesar (12:13–17), about marriage and the resurrection (12:18–27), and about the greatest commandment (12:18–34). Next Jesus puts a question to his opponents (12:35–37). Citing Psalm 110:1, he sets them an exegetical conundrum: How can the Messiah be both David's son and his "Lord"? The controversies

conclude with a short polemic against the scribes (12:38–44). Then Jesus highlights the piety of a widow who gives all that she has (12:41–44).

A long discourse, the longest single speech of Jesus in the Gospel, follows,
prompted by Jesus' prediction of the temple's destruction and the disciples'
question arising from it (13:1–4). Seated on the Mount of Olives and overlooking the temple, Jesus warns of woes and suffering to come and tells of the
coming of the Son of Man in clouds with great power and glory (13:5–37).

Mark's account of the passion commences with the narration of the plot to
kill Jesus (14:1–2). The incident in which an anonymous woman anoints Jesus,
an act that Jesus interprets as an anticipation of his burial (14:3–9), precedes
Judas's meeting with the chief priests (14:10–12), at which he offers to hand
over his master to them. Jesus then holds a Passover meal with his disciples
(14:12–31), during which he predicts his betrayal, his denial by Peter, and his
abandonment by all his disciples (14:17–31). The evangelist relates the agony
in Gethsemane (14:32–42), in which Jesus' resolve to do God's will is tested.
This is immediately followed by Jesus' betrayal and arrest (14:43–52). The
trial before the Jewish authorities (14:53–65) is recounted in close conjunction with the story of Peter's denial (14:54, 66–72). Upon his answer to the
direct question of the high priest, Jesus is condemned to death. He is handed
over to Pilate, whose attempt to release him comes to nothing (15:1–15). Jesus
is cruelly mocked by the soldiers (15:16–20) before being led away to execution. The crucifixion scene is the climax of Mark's narrative. Jesus dies alone
and in anguish, forsaken even by God. But his death prompts the confession
of the centurion, which brings out the christological significance of the event
(15:39). Mark mentions the presence of women at the scene (15:40–41) before
telling of Jesus' burial in a tomb hewn out of rock (15:42–47).

Epilogue

The Gospel ends with the story of the empty tomb being discovered by the
women (16:1–8). A "young man" (most likely an angel) at the tomb tells the
women that Jesus has been raised; he instructs them to tell the disciples to go
to Galilee, where they will see Jesus. The women flee the tomb, saying nothing to anyone.

As modern translations of the Bible indicate, the ending of Mark is prob-
lematic. The longer ending (16:9–20), with postresurrection appearances and
a commission, does not appear in the most reliable manuscripts. The text
differs in style from the rest of the Gospel. A shorter ending, in which the
women report back to Peter's companions, is also attested, but it is clearly a
later addition created to give the Gospel a more satisfactory conclusion (in
some manuscripts the shorter ending is combined with the longer one). The

oldest and most reliable manuscripts thus end at 16:8. Some scholars think that the original ending of the Gospel was somehow lost, but others believe that the evangelist actually intended his Gospel to conclude at 16:8, with the comment "and they said nothing to anyone, for they were afraid." While this statement looks distinctly anticlimactic, it is not an unfitting ending to Mark's narrative, given the evangelist's sense of irony (see below).

STYLE

Mark's writing style is simple and direct.[3] He has few long complicated sentences. Mark writes in a storytelling, verbal style, rather than in the literary Greek of his time. The evangelist tends to write paratactically (parataxis is the use of coordinate clauses; literary Greek prefers subordinating constructions), linking sentences with the Greek conjunction *kai*, "and." Mark's extensive use of the word "and" at the beginning of sentences is not very evident in modern versions of the Bible but can be seen in older, more literal translations such as the KJV (King James Version) or ASV (American Standard Version). Sometimes Mark omits conjunctions, a phenomenon called "asyndeton" (Greek prefers connected sentences). The evangelist also makes frequent use of the "historic present," which is the employment of the present tense for past action (my trans.: e.g., "the Spirit *drives* him out into the wilderness," 1:12; "they *go into* Capernaum," 1:21; "they *tell* him about her," 1:30). Mark uses a less sophisticated Greek style than other Gospels, but his constant recourse to the historic present adds to the vividness and drive of his narrative (like reading "live" commentary). There are 151 instances of the historic present in Mark (compared with 93 in Matthew and 11 in Luke),[4] though they are virtually undetectable in modern Bible translations, since they are normally rendered as past tenses.

Although his Gospel is the shortest, Mark is actually the wordiest of the Synoptic writers. In parallel passages across the triple tradition, Mark's account is usually the longest.[5] For example, the story of the stilling of the storm consists of 120 Greek words in Mark, 73 in Matthew, and 94 in Luke.[6] Mark's superfluous wording is exemplified by his use of double expressions, by which he says the same thing twice, such as "when evening came, when the

---

3. On Mark's Greek style, see Nigel Turner, *Style*, vol. 4 of *A Grammar of New Testament Greek*, by James Hope Moulton, W. F. Howard, and Nigel Turner (Edinburgh: T&T Clark, 1976), 11–30.

4. Ibid., 20; Mark L. Strauss, *Four Portraits, One Jesus: An Introduction to Jesus and the Gospels* (Grand Rapids: Zondervan, 2007), 173.

5. Robert H. Stein, *The Synoptic Problem: An Introduction* (Grand Rapids: Baker Book House, 1987), 49–51. This shows that Mark cannot be viewed as an abridgement of Matthew, as Augustine thought.

6. Ibid., 50.

sun was set" (1:32, my trans. in this sentence); "in the morning, while it was still very dark" (1:35); "hungry and in need of food" (2:25).[7] Modern translations sometimes smooth out these "redundancies." Another characteristic feature of Mark's style is his fondness for using short informative comments introduced by the Greek word *gar*, meaning "for," such as "for they were fishermen" (1:16); "for he taught them as one having authority" (1:22).[8]

Mark's vocabulary is relatively limited: he uses a total of 1,270 words, of which around 80 are New Testament hapax legomena (said once), words occurring only once in the New Testament.[9] He is especially fond of the Greek adverb *euthys*, often translated as "immediately" (e.g., 1:10, 12, 18, 20, 21). This is perhaps his most characteristic word. It occurs around 42 times in the Gospel; by contrast, it appears just five times in Matthew (though Matthew uses a related word, *eutheōs*, 13 times), once in Luke, and three times in John. Mark's habitual deployment of the term "immediately," particularly in the first half of the Gospel, helps to gives this section of the narrative an urgent feel. Mark also makes extensive use of the Greek word *polys* meaning "many," "much," "great," and so forth. Other favorite words are "gospel" (e.g., 1:1, 14, 15; 10:29); "began" (1:28, 31, 45; 2:23; etc.); "again" (e.g., 2:13; 3:1, 20); "amazed" (e.g., 1:27; 2:12); "all" (e.g., 1:5, 32, 37).

That Mark translates into Greek several Aramaic phrases (e.g., *Boanērges*, *Talitha koum*, *Korban*; see 3:17, "Boanerges"; 5:41, "Talitha cum"; 7:11, "Corban"; 7:34) and explains Jewish customs (e.g., 7:3–4, 11) may well indicate that the Gospel was written with a Gentile audience in mind. In parallel passages in Matthew and Luke, Aramaic expressions are nearly always missing (exceptions are Matt. 27:33, 46; Mark 15:22, 34). The Gospel also contains some Latin loanwords (e.g., *quadrans* for "penny" in 12:42). "Latinisms" (Latin words and constructions) are more frequent in Mark than in other New Testament writings except the Pastoral Epistles.[10]

NARRATIVE TECHNIQUE

Mark's most characteristic literary device is "intercalation," his "sandwiching" technique. The story of the raising of Jairus's daughter, for example, is

---

7. On Mark's redundancies, see ibid., 58–62. Mark's double expressions may correspond to Hebrew parallelism, as evident in the poetic style of the psalms: see Turner, *Style*, 19–20.

8. On Mark's *gar* clauses, see Stein, *Synoptic Problem*, 83.

9. Turner, *Style*, 28.

10. Ibid., 29–30. The relative frequency of Latinisms has sometimes been taken as supportive of early church tradition associating this Gospel with Rome, but as Turner points out (ibid., 29), the influence of Latin on Mark's language "could have happened as well in the Roman provinces."

inserted within the story of the healing of the woman who suffered from hemorrhage (5:21–43). Jesus' cleansing of the temple is sandwiched between the cursing of the fig tree and its withering (11:12–25). By linking two stories by means of intercalation, Mark intends that one should illuminate the other.[11]

Mark has a liking for triads or groups of three.[12] For example, there are three predictions of the passion (8:31–38; 9:31; 10:32–34); at the garden of Gethsemane, three times Jesus finds his disciples asleep (14:37, 40, 41); Peter denies Jesus three times (14:68, 70, 71); three intervals of three hours are narrated in the crucifixion (15:25, 33, 34). Repetition often conveys emphasis, and Mark's triads tend to relate to his own narrative emphases, especially the suffering of Jesus and the failings of the disciples. The triadic pattern involves a progressive development, with the third member of the series revealing "the dynamic of that entire series."[13]

The evangelist displays an interest in tiny descriptive details. In the story of the healing of the paralyzed man in 2:1–12, we are told that so many people had gathered around the house in which Jesus was staying that there was no room left, "not even in front of the door" (2:2). We read of how the four men carrying the paralyzed man "dug through" (2:4) the roof in order to lower the mat on which he lay. In the story of the demon-possessed man in 5:1–20, Mark states that when some people had tried to restrain the poor wretch with chains and shackles, he "wrenched apart" the chains and "broke in pieces" the shackles (5:4). Mark's recounting of such details has sometimes been interpreted as showing his dependence on eyewitness testimony, but this is not certain. What it does exemplify is the evangelist's ability to produce a memorable story with many visual elements.

Recent study has drawn attention to the heavy presence of irony in Mark's narrative.[14] There is situational irony, involving a disjunction between intention and result, as in the many times people break Jesus' commands to keep silent. Jesus tells the leper whom he has cleansed not to say anything to anyone but to go to the priest and offer the appropriate sacrifice for his cleansing. However, Mark comments: "He went out and began to proclaim it freely, and to spread the word, so that Jesus could no longer go into a town openly" (1:45). Here we have an ironic contrast between what Jesus (apparently) wants to happen and what actually happens. There is situational irony too in Mark's depiction of the disciples (see further below): those who have been given the

11. Compare David Rhoads and Donald Michie, *Mark as Story: An Introduction to the Narrative of a Gospel* (Philadelphia: Fortress Press, 1982), 51. For other instances of intercalation, see Mark 3:20–35; 6:7–32; 14:1–11; 14:12–25, 53–72.

12. Ibid., 54–55.

13. Ibid., 55.

14. See esp. Jerry Camery-Hoggatt, *Irony in Mark's Gospel: Text and Subtext*, SNTSMS 72 (Cambridge: Cambridge University Press, 1992).

secret of the kingdom of God turn out to be as blind to God's purposes as those on the outside. The ending of Mark's Gospel is also ironic.[15] Whereas earlier in the Gospel, Jesus had issued commands to silence that were broken, here the women are commanded by the divine messenger to go forth and tell, but they remain silent (16:8)!

NARRATIVE TIME

Mark gives the general impression of forward movement through time, but he is not necessarily presenting a series of episodes in strict chronological succession. The conflict stories of 2:1–3:6 are most likely grouped according to their form, as are the miracle stories of 4:35–5:20 and the controversy stories of 11:27–12:44. In terms of duration, time moves at almost breakneck speed in the first half of the Gospel, the fast pace reinforced by the frequency of the word "immediately." With Jesus' arrival at Jerusalem, at 11:1, narrative time slows down markedly; the first part of the narrative has been impatient to arrive at what follows.

As Mark narrates the ministry of Jesus in the first part of the Gospel, he shows little concern to quantify the passing of time. Some time notes are given ("forty days," 1:13; "when the Sabbath came," 1:21; "that evening," e.g., 1:32), yet on the whole the evangelist is unconcerned with chronological specificity. But from 11:1 onward, the evangelist gives a day-by-day account of events (11:12, 19, 20; 14:1, 12, 17). These temporal notes form the basis of the Christian Holy Week.[16] Mark also carefully relates the passing of time on the day of crucifixion (15:1, 25, 33, 34, 42). The slowing down and detailing of time from 11:1 onward coincides with the narrative emphasis on Jesus' passion.

NARRATIVE SPACE

Mark's narrative displays a clear pattern of movement.[17] Jesus comes from Galilee to the river Jordan, where John baptizes and where the inciting incident of the core story takes place (1:9–11). Jesus immediately heads into the wilderness, where he is tempted (1:12–13). He then returns to Galilee to begin his ministry (1:14). He moves around the region of Galilee, conducting the bulk of his ministry in this area (1:16–7:23). Then he travels north and

15. Rhoads and Michie, *Mark as Story*, 81.
16. Richard A. Burridge, *Four Gospels, One Jesus? A Symbolic Reading* (London: SPCK, 1994), 53.
17. See further Rhoads and Michie, *Mark as Story*, 68–72.

east (7:24–9:29) before coming back to Galilee (9:30–52). From Capernaum in Galilee, he moves through Judea and the Transjordan (10:1), reaches Jericho, and finally arrives at Jerusalem (11:1), where the rest of the story plays out. This pattern of movement gives prominence to the story's climax and drives the reader toward the denouement in Jerusalem.[18]

Prominent settings in Jesus' ministry, before the arrival in Jerusalem, are houses (e.g., 1:29; 2:15; 7:17, 24; 9:33), the seaside (e.g., 1:16; 2:13; 3:7), the sea (4:35–41; 6:45–52; 8:13–21) and synagogues (1:21, 39; 3:1; 6:2). Mark seems to lay mild emphasis on the house as the scene of private teaching (7:17; 9:28; 10:10), which probably links with his secrecy theme (see below). Mountains also figure occasionally as settings (3:13; 9:2; cf. 13:3). In the prologue, the "wilderness" is significant (1:3, 4, 12, 13).

When Jesus reaches his destination in Jerusalem, the temple looms large in the narrative. It is the scene of a dramatic action by Jesus (11:15–19), prompting a resolution to kill him, the setting for teaching and disputations (11:27; 12:35; 13:1; 14:49), and the subject of a prophecy of destruction (13:2; cf. 14:58). Mark's attitude toward the temple is a matter of debate. The temple incident of 11:15–19 seems to exhibit a concern on Jesus' part to restore the temple to its proper function, but the framing of the incident within the story of the cursing and withering of the fig tree (11:12–14, 20–21) seems to interpret it as an acted parable of judgment. Like the fig tree, the temple is found barren. As the fig tree withers, so the temple will be laid to waste. In 13:1–2, Jesus explicitly prophesies the temple's destruction.

THE CHARACTERIZATION OF JESUS

More so in Mark than in any of the other Gospels, there is mystery surrounding the figure of Jesus. People wonder who he is (4:41; 6:3; 8:27, 29; 11:28; 14:61; 15:2), and Jesus often tells those who have knowledge of his identity to keep quiet about it (1:25, 34; 3:12; 8:30; see discussion below, under "Secrecy Theme").

Jesus' identity is made known in the Gospel primarily by the titles used of him.

The Titles Used for Jesus

Messiah. The Gospel incipit (the opening words) identifies Jesus as *Christos*, the Greek translation of the Hebrew *mashiakh*, "Messiah," which means

18. Compare ibid., 72.

"anointed one." Kings, prophets, and priests of Israel were anointed to their roles. An anointed figure, acting as God's agent, figured heavily in Jewish hopes of the period (though not all Jews were awaiting a messiah). Jewish messianic expectation was varied, but the predominant hope was for a (human) king in the line of David (cf. 2 Sam. 7:12–16).[19] The Davidic messianic hope is reflected in Mark's Gospel (10:47–48; 12:35–37) and is the background to Jesus' self-identification. Jesus does not, though, conform to the warrior-deliverer role of the Davidic Messiah (cf. *Psalms of Solomon* 17:22–25).

The title "Christ," for "Messiah," occurs at strategic points (in Gk.): in Peter's confession (Mark 8:29); at the trial (14:61); during the crucifixion (15:32). Peter's confession, "You are the Christ," occupies a pivotal role in the narrative; the first half of the Gospel leads up to it. Jesus does not reject the messianic identification, but he rebukes Peter for his incomplete understanding of what it means. He is not the Davidic warrior-deliverer Messiah, but the suffering Son of Man.[20] Jesus wants his messianic status to remain secret for now (see below on secrecy); however, near the end of the Gospel, when the high priest asks Jesus whether he is the Messiah, he replies with an unequivocal, "I am" (14:62). The time for secrecy is over. This sort of definite response is distinctive to Mark. During the crucifixion, the title "Messiah" is applied to Jesus mockingly by the chief priests and scribes. But what is said in mockery ironically expresses the truth.

Son of God. The title "Son of God" is used for Jesus in the Gospel's opening verse, but several important manuscripts do not have the phrase, so we cannot be sure whether it goes back to the original text of Mark or whether a copyist inserted it later. Even so, Jesus is identified as God's Son very early in the Markan narrative: at Jesus' baptism, the voice of God claims him as God's beloved son (1:11). On two separate occasions in the course of Jesus' dynamic ministry, demons address him as Son of God (3:11; 5:7); this title thus indicates that he has power over the demons. In the first instance, the attestation is accompanied by prostration and crying out; in the second, the demons acknowledge Jesus' supernatural ability to torture them. At the transfiguration, Jesus again is called God's Son (9:7). Jesus implicitly identifies himself as God's "beloved" Son in the parable of the Vineyard (12:6), and he refers to himself in absolute terms as "the Son" at the end of the eschatological discourse (13:32). At the trial, he admits before the high priest that he is "the Son of the Blessed One" (14:61). Finally, at the cross, after Jesus' death,

---

19. James D. G. Dunn, *Jesus Remembered*, vol. 1 of *Christianity in the Making* (Grand Rapids: Wm. B. Eerdmans Publishing Co., 2003), 619–22.

20. Joel Marcus, *Mark: A New Translation with Introduction and Commentary*, vol. 2, *Mark 8–16*, AB 27A (New York: Doubleday, 2009), 612.

the Roman centurion publicly announces, "Truly, this man was God's Son" (15:39). Coming at the climax of his narrative, the confession represents what is for this evangelist the highest view of Jesus.

One must be careful not to read back into the Gospel a full Trinitarian understanding of Jesus as God's Son, for "the Son" as second person of the Trinity is a Christology that postdates the Gospel and is given creedal expression in the Nicene and Chalcedonian creeds.

In the Old Testament, angelic beings (Gen. 6:2), the nation (Exod. 4:22), and the king (2 Sam. 7:14; Ps. 2:7) are called God's sons. By the first century, there is evidence that Jews were beginning to speak of the expected messiah as God's Son.[21] Indeed, in Mark's Gospel, the classifications "Messiah" and "Son of God" overlap. In 14:61, "Son of the Blessed One" is clearly a messianic title. Yet in some passages, especially 13:32 and 15:39, the title God's Son seems to involve Jesus' transcendent status (in 13:32, "the Son" is placed above the angels).

Lord. This title is used for Jesus relatively infrequently in Mark by comparison with the other Gospels. In Greek usage, the underlying word *kyrios* could be used simply as a term of respect, meaning "sir," or as a term for someone with authority over others, such as "master" (e.g., slave master or master of the household). The Syro-Phoenician woman calls Jesus *kyrios* in 7:28; here the title has the sense "sir." Jesus refers to himself as "lord of the Sabbath" in 2:28, meaning that he has authority over the sacred day. However, *kyrios* was also applied to Greco-Roman divinities, and Greek-speaking Jews used it of God. In the Septuagint, the Greek translation of the Hebrew Scriptures, *ho kyrios*, "the Lord," is the standard designation for God. The citation of Isaiah 40:3 in Mark 1:2–3 implicitly identifies Jesus with the Lord God of Israel. Twice Jesus speaks of "the Lord" (5:19; 11:3) ambiguously, perhaps with reference to himself or to God.

Son of Man. This is the most frequently used christological title in the Gospel, appearing fourteen times. It is only found in statements made by Jesus (cf. the questions in John 12:34). The background to this title is greatly debated.[22] In the Old Testament, "son of man" is a designation for a human being, a "mortal" (e.g., Ezek. 2:1; 3:1). In Aramaic, the language of Jesus, the expression "son of man" was an indirect way of speaking of oneself. In Daniel 7:13–14, though, we read of a mysterious "one like a son of man" (RSV), "coming with the clouds of heaven"; he enters God's presence and is given dominion. In the Gospels, "Son of Man" is a title, which Jesus uses of himself

21. See the Dead Sea Scrolls texts 4QFlor 1.10–13; 4Q246; cf. Joel Marcus, *Mark: A New Translation with Introduction and Commentary*, vol. 1, *Mark 1–8*, AB 27 (New York: Doubleday, 2000), 162.
22. See the summary in Dunn, *Jesus Remembered*, 724–37.

(and with exclusive regard to himself). The title is found only twice in the first half of Mark's Gospel (2:10, 28), in both instances, with reference to Jesus' authority on earth. In the second half of the narrative, it is predominantly used in connection with Jesus' impending suffering, rejection, and resurrection (8:31; 9:9, 12, 31; 10:33, 45; 14:21, 41). On three occasions it is used in an eschatological connection, with reference to the future coming of the Son of Man (8:38; 13:26; 14:62). These three sayings plainly allude to the enigmatic "one like a son of man" in Daniel 7:13–14.

Other titles. Mark has a proportionally high number of references to Jesus as "teacher" (12 in all: e.g., 4:38; 5:35; 9:17). The evangelist's stress on Jesus' role as a pedagogue is particularly striking in view of the fact that he does not include as much of Jesus' teaching as do the other Gospel writers. Jesus is called "teacher" by both outsiders (9:17; 10:17, 20; 12:14, 19, 32) and his own disciples (4:38; 9:38; 10:35; 13:1).

Jesus is popularly regarded as a "prophet" (8:28; cf. 6:15; 14:65). On one occasion, Jesus portrays himself as a prophet (6:4). Aspects of his ministry recall the activity of Elijah and Elisha (e.g., the feeding of the five thousand calls to mind a similar but smaller-scale miracle performed by Elisha in 2 Kgs. 4:42–44; see chap. 8 below). In the transfiguration, Jesus is implicitly identified as the "prophet like [Moses]" (Deut. 18:15; see chap. 10 below), a quasi-messianic figure.[23] The general category of prophet, though, is clearly viewed by Mark as less than adequate for conveying Jesus' significance (8:27–30).

Blind Bartimaeus addresses Jesus with the messianic title "Son of David" (10:47–48). The title "King of the Jews" occurs with some frequency in Mark 15 (vv. 2, 9, 12, 18, 26). Those who use the title, or its variant "King of Israel" (15:32), do so ironically, indicating that they believe it to be an inappropriate designation for Jesus. It is applied to him accusingly and mockingly. Jesus himself is evasive when Pilate asks him, "Are you the King of the Jews?" (15:2).[24] Jesus is indeed Israel's king, but not the warrior king of popular messianism.

Characterizational Emphases

Mark shows particular interest in Jesus' emotions. Jesus goes through a gamut of emotions in this Gospel. He experiences compassion (1:41; 6:34), love (10:21), grief (3:5), wonder (6:6), indignation (10:14), and anger (1:43; 3:5; 9:25). He suffers anguish as he looks ahead to his death (14:33–34), and his only utterance at the crucifixion is the cry of abandonment (15:34).

---

23. Ibid., 656.
24. Pilate's question appears in all four Gospels, and in all four Jesus replies evasively.

While references to Jesus' emotions might underline his humanity,[25] Mark also seems to lay strong emphasis on Jesus' "divine" qualities.[26] Jesus exercises powers and prerogatives that characteristically belong to God: forgiving sin (2:5), knowing others' thoughts (2:8), exercising lordship over the Sabbath (2:28), stilling the storm (4:35–41), walking on the water (6:45–52). The ascription of such abilities to Jesus is not unique to Mark, but it is a particularly noticeable feature of Mark's christological portrait.

The second half of the Gospel gives prominence to the suffering of Jesus.[27] Again, emphasis on Jesus' suffering is not uniquely Markan, but the extent to which the suffering role of Jesus (influenced to some extent by the notion of the Suffering Servant, portrayed in Isa. 52:13–53:12) dominates the narrative from 8:31 onward is striking.

In comparison with the other Gospels, there is a "rawness" to Mark's portrayal of Jesus. Commands issued by Jesus are directly disobeyed; Jesus is unable to perform miracles in his hometown; he makes two attempts at healing a blind man; and so forth. Mark senses no theological difficulty in Jesus' subordinating himself to John or submitting to a baptism of repentance for the forgiveness of sin (see chap. 7). He neglects to tell us the outcome of Jesus' temptation. And he offers no appearance of the risen Jesus. The rawness of Mark's portrait of Jesus is not without attraction for many contemporary readers because it shows Jesus untamed and uncut.

THE CHARACTERIZATION OF THE DISCIPLES

As noted in chapter 2, all the evangelists portray the disciples with conflicting traits. While Mark acknowledges the positive features of the disciples (they are called, commissioned, made privy to the mystery of the kingdom, etc.), he accentuates their failings. Of all the evangelists, Mark offers the most uncomplimentary portrait of Jesus' disciples. They fail to understand Jesus' parables (4:11–13, 33–34; 7:18); they are lacking in faith (4:40; 11:22–24); they do not perceive Jesus' ability to feed the multitudes miraculously (6:34–44; 8:1–10); they answer Jesus sarcastically (6:37); they do not perceive the meaning of the miracles (6:52; 8:14–21); they are hard-hearted (6:52); they are unable

---

25. However, we need to be careful about assigning emotion only to the human side of a human/divine distinction. In the OT, God displays emotion.

26. Compare Strauss, *Four Portraits*, 195.

27. Theodore J. Weeden (*Mark: Traditions in Conflict* [Philadelphia: Fortress Press, 1971]) argues that the emphasis on Jesus' suffering is used by Mark to moderate the view of Jesus as a wonder-working divine man, which dominates the first half of the Gospel. But it is not clear that Mark is deliberately trying to correct a christological imbalance.

to fulfill their assigned task (9:14–29). Jesus rebukes Peter for his inability to accept the necessity of Jesus' suffering (8:33). Judas betrays him (14:10–11, 43–46), Peter denies him (14:54, 66–72), and at the crucial moment all of them flee (14:50). Unlike the other evangelists, Mark does not narrate the restoration of the disciples (though he records Jesus' prediction that they will see him in Galilee after the resurrection; 14:28).

Mark's more negative portrait of the disciples has occasioned much discussion. Some think that the evangelist uses the dullness of the disciples to teach readers about the true nature of discipleship; thus their failures serve a positive pastoral purpose. More likely, as Burridge argues,[28] their misapprehension is meant to accentuate the inscrutability of Jesus.

THE CHARACTERIZATION OF THE RELIGIOUS AUTHORITIES

Across the Synoptic Gospels, there are five main groups of religious authorities:[29] the Pharisees, the scribes, the chief priests, the elders, the Sadducees. The Pharisees constituted a lay movement devoted to the observance of Torah. The scribes were a professional class of experts in Torah. The chief priests, based in Jerusalem, controlled the temple and held significant political power under the Romans. The chief priests formed the core membership of the ruling council, the Sanhedrin. The elders appear to have been lay members of the Sanhedrin. The Sadducees were an aristocratic group, tied to the temple and the priesthood.

The Pharisees figure mainly in the first half of the narrative. Conflicts with the Pharisees arise over Jesus' associations with sinners (2:16), Sabbath observance (2:24; 3:2), and washing hands (7:5). The Pharisees try to ensnare Jesus, asking for a sign from heaven (8:11) and questioning him about divorce (10:2) and the payment of tax (12:13–17). The early confrontations lead the Pharisees to conspire with the Herodians (apparently supporters of the Herodian dynasty and thus complicit with Roman policy)[30] on how to destroy Jesus (3:6). The Pharisees are not mentioned in Mark's narrative after 12:13; they are not directly incriminated in the conspiracy to have Jesus killed.

28. Burridge, *Four Gospels*, 48.

29. On the Jewish leaders in Mark, see Marcus, *Mark*, 2:1099–1103, 1121–23.

30. On the Herodians, see further Harold W. Hoehner, "Herodian Dynasty," in *Dictionary of Jesus and the Gospels*, ed. Joel B. Green, Scot McKnight, and I. Howard Marshall (Leicester: InterVarsity Press, 1992), 317–26, here 325.

The scribes are the most frequently mentioned adversarial group in Mark's Gospel (some 20 times).[31] The scribes are linked with the Pharisees in the disputes about eating with sinners and eating with defiled hands (2:16; 7:1–2). On several occasions, they question Jesus' authority (2:6; 3:22; 11:27). Following Jesus' cleansing of the temple, they seek to destroy him (11:18), and they participate alongside the chief priests in the plot that brings about his death (14:1, 43, 53). They join with the chief priests in mocking Jesus as he hangs on the cross (15:31). Jesus condemns the scribes for their ostentatious clothing, love of honor, outward show of piety, and exploitation of widows (12:38–40). Yet one scribe who engages with Jesus wisely is said to be close to the kingdom of God (12:34), a comment distinctive to Mark.

The chief priests emerge as Jesus' main opposition in Jerusalem (e.g., 11:18, 27; 14:1, 10), though their role as opponents is anticipated in the passion predictions (8:31; 10:33). They are stirred to action against Jesus after he "cleanses" the temple, motivated by fear (11:18). They conspire with the scribes to engineer his arrest and execution (14:1). The high priest, the leader of the chief priests, elicits from Jesus the confession that secures his condemnation (14:61–63). The chief priests accuse Jesus before Pilate (15:3) and then stir up the crowd to have him release Barabbas instead of Jesus (15:31). They deride Jesus on the cross (15:31–32).

The elders are mentioned only seven times (7:3, 5; 8:31; 11:27; 14:43, 53; 15:1), always in association with the scribes and chief priests; like the chief priests, they are always hostile to Jesus.

The Sadducees appear only in the conflict story of 12:18–27, in which they question Jesus about the resurrection of the dead, a belief to which they do not hold. Jesus' trumps their trick question with his clever reply.

THEMES

The central theme of Jesus' preaching in Mark's Gospel, as in all the Synoptic Gospels, is the kingdom of God (the actual phrase occurs 14 times in the Gospel).[32] The kingdom of God in the teaching of Jesus is to some extent a realm (hence it can be "entered": 10:14–15, 23–25), but it is more the manifestation of God's sovereignty. In 1:15 Jesus announces that "the kingdom of God has come near," indicating the imminence of God's dominion. Other

---

31. On the scribes in Mark, see Graham H. Twelftree, "Scribes," in Green, McKnight, and Marshall, *Dictionary of Jesus and the Gospels*, 732–35, here 734.

32. On the kingdom theme in Mark, see I. Howard Marshall, *New Testament Theology: Many Witnesses, One Gospel* (Downers Grove, IL: InterVarsity Press, 2004), 78–81.

sayings imply the presence of the kingdom. The parable of the Mustard Seed in 4:30–32, for instance, indicates the presence and growth of the kingdom on earth. Yet the full manifestation of the kingdom lies in the future (14:25; 15:43).

The Secrecy Theme

In Mark's Gospel, Jesus expresses a particular concern for secrecy.[33] He issues commands of silence to demons (1:24–25, 34; 3:12), his disciples (8:30; 9:9), and those who experience or witness his healing (1:43–44; 5:43; 7:36; 8:26). He tries to avoid public attention (7:24; 9:30–31), seeks seclusion for himself and his disciples (1:35; 6:30–31), and often speaks to them in private (4:10, 34; 7:17; 9:28; 13:3). In parallel passages in Matthew and Luke, the secrecy element is often missing.

The emphasis on concealment in Mark is commonly known as "the messianic secret," following Wilhelm Wrede's influential book by that title published in 1901. The secrecy theme in Mark probably reflects a genuine historical concern on the part of Jesus: to avoid messianic enthusiasm engulfing his mission. It probably also reflects a theological conviction on the part of the evangelist: one cannot properly understand who Jesus is until his death and resurrection (cf. 9:9). Thematically, the messianic secret fits hand in hand with the portrayal of the disciples, who do not understand who Jesus is, and with the irony of the Gospel, that readers do know who Jesus is.

Despite its common usage in studies of Mark's Gospel, the term "messianic secret" is a little misleading since only one of the texts evincing the secrecy theme in the Gospel is explicitly about Jesus' messiahship (8:30). Also, the imposition of secrecy is not thoroughgoing: Jesus often heals openly. In 5:19 he positively encourages the demoniac to go out and tell others about the miracle. In 10:48 it is the crowd and not Jesus who tries to silence blind Bartimaeus. Jesus accepts the beggar's public identification of him as "Son of David." It is difficult to discern a consistent rationale for this fluctuation between secrecy and openness. There is also variation in the responses to Jesus' commands to silence. Sometimes Jesus' commands are observed; sometimes they are broken. Yet there is a pattern. Injunctions to silence relating to Jesus' *activity* are sometimes broken (1:44–45; 7:36). Silence about his *identity* invariably is kept (1:24–25, 34; 3:12; 8:30; 9:9). The secrecy relating to Jesus' identity is consistently maintained in the Galilean ministry. It is partly lifted as Jesus approaches and enters Jerusalem (10:48); the veil is removed altogether at his confession before the high priest (14:62).

33. Marcus, *Mark*, 2:525.

Radical Discipleship

Discipleship is a theme common to all the Gospels, but it is particularly important in Mark.[34] The evangelist's emphasis on discipleship comes out in 8:31–10:52, which contains a number of short blocks of teaching on the subject (8:34–38; 9:33–37, 41–50; 10:23–31, 35–45). The material is not distinctive to Mark, but since he includes fewer of Jesus' teachings than any of the other evangelists, it receives greater prominence in this Gospel. The sayings bring out the radical nature of discipleship: following Jesus involves self-denial (8:34), servility (9:35), renouncing riches (10:23), and suffering (8:34; 10:37–38). Mark thus accentuates the costliness of discipleship, though it is made clear that the rewards will more than compensate disciples for what is lost (10:29–30).

Imminent Eschatology

The longest single speech of Jesus in the Gospel is the eschatological discourse of Mark 13.[35] It is obvious that the subject matter is of some importance to Mark, though both Matthew and Luke include more eschatological material. Mark's version of the discourse ends distinctively on an imminent note. Jesus (speaking, it appears, directly to readers of the Gospel, thus breaking the "fourth wall")[36] issues a call to vigilance: "What I say to you I say to all: Keep awake" (13:37). We are thus given a strong impression of the nearness of the *parousia* (Christ's return). The other three Gospels all betray some sense of delay in Christ's return (yet even Mark makes clear that only God knows the day and hour; 13:32).

CONCLUSION

Of the four Gospels, it is Mark's that most clearly displays the basic story common to them all, beginning with the ministry of John the Baptist and ending with the resurrection, with few embellishments. Yet Mark's telling of the shared story has a discernable individuality: the rawness of the Christology, the warts-'n'-all portrayal of the disciples, the accent on radical commitment,

---

34. See further Ernest Best, *Following Jesus: Discipleship in the Gospel of Mark*, JSNTSup 4 (Sheffield: JSOT Press, 1988).

35. This discourse has spawned an enormous amount of scholarly literature. See Timothy J. Geddert, *Watchwords: Mark 13 in Markan Eschatology*, JSNTSup 26 (Sheffield: JSOT Press, 1989).

36. The "fourth wall" is the imaginary wall between the dramatis personae (the characters in a dramatic work) and the audience. Breaking the fourth wall is when a character speaks directly to the audience.

the emphasis on concealment, the disturbing ending. Such idiosyncrasies make Mark's Gospel the edgiest of the four.

FOR FURTHER READING

Best, Ernest E. *Mark: The Gospel as Story*. Edinburgh: T&T Clark, 2000.

Boring, M. Eugene. *Mark: A Commentary*. New Testament Library. Louisville, KY: Westminster John Knox Press, 2006.

France, Richard Thomas. *The Gospel of Mark*. New International Greek New Testament Commentaries. Grand Rapids: Wm. B. Eerdmans Publishing Co., 2002.

Hare, Douglas R. A. *Mark*. Westminster Bible Companion. Louisville, KY: Westminster John Knox Press, 1996.

Hooker, Morna D. *The Gospel according to St Mark*. Black's New Testament Commentaries. London: A&C Black, 1991.

Marcus, Joel. *Mark: A New Translation with Introduction and Commentary*. Vol. 1, *Mark 1–8*. Vol. 2, *Mark 8–16*. Anchor Bible 27–27A. New York: Doubleday, 2000–2009.

Martin, Ralph P. *Mark: Evangelist and Theologian*. Exeter: Paternoster Press, 1972.

Rhoads, David, and Donald Michie. *Mark as Story: An Introduction to the Narrative of a Gospel*. Philadelphia: Fortress Press, 1982.

Smith, Stephen H. *A Lion with Wings: A Narrative-Critical Approach to Mark's Gospel*. Sheffield: Sheffield Academic, 1996.

Telford, William R. *The Theology of the Gospel of Mark*. Cambridge: Cambridge University Press, 1999.

Williamson, Lamar, Jr. *Mark*. Interpretation. Louisville, KY: Westminster John Knox Press, 2009.

Wright, N. T. *Mark for Everyone*. Louisville, KY: Westminster John Knox Press, 2004.

4

The Gospel according to Matthew

Matthew's narrative closely resembles that of Mark. It is generally accepted that Matthew drew extensively on the work of his forerunner in composing his Gospel. He incorporates the large bulk of Mark's Gospel, adding to the beginning a genealogy and a birth and infancy narrative, and to the end some postresurrection appearances and a commission to worldwide mission. He records much more of Jesus' teaching, including the Sermon on the Mount, which is without parallel in Mark (but partially paralleled in Luke's Sermon on the Plain; see chap. 5 below). With his addition of a birth and infancy account, Matthew makes his Gospel conform more closely to the format of ancient biography.

Matthew's characterization of Jesus gives prominence to the way in which, in his person and in his activity, he brings to realization Old Testament hopes and ideals. Matthew portrays Jesus as the expected Messiah. As such, he is "Son of David" and "King of the Jews." The evangelist also presents him as the new Moses, the shepherd, the Lord's Servant, and wisdom incarnate, drawing on Old Testament types and figures. Through formal citations of Old Testament texts, Matthew shows how events in Jesus' life fulfill Scripture, though often in unexpected ways. Matthew emphasizes the divine sonship of Jesus, and only Matthew among the evangelists calls Jesus "Emmanuel," meaning "God with us."

TEXTUAL STRUCTURE

Although Matthew's Gospel is the most carefully structured of the four Gospels, there is no agreed understanding of Matthew's plan. It is commonly recognized that the Gospel has five major stretches of teaching: chapters

5–7, 10, 13, 18, 24–25. There is extended teaching of Jesus elsewhere in the Gospel (12:25–45; 21:28–22:14; chap. 23),[1] but what is significant about these five blocks is that they are clearly flagged. The same formula is found at the end of each them: "when Jesus had finished saying these things/parables" (7:28; 11:1; 13:53; 19:1; 26:1). At the conclusion of the final sermon, we read: "When Jesus had finished saying *all* these things" (26:1, emphasis added). It seems evident that Matthew intends these didactic sections to be viewed as distinct discourses intersecting the narrative development. The Gospel thus seems to follow a pattern of alternating narrative and discourse, stories of Jesus' actions intercalated with blocks of Jesus' teaching. B. W. Bacon has proposed an outline for the Gospel on this basis.[2] He links narrative and discourse in pairs and delineates five main sections, which he calls "books": chapters 3–7, 8–10, 11–13, 14–18, 19–25. Bacon argues that the five books that make up the body of the Gospel were patterned after the Pentateuch, the five books of Moses. This outline is attractive, but it has failed to win common assent largely because it relegates the birth and infancy narrative and the passion and resurrection narrative to the status of prologue and epilogue respectively.[3]

Jack Kingsbury divides up the Gospel differently.[4] His approach is based on another structural marker in the Gospel: the phrase "from that time on Jesus began to . . ." The formula occurs in 4:17, at the beginning of Jesus' ministry, and in 16:21, just after Peter's confession, where Jesus begins to teach his disciples about his impending death. Kingsbury thus divides Matthew's Gospel as follows: 1:1–4:16; 4:17–16:20; 16:21–28:20. This breakdown of the text gives Matthew the same bipartite structure as Mark, with 1:1–4:16 as an extended introduction. However, Peter's confession is not quite as pivotal in Matthew's Gospel as it is in Mark. Also, the breaks between 11:1 and 11:2 and between 20:34 and 21:1 seem just as important within Matthew's developing narrative as those between 4:16 and 4:17 and between 16:20 and 16:21. A more satisfactory approach, therefore, may be to divide the text into five main sections as follows:[5]

---

1. Matthew 23 is sometimes taken along with chaps. 24–25 as constituting a single discourse, but 24:1–2 marks a clear shift between what precedes and what follows.

2. Benjamin W. Bacon, *Studies in Matthew* (London: Constable, 1930); cf. W. D. Davies and Dale C. Allison Jr., *The Gospel according to Saint Matthew*, 3 vols. (Edinburgh: T&T Clark, 1988–97), 1:59.

3. Dale C. Allison Jr., *The New Moses: A Matthean Typology* (Minneapolis: Fortress Press, 1993), 293–98.

4. Jack Dean Kingsbury, *Matthew: Structure, Christology, Kingdom* (Philadelphia: Fortress Press, 1975), 7–25.

5. As Frank J. Matera, *New Testament Christology* (Louisville, KY: Westminster John Knox Press, 1999), 28.

Within these divisions, one may acknowledge the alternation of teaching and narrative that Bacon and others have highlighted.

PLOT

Since Matthew's narrative is very close to that of Mark, we may skim over some parts of it that replicate Mark's plot.

Birth, Infancy, and Preparation for Ministry (1:1–4:17)

Matthew begins with a genealogy (1:2–17), which is designed to show that Jesus is a descendant of David (through his adoptive father, Joseph), thereby establishing his messianic credentials. The genealogy divides neatly into three units of fourteen generations: from Abraham to David, from David to the exile, from the exile to Jesus.

After the genealogy, Matthew gives an account of Jesus' miraculous conception and birth (1:8–25), focusing on Joseph and his dilemma. Joseph learns that Mary, to whom he is betrothed, is pregnant. He wants to break their engagement but does not want to expose her to public shame. The angel of the Lord appears to him in a dream and explains that Mary's unborn child has been conceived from the Holy Spirit. Joseph should not be afraid, then, to marry her. He is told to name the child "Jesus" because he will save his people from their sins (1:21). Joseph takes Mary as his wife, and Jesus is born. The arrival of the magi in Jerusalem, seeking "the child who has been born king of the Jews" (2:2), prompts the first conflict in the narrative, as Herod tries to destroy the infant. Herod's plan to kill the child foreshadows the final plot to do away with Jesus. After being warned in a dream of Herod's murderous intent, Joseph takes Jesus and Mary and escapes with them to Egypt. After Herod's death, the family return to Israel, settling in Nazareth (2:23).

The narrative jumps forward in time to the ministry of John the Baptist (3:1–12) and the appearance of the adult Jesus. Matthew includes a summary of John's preaching of repentance. At his baptism, Jesus is declared to be God's Son (3:13–17). In the temptation (4:1–11), which is described at greater length than in Mark's Gospel, Jesus sonship is tested and proved. Matthew then narrates Jesus' move to Capernaum to make his home there (4:12–16).

Ministry of Teaching, Preaching, and Healing (4:17–11:1)

The preparation complete, the ministry begins. As in Mark, the ministry of Jesus commences with his proclamation of the kingdom. The evangelist narrates the call of the first disciples (4:18–22) before giving an epitome of Jesus' activity (4:23–25).

At this point, Matthew gives us the first of the five major discourses that mark out his Gospel. The Sermon on the Mount is a carefully structured unit. Its teaching begins with the Beatitudes (or blessings, 5:3–12) and turns to the theme of witness in the world (5:13–16). Jesus next asserts that he has come to fulfill the law (5:17–20); then, in a series of antitheses ("You have heard that it was said, . . . but I say to you, . . ."; 5:21–48), he issues higher demands than the law requires. After this he gives instruction on the practice of righteousness (6:1–18), which leads into teaching that relativizes earthly treasures and concerns (6:19–34). Sayings follow on judging others and asking from God (7:1–12). The sermon draws to conclusion by setting forth two ways (7:13–27). Hearers are divided into two camps: those who hear Jesus' words and act on them, and those who hear his words but do not act on them. Matthew records the crowds' amazement at Jesus' teaching and the authority with which he speaks (7:28–29).

From teaching, the evangelist turns to narrative action. The evangelist records ten miracles (chaps. 8–9), in three groups of three (the raising of the synagogue leader's daughter and the woman with a hemorrhage are narrated as one episode; 9:18–26). Matthew also narrates the call of Matthew (9:9) and describes emerging conflict with the religious authorities (9:2–8, 10–13, 34).

Jesus appoints twelve disciples and sends them out to carry on his mission of preaching and healing (10:1–4). The commissioning of the Twelve is the occasion for the second major speech of the Gospel, the mission discourse (10:5–11:1). The address moves from instructions for the mission at hand (10:5–15) to warnings of future suffering and persecution (10:16–25), then to more general teaching on discipleship (10:26–42). A further summary of Jesus' activity (11:1) forms a transitional conclusion.

Expanding Ministry, Growing Opposition (11:2–16:20)

The next stage of the developing plot begins with John the Baptist's question to Jesus from prison (11:2–6): "Are you the one who is to come, or are we to wait for another?" In answering the question, Jesus refers to his mighty deeds, which realize prophetic and messianic hopes (see chap. 5 below, on Luke's parallel to this passage). Jesus next speaks about John and his place in God's plan, identifying the Baptist as the expected Elijah (cf. Mal. 4:5–6). He denounces "this generation" for rejecting both John's solemn message and his own more-festive style of ministry (11:16–19). Jesus implies that his messianic works are the works of personified wisdom (11:19; see below). He condemns the cities Chorazin and Bethsaida for their failure to repent (11:21–24). Then he issues a profound statement on the Father and the Son (11:25–27) and invites all who are weary to come and find rest (11:28–30).

From this point onward, the festering conflict intensifies. Matthew narrates two incidents involving conflict over the Sabbath (12:1–14), after which the Pharisees resolve to kill Jesus. A summary of Jesus' healing activity is then given (12:15–21). The evangelist cites Isaiah 42:1–4 (the longest quotation in the Gospel) to show that Jesus fulfills the role of the Lord's Servant. Further confrontation with the Pharisees follows (12:22–45). The arrival on the scene of Jesus' mother and brothers prompts teaching about his true family (12:46–50).

This takes us to the third main discourse of the Gospel, falling at the midway point of the narrative. The discourse presents a set of parables on the kingdom theme. Again, the teaching is highly structured, falling into two fairly even parts, one addressed to the crowds in public (13:1–35), the other to the disciples in private (13:36–52). Jesus tells seven parables in all: the Sower (13:1–9, interpreted in 13:18–23); the Weeds (13:24–30, interpreted in 13:37–43); the Mustard Seed (13:31–32); the Leaven (13:33); the Treasure (13:44); the Pearl (13:45–46); the Net (13:47–50).

From extended teaching, Matthew again returns to Jesus' activity, beginning with Jesus' preaching and rejection in his hometown (13:54–58). The stretch of narrative from 13:54 to 16.20 broadly parallels Mark 6:1–8.30. Although Peter's confession at Caesarea (16:13–20) is less pivotal in Matthew's Gospel than in Mark's, it nevertheless constitutes a peak point in the narrative.

From Galilee to Judea (16:21–20:34)

The first passion prediction (16:21–23), following straight on from Peter's confession, signals a shift in the narrative development. Jesus' impending death now comes more clearly in view (two further passion prophecies are given within a short narrative space: 17:12, 22–23). Matthew's plot from 16:21–17:23 follows Mark's sequence (Mark 8:31–9:32). The story of the coin found in a fish's mouth in 17:24–27, though, is distinctive to Matthew.

The fourth major discourse of the Gospel is next in the narrative order (18:1–19:2). It deals with communal relations and envisages a "church" setting (18:17). The sermon begins with a literal reference to children (18:2–5), but the thought turns to community members metaphorically conceived as children (18:6–14). Attention then moves to community discipline (18:15–20).

The sermon concludes with the parable of the Unforgiving Servant, underlining Jesus' call for ongoing forgiveness (18:21–35).

With this discourse, we come to the end of the Galilean ministry. Jesus leaves Galilee and enters Judea, beginning his fateful journey to Jerusalem (19:1). Again the plot largely follows that of Mark, with some distinctive Matthean material: Jesus' teaching on eunuchs and celibacy (19:10–12), the parable of the Laborers in the Vineyard (20:1–16). The healing of *two* blind men as Jesus leaves Jericho (Mark has only one), on his way to Jerusalem, brings this section of the narrative to a close (20:29–34).

Jerusalem, Passion, and Resurrection (21:1–28:20)

Jesus' arrival in Jerusalem signals the beginning of the end. He enters the holy city in a kingly fashion (21:1–11), recalling the identification of Jesus as "king of the Jews" in the birth narrative (2:2) and pointing forward to his crucifixion as "King of the Jews" (27:37). Matthew cites Zechariah 9:9 to make explicit Jesus' fulfillment of messianic prophecy. Jesus enters the temple and drives out those buying and selling (21:12–13). He conducts healings, and children hail him as "Son of David" (21:14–17). A further symbolic action follows: the cursing of the fig tree, which withers immediately (21:18–22). Matthew then relates a series of controversies, questions, and parables, which parallel and expand on Mark 11:27–12:40. Jesus constantly trumps and disgraces his opponents. The cycle is brought to a close with the comment "No one was able to give him an answer, nor from that day did anyone dare to ask him any more questions" (22:46). After this, Jesus launches into a tirade against the scribes and Pharisees (chap. 23). The woes against the religious authorities are followed by the final discourse of the Gospel, the eschatological discourse, delivered on the Mount of Olives (chaps. 24–25). Matthew's version of this speech is lengthier than the Markan equivalent (Mark 13). In his extension of Mark's eschatological discourse (24:37–25:46), Matthew includes several parables, two of which (the Ten Virgins, 25:1–13; the Sheep and the Goats, 25:31–46) are unique to him.

With the conclusion of the fifth discourse, we come to the passion account proper. It begins with a passion prediction distinctive to Matthew (26:1–2), but events proceed more or less as they are narrated in the Markan Gospel, from the plot to kill (26:3–5) to the handing over of Jesus to Pilate (27:1–2). The narrative flow is interrupted by the report of the remorse and suicide of Judas (27:3–10). Matthew's account of the trial before Pilate (27:11–26) uniquely includes the warning sent to Pilate by his wife. Jesus' death on the cross is accompanied by dramatic events (see chap. 11 below).

After recounting the burial of Jesus, Matthew reports that the tomb is sealed with a great stone and a guard placed to secure the site (27:62–66). After his account of the empty tomb being discovered (28:1–8; see chap. 12 below), Matthew narrates two appearances of the risen Jesus. The first is to the women who visit the sepulchre (28:8–10); the second is to the disciples on a mountain in Galilee (28:16–20). In between, we read how the soldiers were bribed to say that the disciples stole the corpse of Jesus while they were asleep (28:11–15). Jesus' final words in the Gospel declare his resurrection authority. He commissions his followers to go to all the nations and make further disciples. They are to teach his commands and baptize them "in the name of the Father and of the Son and of the Holy Spirit" (28:19). And his presence will be with them "to the end of the age" (28:20).

STYLE

Matthew's Greek style has been described as rather lacking in distinction.[6] It is smoother than Mark's style. The evangelist tends to connect sentences with the Greek conjunction *de* rather than *kai*, and he favors the simple past tense above the historic present that Mark loves. These preferences make for "better" Greek (by the literary standards of the time). While Matthew's Greek style is superior to Mark's, it is less sophisticated than Luke's.[7]

Matthew has a total vocabulary of some 1,690 words, of which 112 are New Testament hapax legomena, occurring only once and thus unique to this Gospel.[8] The evangelist makes frequent use of the Greek temporal adverb *tote*, meaning "then," "at that time" (it occurs in Matthew around ninety times; there are only six instances of it in Mark, fifteen in Luke, and ten in John). Matthew often uses the word to mark the beginning of a new paragraph or section (e.g., 2:7, 16; 3:13; 4:1). Another frequently occurring Greek word is the interjection *idou* meaning "behold" (rendered variously in the NRSV as "look," "see," "suddenly," and sometimes not directly translated at all). There are over sixty instances of it in the Gospel. Often it is found in the formulation *kai idou*, "and behold" (a septuagintal expression, reminiscent of the Hebrew Scriptures). Other favorite words demonstrate particularly Matthean themes: "fulfill" (e.g., 1:22; 2:15, 17, 23), "righteous" (e.g., 1:19; 5:45), "righteousness"

---

6. Davies and Allison, *Matthew*, 1:72.
7. For features of Matthew's Greek style, see Nigel Turner, *Style*, vol. 4 of *A Grammar of New Testament Greek*, by James Hope Moulton, W. F. Howard, and Nigel Turner (Edinburgh: T&T Clark, 1976), 31–44.
8. Ibid., 43.

(e.g., 3:15; 5:6, 10, 20), "hypocrite" (e.g., 6:2, 5, 16), "little faith" (*oligopistos*, as in 6:30; 8:26).[9]

NARRATIVE TECHNIQUE

Matthew has a special liking for numbers and numeric patterns.[10] There are many triads in his Gospel (some of which are derived from Mark), such as three fourteens in the genealogy (1:2–17), three angelic messages to Joseph in dreams (1:20; 2:13; 2:19), three gifts of the magi (2:11), three temptations (4:1–11). There are also many instances of the number "two" (e.g., 2:16; 4:18, 21; 6:24; 8:28; 9:27). Underlying Matthew's interest in the number "fourteen" in the genealogy is probably the principle of gematria, an ancient form of numerology by which names are given numerical values. In Hebrew, the numeric value of the consonants in the name "David" ($d + w + d$) is fourteen. The division of Jesus' teaching into five main discourses is probably a numerical allusion to the five books of Moses, which in turn is a gesture toward Jesus' fulfillment of the law and his role as the new Moses (see below).

A literary device frequently employed by the evangelist is repetition.[11] His use of this strategy is evident in the genealogy (the repetition of the word "begat," translated as "the father of" in NRSV); the beatitudes ("Blessed are . . ."); the antitheses ("You have heard that it was said, . . . , but I say to you . . ."; 5:21–48); the parables of the kingdom ("The kingdom of heaven is like . . ."; 13:44–47); the woes against the scribes and Pharisees ("Woe to you . . ."; 23:1–36). As noted above, Matthew uses the same formula ("When Jesus had finished saying these things") after each of his five blocks of teaching.

The most striking of Matthew's repeated formulas is the fulfillment statement "This took place to fulfill what had been spoken by the Lord through the prophet." The formula, which slightly varies in expression, is used ten times in total (1:22–23; 2:15, 17–18, 23; 4:14–16; 8:17; 12:17–21; 13:35; 21:4–5; 27:9–10).[12] The frequent use of the citation formula is a significant literary device in its own right. Other Old Testament passages are cited without such formulas (e.g., 2:5–6; 3:3; 5:17; 10:34–35).

---

9. For a fuller list of Matthew's favorite words and expressions, see Davies and Allison, *Matthew*, 1:74–80.

10. Ibid., 1:85–87; Davies and Allison note that rabbinic texts are filled with numbers and numerical patterns and suggest that Matthew's penchant for numerical patterning places him in the rabbinic world.

11. Ibid., 1:88–92.

12. Ibid., 3:573–74.

In keeping with his organized approach, the evangelist sometimes provides a heading sentence at the beginning of sections (e.g., 1:18; 6:1; 7:1; 11:20) and a summarizing statement at the end of units (e.g., 5:48; 6:34; 7:12).[13]

NARRATIVE TIME

Matthew's constant use of the temporal adjective *tote* might suggest a concern for chronological precision, but only sometimes does it have a strict temporal force (meaning "next in temporal order"). More often it serves as a loose connective. The narrative follows a broad chronological sequence, but it is clear that much of the material has been arranged according to form and topic. Chapters 8–9, for instance, group together ten miracle stories, and chapter 13 brings together seven parables on the theme of the kingdom. Many scholars think that the Sermon on the Mount is a selection of Jesus' teachings compiled by the evangelist himself rather than a single sermon delivered on a particular occasion.

The alternation between action and extended speech modulates the pace of storytelling. As in Mark's Gospel, narrative time slows down significantly when Jesus reaches Jerusalem.

Matthew dates the birth of Jesus to the time of King Herod (2:1) and the move of the holy family to Nazareth to the reign of Archelaus (2:22). Like Mark, Matthew does not carefully mark the passing of time in his account of Jesus' ministry, but as in Mark's Gospel, time notes become more pronounced once Jesus arrives in the capital (21:17–18, 23; 26:1–2, 17, 20; 27:1, 45–46, 57, 62; 28:1).

NARRATIVE SPACE

After the birth narrative (with the movement from Bethlehem to Egypt, back to Israel, and settlement in Nazareth), Matthew's narrative follows the geographical progression exhibited in Mark: baptism in the Jordan, ministry in Galilee, withdrawal to the north, travel through Judea and Jericho, then arrival, ministry, and crucifixion in Jerusalem. The Gospel ends, though, in Galilee (28:16–20). Galilee is identified in Matthew as "Galilee of the Gentiles" (4:15; cf. Isa. 9:1). It is appropriate, therefore, that the commission to take the gospel to all nations takes place there.

13. Ibid., 1:93.

As in Mark, houses (e.g., 2:11; 8:14; 9:10, 23, 28), the sea/seaside (e.g., 4:13, 18; 8:23–27, 32) and synagogues (4:23; 9:18, 35; 12:9; 13:54) are prominent narrative locations in the Galilean ministry. In Matthew, synagogues are more sharply distinguished as "their synagogues": 4:23; 9:35; 10:17; 12:9; 13:54; 23:34 ("your"). This may reflect a situation in which Matthew's immediate addressees consider themselves, or are beginning to see themselves, as socially distinct from the Jewish community or at least other Jews.

The temple is a significant narrative location in the final section of the Gospel (21:12, 14, 15, 23; 24:1–2). Matthew's view of the temple, like Mark's, is the subject of scholarly debate. Matthew portrays Jesus as paying the temple tax (17:24–27), but Jesus seems to pay this tax as a concession rather than out of genuine conviction. In 24:15, Jesus speaks reverentially of the temple as "the holy place," but in the context of a prophecy about its defilement. Matthew is clear that the temple is destined to be destroyed (24:2). To prophesy the temple's destruction might seem to be anti-Jewish (on Matthew's alleged anti-Judaism, see below), but such prophecy is well established in Jewish scriptural tradition (Jer. 7). Also, Matthew is aware that the temple actually was destroyed in 70 CE, and this saying reflects commentary on that event.

Mountains are especially significant in Matthew's Gospel. The third temptation takes place on a very high mountain (4:8); a major sermon is delivered on a mountain (5:1) and is traditionally called the "Sermon on the Mount"; Jesus goes up a mountain to pray (14:23; cf. Mark 6:46); he is transfigured on a mountain (Matt. 17:1; cf. Mark 9:2). Healings take place on a mountain (Matt. 15:29–31), where four thousand are fed (15:32–39). Jesus enters Jerusalem over the Mount of Olives (21:1; cf. Mark 11:1), from where he delivers his eschatological discourse (24:3; cf. Mark 13:3) and to where he and the disciples go after their final meal (26:30; cf. Mark 14:26). The risen Jesus commissions his followers on a mountain in Galilee (28:16–20). The emphasis on mountains in this Gospel relates to some extent to the evangelist's view of Jesus as a new Moses (see below).

THE CHARACTERIZATION OF JESUS

Following the pattern of the previous chapter (on Mark), we will look first at Matthew's christological titles and then at his characterization of Jesus.

The Titles Used for Jesus

Messiah. Jesus is identified as the Messiah at the commencement of the Gospel (1:1), and his messianic status is reiterated in the genealogy (1:16–17) and birth narrative (1:18; cf. 2:4). John the Baptist hears in prison "what the Messiah was doing" (11:2). Peter confesses Jesus as the Messiah (16:16). In Matthew's version of this episode, Jesus praises Peter's acclamation and orders the disciples "not to tell anyone that he was the Messiah" (16:20). To the high priest's demand "Tell us if you are the Messiah, the Son of God," Jesus replies, "You have said so." The answer sounds evasive, but it has an affirmative sense (cf. 26:25). After his condemnation by the high priest, Jesus is mocked as a would-be Messiah (26:68, only in Matthew). The title "Messiah" is also applied to Jesus in derisory fashion by Pilate (27:17, 22, both references only in Matthew).

Son of God. Jesus is identified as God's Son in the birth and childhood narrative. In the return of the holy family to Nazareth, Matthew finds the fulfillment of Hosea's prophecy: "Out of Egypt I have called my son" (2:15; cf. Hos. 11:1). At the baptism the divine voice publicly announces, "This is my beloved Son." Satan addresses Jesus as God's Son at the temptation (Matt. 4:3, 6; paralleled in Luke). Jesus is recognized as God's Son by the demons in the story of the Gadarene demoniacs (8:29). Jesus speaks of his unique relationship to God, as "the Son" to "the Father" (Matt. 11:25–27 = Luke 10:21–22). Uniquely in Matthew, Jesus is identified as Son of God after his walking on the water (Matt. 14:33) and in the messianic confession at Caesarea Philippi (16:16). Jesus implicitly identifies himself as God's Son in the parable of the Vineyard (21:33–46) and refers to himself as "the Son" in the eschatological discourse (24:36). At Jesus' trial the high priest asks him if he is "the Messiah, the Son of God" (26:63). Uniquely in Matthew, Jesus is mocked on the cross as Son of God; the centurion and the soldiers call him God's Son (27:40, 43). At the conclusion of the Gospel, in the Great Commission, exclusive to Matthew, Jesus refers to himself as the divine Son in using the proto-Trinitarian formula "Father and Son and Holy Spirit" (28:19).

As we noticed in the Gospel of Mark, it is important to emphasize that "Son of God" is not necessarily a divine title in Matthew. In some passages it is clearly a messianic title (8:29; 26:63), and in 2:15, the notion of God's Son involves an Israel typology, claiming Israel as God's son. But in other contexts, especially 28:19, the ascription of divine sonship to Jesus clearly indicates his transcendent status.

Lord. The title *kyrios*, "Lord," is frequently used for Jesus in Matthew. Jesus is first identified as "the Lord" implicitly in the citation of Isaiah 40:3 in Matthew 3:3. In many instances thereafter, *kyrios* is a respectful term of address or bears the sense "master" (8:2, 6, 8, etc.). The formulations "Lord, save us/me" (8:25; 14:30) and "Have mercy, Lord" (15:22; 17:15; 20:30, 31), directed at Jesus, echo invocations to God in the psalms (e.g., Pss. 11:1; 106:47; 6:3;

30:10).[14] These formulations are distinctively Matthean. In a saying in the eschatological discourse (Matt. 24:42), Jesus refers to himself as "your Lord," casting himself in the role of God at his eschatological coming (this element of the saying also is distinctively Matthean). Uniquely Matthean are scenes of judgment in which people call on Jesus as Lord (7:21; 25:37, 44).[15]

Son of Man. The term is used some thirty times in Matthew's Gospel, from 8:20 onward. As in all the Synoptics, the term is used with respect to the earthly activity of the Son of Man (e.g., 8:20; 9:6); the suffering, death, and resurrection of the Son of Man (e.g., 12:40; 17:9, 12, 22); and the future role of the Son of Man. Matthew lays particular emphasis on the eschatological role of the Son of Man. Only Matthew speaks of the *parousia* of the Son of Man (24:3, 27, 37, 39), a term used elsewhere in the New Testament for the second coming of Jesus (e.g., 1 Cor. 15:23; 1 Thess. 2:19). Also distinctively Matthean is the picture of the Son of Man seated on his glorious throne (Matt. 19:28; 25:31).

Other titles. As in Mark, "teacher" is a frequently used title for Jesus (e.g., Matt. 8:19; 9:11; 10:24, 25). In Matthew, though, Jesus actually *does* a lot of teaching. One may rightly conclude that Jesus' role as authoritative teacher is a significant aspect of Matthew's characterization of Jesus. Even so, it is striking that Jesus is never called "teacher" by his closest followers. Furthermore, only Judas calls Jesus "rabbi" in Matthew's Gospel (26:25, 49).[16]

The populace regards Jesus as a "prophet" (14:5; 16:14; 21:11, 46). To some extent his ministry is prophetic in style. Jesus refers to himself as a prophet (13:57). As in Mark, the prophetic categorization within Matthew represents a lower estimation of Jesus (16:13–17), though the implicit designation of Jesus as the prophet like Moses (Deut. 18:15) in Matthew 17:5 clearly has christological significance.

The messianic title "Son of David" is especially prominent in Matthew. It is used for Jesus eight times in this Gospel (1:1; 9:27; 12:23; 15:22; 20:30, 31; 21:9, 15; cf. 22.42). The title coheres with Matthew's traditional expectation of a Messiah from David's line who would exercise royal functions. Those who address Jesus as "Son of David" are often those in need (9:27; 15:22; 20:30; 21:15).[17] The title "King of the Jews/Israel" is applied to Jesus in mockery in the trial and crucifixion (27:11, 29, 37, 42) but affirmatively in

---

14. Simon J. Gathercole, *The Pre-Existent Son: Recovering the Christologies of Matthew, Mark, and Luke* (Grand Rapids: Wm. B. Eerdmans Publishing Co., 2006), 246.

15. Ibid.

16. "Rabbi" is the Greek form of a Hebrew word meaning "my great one." It became the specialized term for an ordained Jewish teacher. In Jesus' day, it seems to be have been applied to teachers but not as a technical term. See Marcus, *Mark*, 2: 633.

17. David R. Bauer, "Son of David," in *Dictionary of Jesus and the Gospels*, ed. Joel B. Green, Scot McKnight, and I. Howard Marshall (Leicester: InterVarsity Press, 1992), 766–69, here 769.

the birth narrative (2:2). The triumphal entry marks the coming of Israel's king to Jerusalem (21:5).

In 12:18–21, citing Isaiah 42:1–4, Matthew explicitly identifies Jesus as the Lord's "Servant" of the book of Isaiah.[18] In 1:23, he is identified as "Emmanuel, . . . God is with us." The epithet is derived from Isaiah 7:14. Care must be taken not to read back—into either the original passage in Isaiah or its citation by Matthew—christological ideas that belong to later church doctrine. But Matthew's clear implication is that Jesus manifests or focalizes the presence of God on earth: thus in 18:20 and 28:20 Jesus promises his own presence among his followers.

Characterizational Emphases

Matthew presents Jesus, to a significant extent, as a new Moses.[19] There are clear parallels between Jesus and Moses, especially in the early chapters of the Gospel. Both are threatened by an evil ruler (Pharaoh, Herod), survive when infants of their age are massacred, and spend time in Egypt (Exod. 2; Matt. 2). Like Moses, Jesus fasts for forty days and nights (Exod. 34:28; Matt. 4:2).[20] As Moses ascended Mount Sinai to receive the law, Jesus delivers his first great speech (and stricter interpretation of the law) on a mountain (5:1). Allusions to Moses continue as the narrative proceeds. The final scene of the Gospel, unique to Matthew, has Jesus, just like Moses, ending his earthly activity on a mountain. As noted above, the five main discourses of the Gospel seem to allude to the five books of Moses,

Matthew also presents Jesus as a shepherd.[21] In the birth and infancy narrative (2:6), Jesus is spoken of as a ruler come forth "to shepherd my people Israel" (picking up 1 Chr. 11:2; cf. Mic. 5:2–5). Jesus is said to have compassion on the crowd because they are "like sheep without a shepherd" (9:36; cf. Mark 6:34). In the eschatological discourse, the Son of Man is portrayed as a shepherd, separating people "as a shepherd separates the sheep from the goats" (25:32). Jesus speaks of his coming death as the smiting of the shepherd (Matt. 26:31; cf. Mark 14:27; citing Zech. 13:7). The portrayal of Jesus as a shepherd is related to the new-Moses characterization in that Moses was remembered as a shepherd (Isa. 63:11; also Matt. 9:36 alludes to Num. 27:17,

18. See further Richard Beaton, *Isaiah's Christ in Matthew's Gospel* (Cambridge: Cambridge University Press, 2002).

19. Allison, *New Moses*. All four Gospels display a Jesus-Moses parallel: the Synoptic Gospels clearly in the transfiguration story (see chap. 10 below), the Fourth Gospel in the discourse on the "bread of life" (6.22–59; cf. John 1:17).

20. Davies and Allison, *Matthew*, 1:358.

21. John Riches, "Matthew for the Church's Year," *Expository Times* 122, no. 2 (November 2010): 73–81, here 78.

of Moses and Joshua), and also links Jesus to David, who was a shepherd (1 Sam. 17:15, 34–35). Additionally, it connects Jesus with the LORD God, who in the Old Testament is supremely the "Shepherd of Israel" (Ps 80.1; Jer. 31.10; etc.).

In Matthew 12:42 and 13:54, Jesus' wisdom is highlighted, characterizing him as a wise man or sage. In the Old Testament (esp. Prov. 8:22–31) and early Jewish writings, God's wisdom is spoken of as if it were a distinct person. In Matthew 11:28–30, Jesus speaks remarkably like personified wisdom in Sirach 51:23–26. That Jesus plays the part of personified divine wisdom is strongly suggested in Matthew 11:2–19. The reference to "the works of the Messiah" (Gk.) at the beginning of the section (11:2) matches the reference to the works of wisdom at the end of it (11:19).[22]

Matthew places particular emphasis on Jesus as the object of worship (2:11; 8:2; 9:18; 14:33; 15:25; 20:20; 28:9, 17; outside of Matthew, we read of Jesus being "worshiped" only in Luke 24:52 and John 9:38). The Greek word *proskyneō* can simply mean "to fall before," but in certain instances, it does seem to mean worship in the full sense of prostrating oneself before the divine (Matt. 14:33; 28:17).

THE CHARACTERIZATION OF THE DISCIPLES

Matthew's portrayal of the disciples is more complimentary than Mark's.[23] Where Mark says that the disciples do not understand Jesus' words (Mark 4:13; 6:52; 8:21; 9:10), Matthew either has no reference to their lack of understanding or states that the disciples *do* understand (13:16–17, 51; 16:12). The disciples' understanding is also emphasized in 13:51, as Jesus concludes the parables on the kingdom of heaven. Whereas Mark highlights their lack of faith (4:40), Matthew picks up on the "little faith" that they do have (6:30; 8:26; 14:31; 16:8; 17:20).[24] Even so, while Matthew focuses less on the failure of the disciples, he certainly does not gloss over their negative actions (e.g., 15:23; 16:23; 19:13–15).[25]

22. On Matthew's wisdom Christology, see Fred W. Burnett, *The Testament of Jesus-Sophia: A Redaction-Critical Study of the Eschatological Discourse in Matthew* (Washington, DC: University Press of America, 1981); and Celia M. Deutsch, *Lady Wisdom, Jesus, and the Sages: Metaphor and Social Context in Matthew's Gospel* (Valley Forge, PA: Trinity Press International, 1996).

23. Richard A. Burridge, *Four Gospels, One Jesus?* (London: SPCK, 1994), 83–85; Mark L. Strauss, *Four Portraits, One Jesus: An Introduction to Jesus and the Gospels* (Grand Rapids: Zondervan, 2007), 242–43.

24. Burridge, *Four Gospels*, 84.

25.See further Jeannine K. Brown, *Disciples in Narrative Perspective: The Portrayal and Function of the Matthean Disciples* (Atlanta: Society of Biblical Literature, 2002), who lays emphasis on the disciples' shortcomings.

Matthew has a special interest in Peter. He is prominent in two passages unique to the Gospel (17:24–27; 18:21–22). In the incident at Caesarea Philippi, a blessing is pronounced upon him on account of his christological confession; Jesus then tells Peter that he is the rock upon whom the church will be built (16:17–20). Jesus' statement is a play on words, since the name Peter means "rock/stone." According to some interpreters, Jesus is not saying that *Peter* is the rock but that the rock is his confession. But it is more natural to take Peter himself as the rock. By designating Peter as the rock of the church, Jesus is assigning him an important role in the church's foundation (cf. Eph. 2:20).[26] Although Matthew accentuates the preeminence of Peter among the disciples, he does not hide his faults (e.g., 14:29–31; 16:23; 26:69–75).

THE CHARACTERIZATION
OF THE RELIGIOUS AUTHORITIES

The religious leaders are portrayed in a strongly negative fashion. The Pharisees are mentioned frequently in Matthew (some 29 times), and they are always hostile to Jesus (e.g., 9:11, 34; 12:2, 14, 24, 38). Jesus is equally scathing about them, especially in the woes of chapter 23, where he calls them hypocrites, snakes, and whitewashed tombs and accuses them of greed, love of honor, and self-indulgence. Yet Jesus grants that the Pharisees and scribes "sit on Moses' seat," and he tells the crowds and his disciples to do and follow what they teach (23:2). In Matthew, the Pharisees are involved alongside the chief priests in the final plot to do away with Jesus (27:62).

The scribes frequently are associated with the Pharisees (5:20; 12:38; 15:1; 23:2, 13–39), the chief priests (2:4; 16:21; 20:18; 21:15; 27:41) and elders (16:21; 26:57; 27:41). Again, their profile in the Gospel is negative, though there are a few chinks of light (8:19; 13:52; 23:2).

The chief priests make a brief appearance in the birth and infancy narrative (2:4) and are mentioned in the passion predictions (16:21; 20:18), but otherwise they figure as narrative participants only in the passion narrative (e.g., 21:15, 23, 45). They are regularly associated with "the elders" (16:21; 21:23; 26:3, 47; 27:1, 3, 12, 20; 27:41; 28:12) and are always hostile to Jesus. The chief priests and the elders devise the plan to bribe the soldiers (28:12).

The elders are mentioned more frequently in Matthew than in any of the other Gospels (11 times). In Matthew they are called "the elders of the

26. In Roman Catholic interpretation, Peter's role as the rock of the church is an important basis of papal authority. Peter's apostolic authority is passed in direct lineage to subsequent holders of this office.

people" (21:23; 26:3, 47; 27:1), a designation that portrays them as acting on behalf of the nation.

The Sadducees, who appear only once in Mark (12:18) and in Luke (20:27) and not at all in John, are mentioned seven times in Matthew (3:7; 16:1, 6, 11, 12; 22:23, 34). In Matthew they are almost always linked with the Pharisees (3:7; 16:1, 6, 11, 12; 22:34) and appear as antagonistic (16:1; 22:23).

The more heated nature of the exchanges between Jesus and the religious authorities in Matthew probably reflects growing conflict with the majority Jewish community at the time of writing (at least in Matthew's locality). The Gospel seems to presume a distinction between church and synagogue (referred to, as noted above, as *"their* synagogues"). Matthew's negative portrayal of the Jewish authorities has led some interpreters to label him as "anti-Jewish." The statement attributed to the Jewish crowd in 27:25, "His blood be on us and on our children!" recorded only by Matthew, seems to lend weight to that accusation. It would be a mistake, however, to read later anti-Semitism back into the Gospel. Matthew himself was almost certainly a Jewish Christian, writing for a predominantly Jewish Christian audience, even if these readers had begun to define themselves in opposition to other Jews.[27] The evangelist has given us a thoroughly Jewish Gospel, emphasizing and indeed celebrating the Jewishness of Jesus. The statement of 27:25, in its literary context, has a narrow focus; it does not apply to all Jews for all time (see below on the Gentile mission).

THEMES

The kingdom theme is especially characteristic of Matthew's Gospel. There are more kingdom sayings in Matthew's Gospel than in any of the other three. Around 30 kingdom sayings are unique to Matthew (e.g., 3:2; 5:10, 19, 20; 7:21).[28] Matthew prefers the expression "kingdom of heaven" (32 times) to "kingdom of God" (five times, if counting 6:33). As in Mark, the kingdom is both imminent and present. And as in Mark, the final realization of God's dominion lies in the future (20:21; 25:34; 26:29). The motif of the kingdom is found in each of the main teaching sections in the Gospel (e.g., 5:3, 10, 19; 10:7; 13:11, 19, 24; 18:1, 3, 4; 24:14). Other themes developed by Matthew include the following.

27. For an account of Matthew's primary audience as a community of Jewish followers of Jesus in competition with other Jewish communities, see Anthony J. Saldarini, *Matthew's Christian-Jewish Community* (Chicago and London: University of Chicago Press, 1994).

28. Chrys C. Caragounis, "Kingdom of God/Kingdom of Heaven," in Green, McKnight, and Marshall, *Dictionary of Jesus and the Gospels*, 417–30, here 426.

God as "Your Father"

Jesus speaks of God in an exclusive way as *"my* Father" (e.g., 7:21; 10:32–33; 11:27; 12:50), but he also talks frequently about God as *"your* Father" (e.g., 5:16, 45, 48; 6:1, 4; *"our* father" in 6:9), encouraging his hearers to view God in paternal terms.[29] The formulation "your Father" is not absent from the other Gospels, but it appears much less often (Mark 11:25; Luke 6:36; 12:30). In John's Gospel, only once does Jesus speak to his disciples of God as "your Father" (20:17), and never in John is God called "our Father." The stress on the intimate child-father relationship that Jesus' followers can enjoy with God is thus a particular Matthean emphasis (for John, this intimacy is with Jesus himself).

The Law

Matthew shows more interest in the Jewish law than any of the other Gospel writers. A passage found in this Gospel alone is one of the strongest affirmations of the law in the entire New Testament (5:17–19).

Jesus himself is faithful to the law, and he exhorts others to obey it (8:4; 7:12; 19:17; 22:34–40). He expects his disciples to take gifts to the altar (5:23–24), to give alms (6:1–4), and to fast (6:16–18). In passages that Matthew has in common with Mark, Matthew sometimes has an additional element that lays emphasis on the law (12:12; 19:17; 24:20).

At the same time, Matthew portrays Jesus as standing above the law. This is evident especially in the repeated formula governing the antitheses of 5:21–48, "You have heard that it was said, . . . but I say to you, . . ." In the antitheses themselves, Jesus extends and intensifies stipulations of the law, and in some cases he seems to change the command (as when forbidding oaths, which the law permits; cf. Num. 30:2).

Matthew exhibits a high view of the law and portrays Jesus as the fulfillment of the law (5:17–18). Yet Jesus' teaching is accorded an even greater level of authority: whereas the law endures *until* heaven and earth pass away, Jesus' words "will never pass away" (24:35). In the closing commission, the disciples are told to observe all that *Jesus,* rather than Moses, has commanded them (28:20).[30]

---

29. See further Larry W. Hurtado, "God" in Green, McKnight, and Marshall, *Dictionary of Jesus and the Gospels,* 270–76, here 273.

30. In Marshall's view, Matthew effectively presents Jesus' teaching as a "new" Torah (see I. Howard Marshall, *New Testament Theology: Many Witnesses, One Gospel* [Downers Grove, IL: InterVarsity Press, 2004], 119), but this interpretative judgment exceeds the evidence and undermines Matthew's clear understanding of the enduring importance of the law, even as Jesus reinterprets and strengthens it.

Righteousness

We have already noted Matthew's fondness of the terminology of "righteousness." Righteousness is a key theme of the Sermon on the Mount (5:6, 10, 20; 6:33). For Matthew, righteousness means conformity to God's will. It is lifestyle or mode of behavior. It is not, as in Lutheran interpretation of Paul, a status conferred by God on the basis of faith; rather, for Matthew, righteousness refers to one's good deeds. Righteousness is an entry condition for the kingdom of heaven (5:20). The level of righteousness demanded by Jesus exceeds that of the scribes and Pharisees (5:20) and goes beyond what the Mosaic law requires (5:21–48).[31]

Coming Judgment

Coming judgment is a particularly prominent theme in Matthew's Gospel. Warnings of judgment pervade the teaching of Jesus in this Gospel. In forewarning of judgment, Jesus uses the imagery of fire (e.g., 5:22; 7:19; 13:40) and darkness (8:12; 22:13; 25:30) and speaks of "weeping and gnashing of teeth" (e.g., 8:12; 13:42); the latter image does not appear in Mark or John and is found only once in Luke (13:28). The coming judgment will involve separation, vividly illustrated in the parable (or allegory) of the Sheep and the Goats (25:31–46), in which the Son of Man, acting as a shepherd, divides the animals and assigns them to different destinies, based on their treatment of others.

Fulfillment

All the Gospels are concerned to show how Jesus fulfills Old Testament expectation, but it is a particular burden of this evangelist. In the birth and infancy section of the narrative, the narrator repeatedly notes the fulfillment of Scripture in events he relates: The virginal conception fulfills Isaiah 7:14 (Matt. 1:22–23). Jesus' birth in Bethlehem fulfills Micah 5:2 (Matt. 2:5–6). His return from Egypt fulfills Hosea 11:1 (Matt. 2:15). The massacre of the infants fulfills Jeremiah 31:15 (Matt. 2:17–18). The settling down in Nazareth fulfills prophecy that Jesus "will be called a Nazorean" (Matt. 2:23); a specific prophecy like this does not appear in the Old Testament, but Matthew may have in mind Isaiah 11:1 and its reference to the "branch" (*nezer* in Hebrew) of Jesse, in which case, we have a fulfillment based on wordplay (Nazareth/ Nazorean/*nezer*). Alongside these fulfillments, in this section Jesus' adoptive

---

31. For a summary of the theme of righteousness in Matthew, see Scot McKnight, "Justice, Righteousness," in Green, McKnight, and Marshall, *Dictionary of Jesus and the Gospels*, 413–15.

father, Joseph, is a dreamer, like his namesake in Genesis 37–50, who sheltered his people in Egypt.

Elements of Jesus' ministry are said to fulfill Scripture: His Galilean ministry fulfills Isaiah 9:1–2 (Matt. 4:14–16). His healing activity fulfills Isaiah 53:4 (Matt. 8:17) and Isaiah 42:1–4 (Matt. 12:17). His style of teaching in parables fulfills Psalm 78:2 (Matt. 13:35). His triumphal entry fulfills Zechariah 9:9 (Matt. 21:4–5).

Finally, events in the passion bring about scriptural fulfillment: Jesus' arrest fulfils Scripture (Matt. 26:56; no specific OT text is cited). Judas's return of the blood money and its use to purchase the potter's field fulfill Zechariah 11:12–13 and various passages in Jeremiah (Matt. 27:9).

The fulfillment statements convey the impression that Jesus' life and ministry conform to a predisclosed divine plan. Yet the nature of many of the correlations that Matthew draws is such that fulfillment is only evident in retrospect.

The Gentile Mission

Matthew emphasizes the Jewish priority of Jesus' earthly ministry (15:24). The mission of the disciples is initially restricted to the land and people of Israel (10:5–6). After Jesus' rejection in Jerusalem, however, the gospel is extended to the Gentile world. The commandment to "go . . . and make disciples of all nations" in 28:19, one of the clearest New Testament mandates for worldwide mission, comes at the climax of the Gospel and formally rescinds the prohibition of 10:5–6.

The mission to the Gentiles is foreshadowed in the narrative: the four women mentioned in the genealogy (Tamar, Rahab, Ruth, and the wife of Uriah the Hittite—all were Gentiles);[32] the coming of the magi (2:1–12); the faith of the Roman officer (8:5–13); the supplication of the Canaanite woman (15:21–28). The Gentile mission is predicted in 24:14 and is presupposed in 25:31–46.

The expansion of the mission to include Gentiles does not mean, though, the abandonment of the Jewish people. The Jewish mission evidently continues alongside the Gentile one (cf. 10:23), and Matthew includes a promise of the future redemption of Israel (23:39).[33]

The Church

As noted above, Matthew's Gospel is the only one of the four to use the word "church," *ekklēsia* (16:18; 18:17). Luke has many references to the church,

---

32. Davies and Allison, *Matthew*, 3:171.
33. Ibid., 3:323–24.

but only in his second volume, the Acts of the Apostles, and not in his Gospel. In Matthew's Gospel, Jesus anticipates the formation and development of the church after his death and resurrection. The organized, institutional church of later church history is not in view. Envisaged is rather a community of faith formed around the disciples. Some degree of structure to the community is envisaged (18:15–35), no doubt reflecting patterns in place at the time of writing. Jesus also anticipates small groups gathering in his name (18:20).

CONCLUSION

Matthew tells the shared gospel story in such a way as to bring out its links with Israel's history and its realization of Israel's hopes. Matthew emphasizes Jesus' fulfillment of messianic and other Jewish expectations. Jesus' significance is explicated in terms of Old Testament figures and categories: Moses, the shepherd, the Lord's Servant, divine wisdom, Emmanuel. Matthew's Gospel is the most Jewish Gospel (laying emphasis on the Jewishness of Jesus), but it also provides a powerful endorsement of the mission to the Gentiles. The way it combines continuity with Israel's past and progression into the church's future justifies its status as the First Gospel.

FOR FURTHER READING

Davies, W. D., and Dale C. Allison Jr. *The Gospel according to Saint Matthew*. 3 vols. International Critical Commentary. Edinburgh: T&T Clark, 1988, 1991, 1997.
Hare, Douglas R. A. *Matthew*. Interpretation. Louisville, KY: John Knox Press, 1993.
Harrington, Daniel J. *The Gospel of Matthew*. Sacra pagina 1. Collegeville, MN: Liturgical Press, 1991.
Keener, Craig S. *A Commentary on the Gospel of Matthew*. Grand Rapids: Eerdmans, 1999.
Long, Thomas G. *Matthew*. Westminster Bible Companion. Louisville, KY: Westminster John Knox Press, 1997.
Luz, Ulrich. *The Theology of the Gospel of Matthew*. Cambridge: Cambridge University Press, 1995.
Meir, John P. *The Vision of Matthew: Christ, Church, and Morality in the First Gospel*. New York: Paulist Press, 1979.
Nolland, John. *The Gospel of Matthew*. New International Greek New Testament Commentaries. Grand Rapids: Eerdmans; London: Paternoster Press, 2005.
Powell, Mark Allan. *Chasing the Eastern Star: Adventures in Biblical Reader-Response Criticism*. Louisville, KY: Westminster John Knox Press, 2001.
Riches, John. *Matthew*. Sheffield: Sheffield Academic Press, 1996.

Senior, Donald. *The Gospel of Matthew*. Abingdon New Testament Commentary. Nashville: Abingdon Press, 1997.

Stanton, Graham N. *A Gospel for a New People: Studies in Matthew*. Louisville, KY: Westminster/John Knox Press, 1992.

Wright, N.T. *Matthew for Everyone*, Part 1. Louisville, KY: Westminster John Knox Press, 2004.

———. *Matthew for Everyone*, Part 2. Louisville, KY: Westminster John Knox Press, 2004.

5

The Gospel according to Luke

Like Matthew, Luke has used Mark's Gospel in composing his narrative, but whereas Matthew reproduces almost all of Mark, Luke reprocesses only about half of it.[1] Like Matthew, Luke augments the core story of Jesus with a birth and infancy narrative and with postresurrection appearances, but he goes further than Matthew by writing a second volume, the Acts of the Apostles, in which he narrates the birth and expansion of the church. In recent years there has been a tendency to emphasize the narrative unity of Luke and Acts and to treat them as a single continuous work. However, it is not clear that Luke had Acts in mind when he wrote the Gospel. The fact that Luke renarrates Jesus' ascension at the beginning of Acts (Jesus is carried up into heaven at the end of the Gospel) suggests that the second volume may have been conceived after the writing of the Gospel, as a sequel to it. Taken on its own, Luke's Gospel comfortably fits the category of ancient biography.

Luke's biography of Jesus features Jesus' role as Savior of the world. This Gospel gives particular emphasis to Jesus' lordship, compassion, healing, ministry to the poor, and acceptance of outcasts and sinners. In this Gospel, Jesus is filled with the Holy Spirit and exhibits prayerful dependence on God.

TEXTUAL STRUCTURE

A key structural marker in Luke's Gospel is the announcement of Jesus' turn toward Jerusalem in 9:51. This leads into a long section, sometimes called the

---

1. Luke draws on Mark in three main sections of his Gospel: Luke 3:1–6:19; 8:4–9:50; 18:15–24:11. Surprisingly, he more or less passes over a whole chunk of Mark's Gospel (6:45–8:26), moving straight from the feeding of the five thousand to Peter's confession.

"travel narrative," in which Jesus journeys to Jerusalem. In Mark, the journey is narrated in one chapter (10); Matthew devotes two chapters to it (19–20). In Luke, however, it occupies about ten chapters. The bulk of the travel section is made of up distinctively Lukan material (L) and double tradition.

Luke's narrative falls into four main sections:

1:1–4:13	Birth, Childhood, and Preparation for Ministry
4:14–9:50	Ministry in Galilee
9:51–19:27	Journey to Jerusalem
19:28–24:35	Jerusalem, Passion, and Resurrection

Some scholars see Luke 1–2, the birth and childhood narrative, as a distinct section, separate from 3:1–4:13, but since the evangelist regards the ministry of John the Baptist and the Spirit-anointing of Jesus at baptism as the *beginning* of the gospel story (Acts 10:37), it is better to take the whole of 1:1–4:13 as an extended introduction. The broad structure of the Gospel thus reflects the geographical progression of Jesus' ministry as Luke presents it.

Detecting subdivisions in 4:14–9:50 proves to be tricky. One can find certain groups of material, such as the collection of controversies in 5:12–6:11, but no overall systematic arrangement of the contents.

The travel narrative shows some evidence of topical organization (e.g., the three parables that feature something "lost" in chap. 15), but the key structural markers are three notices that Jesus is "on the way" to Jerusalem: 13:22; 17:11; 18:31. Each notice stands at the beginning of a pericope (another notice occurs in the middle of a saying, 13:33, and is not structurally significant). On the basis of these markers, the journey may be divided into four stages: 9:51–13:21; 13:22–17:10; 17:11–18:30; 18:31–19:28.[2]

PLOT

As when describing Matthew's plot, we may glide through some parts of Luke's plot that directly parallel Mark.

Birth, Childhood, and Preparation for Ministry (1:1–4:13)

The story of Jesus' birth is told in tandem with that of John the Baptist. The angel of the Lord appears to Zechariah in the temple and tells him that he and his barren wife, Elizabeth, will have a child, whom they are to name John.

2. More or less following Judith M. Lieu, *The Gospel of Luke* (Peterborough: Epworth Press, 1997), vi–vii.

The angel then appears to Mary and announces that she will bear a son, who is to be called Jesus. When Mary asks how this can be, since she is a virgin, she is told that the child will be conceived by the power of the Holy Spirit. The expectant mothers, who are related, meet. Elizabeth blesses Mary, and Mary responds with a song of praise. Sometime later, Elizabeth gives birth, and the child is circumcised and named. Zechariah praises God with a canticle that matches Mary's. We then read that "the child grew and became strong in spirit" (1:80).

The birth of Jesus takes place in lowly circumstances, but the awesome significance of the event is made clear in the angels' message to the shepherds: "To you is born this day in the city of David a Savior, who is the Messiah, the Lord" (2:11). The presentation of Jesus in the temple is the scene of a prophetic utterance that points to the conflict that lies ahead: the child Jesus, Simeon declares, is destined to cause division in Israel and will be "a sign that will be opposed" (2:34). A notice of the child's growth is then given (2:40), matching the earlier comment made about John the Baptist. Luke goes on to relate an episode involving Jesus as a twelve-year-old boy (2:41–52), demonstrating the child's extraordinary wisdom and his sense of a special filial bond with God. The birth and childhood narrative concludes with another statement of Jesus' physical maturation (2:52).

Moving ahead in time, the evangelist recounts the ministry of John the Baptist. Like Matthew, Luke reports John's preaching of repentance (3:7–9) yet includes a unique record of John's ethical teaching to particular groups (crowds, tax collectors, and soldiers; 3:10–14). The arrest and imprisonment of John (3:18–20) is narrated before Jesus' baptism (3:21–22). Then Luke includes a genealogy of Jesus in which he traces Jesus' ancestry back to Adam (3:23–38). The divine sonship announced by the voice from heaven at the baptism (3:22) comes under scrutiny in the temptation (4:1–13). Luke's version of this episode matches the lengthier account given by Matthew, with some differences in detail.

The Ministry in Galilee (4:14–9:50)

The preparation for ministry complete, Jesus returns to Galilee, "filled with the power of the Spirit" (4:14), and starts to teach in Galilean synagogues. The first major event of Jesus' ministry in Luke's narrative is the preaching in the synagogue at Nazareth, an event that comes later in Mark and Matthew. In his sermon, Jesus paraphrases Isaiah 61:1–2 and applies the prophecy to himself: "The spirit of the Lord is upon me, because he has anointed me to bring good news to the poor. He has sent me to proclaim release to the captives, and recovery of sight to the blind, to let the oppressed go free, to proclaim the year of the Lord's favor" (Luke 4:18–19). Those present initially react favorably, but the mood quickly changes. Jesus complains that "no prophet is accepted in the prophet's hometown" (4:24) and implies that, like Elijah and Elisha before him, he will meet with rejection in Israel. Full of rage, the townspeople drive Jesus out and intend to throw him off a cliff, but he walks through the crowd and moves on. The negative response he receives in Nazareth presages his rejection and crucifixion in Jerusalem. Following the preaching at Nazareth, Luke shows Jesus as fulfilling Isaiah 61:1–2 by preaching good news (4:42–44), releasing those held captive by demons (4:33–36, 41), and curing people of their infirmities (4:38–40).

The evangelist then turns attention to Jesus' gathering of disciples. The call of Simon Peter, James, and John occurs in the context of a miraculous catch of fish (5:1–11): Jesus' demonstration of power leads to their abandonment of "everything" to follow Jesus (5:11). A little later, we read of the call of Levi (5:27–28) and then of the selection of the Twelve (6:12–16). The gathering of disciples dovetails with the growth of opposition, as seen in a series of controversy stories (5:17–6:11, paralleling Mark 2:1–3:6).

The commissioning of the Twelve is followed by Jesus' Sermon on the Plain (Luke 6:17–49). Its contents parallel parts of Matthew's Sermon on the Mount. It begins with a series of blessings and woes (Luke 6:20–26) and then turns to love of enemies (6:27–36), judging (6:37–42), and bearing good fruit (6:43–46). It closes with the theme of being hearers and doers of the word (6:46–49).

Following the sermon comes the healing of the centurion's slave (7:1–10) and the raising of the widow of Nain's son (7:11–17), the latter found only in Luke. John the Baptist wonders if Jesus is the coming one (7:18–23). Jesus' answer, which lists the works he has been doing, recalls the wording of Isaiah 61:1–2, cited earlier. After giving his reply Jesus elaborates on the role of John the Baptist (Luke 7:24–35). Luke tells of Jesus' anointing by a sinful woman (7:36–50) and then makes mention of women, including Mary Magdalene, who accompany Jesus and the Twelve on their itinerant campaign (8:1–3). The parables of the Sower and Lamp come next (8:4–16). Jesus' statement on his true family (8:19–21) is followed by four powerful miracles (8:22–56, paralleling Mark 4:35–5:43).

The sending out and return of the Twelve (9:1–6, 10a) sandwiches the report of Herod's fear that Jesus is John the Baptist risen from the dead (9:7–9). Luke narrates the feeding of the five thousand (9:10b–17), which he follows with Peter's confession and the final passion prediction (9:18–27). The transfiguration provides further heavenly confirmation of Jesus' identity (9:28–36), and the events that follow (9:37–50) bring the Galilean ministry to a close.

The Journey to Jerusalem (9:51–19:44)

The narrator's comment, that Jesus "set his face to go to Jerusalem" (9:51), signals a new phase in the development. To a large extent the journey to Jerusalem is a structural device, since Jesus does not travel steadily toward the city but moves from place to place. That the goal of Jesus' movements is Jerusalem, however, is clear and repeatedly emphasized (13:22, 33; 17:11; 18:31; 19:11). This travel narrative is dominated by teachings, especially parables (17 in all).

The travel section begins with a story of rejection, as Samaritan villagers refuse to receive Jesus (9:51–56). The cost of discipleship is illustrated by the demands Jesus makes of would-be followers (9:57–62). The sending out and return of the seventy (or seventy-two)[3] messengers (10:1–24) precedes the lawyer's testing of Jesus (10:25–28), which leads into the parable of the Good Samaritan (10:29–37). Teaching on prayer (11:1–13) follows the story of Mary and Martha (10:38–42). Conflict reemerges in the form of the Beelzebul controversy (11:14–23); a little later there is a long polemic against the Pharisees and lawyers (11:37–54, which parallels the woes of Matt. 23). A disparate collection of teachings follows: on fearless confession (12:1–12), on the pursuit of wealth (12:13–34), on eschatological preparedness (12:35–48, 54–56), on the division Jesus causes (12:49–53), on coming judgment (13:1–9). Then we have a Sabbath healing followed by two short parables illustrating the growth of the kingdom (13:10–21).

The second stage of the journey commences with teaching about entering the kingdom (13:22–30). After his lament over Jerusalem (13:31–35), Jesus is found in the home of a Pharisee, which is a scene of healing and teaching (14:1–24). More teaching on the cost of discipleship follows (14:25–35), and then we have three parables of Loss and Recovery (15:1–32). The parables of the Dishonest Manager (16:1–14) and the Rich Man and Lazarus (16:19–31) are separated by sayings on the law and prophets, and on divorce and remarriage (16:16–18). Another set of sayings deals with stumbling, forgiveness, faith, and obedience (17:1–10).

The cleansing of ten lepers (17:11–19) is the first incident of the third leg of the journey (17:11–19). There follows an eschatological section (17:20–38), which anticipates the fuller eschatological discourse that Jesus will deliver in Jerusalem. Then we have the parable of the Persistent Widow (18:1–8) followed by the parable of the Pharisee and the Tax Collector (18:9–14) and sayings on children (18:15–17). The story of the rich young ruler flows into discipleship teaching (18:18–30).

---

3. Ancient manuscripts are divided on the number, with some giving "seventy" and others "seventy-two."

The final stage of the travel section begins with a passion prediction (18:31–34). The healing of a blind beggar comes next (18:35–43), followed by the story of Zacchaeus (19:1–10). The parable of the Pounds (19:11–27) marks the close of the long journey.

Jerusalem, Passion, and Resurrection

Finally Jesus arrives at Jerusalem, his goal. Luke narrates the triumphal entry (19:28–38) and the people's acclamation of Jesus as "the king who comes in the name of the Lord" (19:38). Jesus weeps over the city and foretells its destruction (19:39–44, only in Luke). He cleanses the temple (19:45–46) and teaches there every day (19:47–48). A series of debates follows, ending with a denunciation of the scribes (chap. 20). Luke next narrates the incident involving the widow's gift (21:1–4). Then we have Jesus' eschatological discourse (21:5–36), Luke's equivalent of Mark 13 and Matthew 24–25. In Mark and Matthew, the discourse is delivered on the Mount of Olives, but in Luke's Gospel, it is given in the temple precincts.

The plot to kill Jesus (22:1–2) introduces the passion cycle. Luke narrates the betrayal agreement by Judas (22:3–6), the preparation for the Passover (22:7–13), and the Last Supper (22:14–23). Unlike Mark and Matthew, Luke follows the supper with teaching given by Jesus (22:24–38). Jesus' prayer of anguish at the Mount of Olives (22:39–46) is followed by his arrest (22:47–53). Luke's narration of Peter's denial is distinguished by the poignant moment when Jesus turns and looks at Peter (22:54–61). A scene of mockery (22:63–65) precedes the trial before the Sanhedrin, which takes place in the morning (22:66–71). Jesus is then brought before Pilate (23:1–7). The Jewish leaders make a threefold accusation against Jesus: "perverting our nation, forbidding us to pay taxes to the emperor, and saying that he himself is the Messiah, a king" (23:2). Pilate declares Jesus guiltless (23:4), but his accusers will not back down. Upon learning that Jesus is a Galilean, Pilate sends him to Herod (23:8–12, only in Luke). The latter mocks Jesus but, like Pilate, finds him innocent (23:15). Jesus is sent back to Pilate (23:13–25) who makes two further declarations of Jesus' innocence and tries to release him but in the end hands him over to be executed (23:25). Jesus is led to the place called The Skull (23:26–32) and crucified (23:33–49). Only Luke records the exchange between Jesus and "the penitent thief" (23:39–43). At Jesus' death, the centurion praises God and pronounces Jesus "innocent" or "righteous" (23:47; see further chap. 11 below).

The discovery of the empty tomb by the women (24:1–12) is followed by an appearance of the risen Jesus before two disciples on the road to Emmaus (24:13–35). An appearance to Peter (24:34) is indicated but not narrated.

Then Jesus appears before the group of disciples (24:36–49). He calls them to be witnesses of the gospel and to proclaim repentance and forgiveness of sins to all nations. The commission is sealed with a promise of power from on high, and then Jesus is taken up into heaven (24:50–51). The Gospel closes with the disciples filled with joy and blessing God (24:52–53).

STYLE

Luke's Greek is the most stylish of the four evangelists. The evangelist writes with a very good command of the language, using a large range of constructions, including the optative mood (expressing a wish), rarely used in Koine Greek.[4] His preface, which is one long sentence (1:1–4), is written in fine Greek and is perhaps the most carefully crafted sentence in the New Testament (in terms of stylistic excellence, only Heb. 1:1–4 approaches it). The birth and infancy narrative that follows is written in a Jewish Greek mode, which captures the language and style of the LXX. The rest of the Gospel is written in good Koine Greek, with occasional literary flourishes (e.g., 3:1–2) and numerous septuagintal resonances. Luke thus shows remarkable literary versatility. His stylistic variability is also evident in the way he can match the style of his speeches in the Gospel and Acts to the culture of the speaker (compare the speech of Simeon in Luke 2:29–32 with the speech of Festus in Acts 25:14–21).[5]

Luke uses the largest vocabulary of the four evangelists. The total number of different words used in his Gospel is variously estimated; Joseph Fitzmeyer (following R. Morgenthaler) puts the number at around 2,055.[6] Luke's Gospel also has more New Testament hapax legomena than any other Gospel: around 250 words. As Cadbury has demonstrated, the evangelist exhibits a particular liking for classical words and expressions.[7]

A distinct feature of Luke's style is his lexical variation.[8] In the story of the healing of the paralyzed man in 5:17–26, Luke uses two different Greek

---

4. On Luke's Greek style, see Henry J. Cadbury, *The Style and Literary Method of Luke*, part 1, *The Diction of Luke and Acts* (Cambridge, MA: Harvard University Press, 1919); idem, *The Making of Luke–Acts* (London: MacMillan, 1927), 213–38; Joseph A. Fitzmyer, *The Gospel according to Luke*, vol. 1 (Garden City, NY: Doubleday, 1981), 107–27; Nigel Turner, *Style*, vol. 4 of *A Grammar of New Testament Greek*, by James Hope Moulton, W. F. Howard, and Nigel Turner (Edinburgh: T&T Clark, 1976), 45–63.

5. Turner, *Style*, 59–60.

6. Fitzmeyer, *Luke*, 109.

7. Cadbury, *Style and Literary Method*, 1:4–39.

8. Henry J. Cadbury, "Four Features of Lucan Style," in *Studies in Luke–Acts: Essays Presented in Honor of Paul Schubert*, ed. Leander E. Keck and J. Louis Martyn (London: SPCK, 1968), 91–97.

words for "bed" (*klinē* and *klinidion*); in speaking of John the Baptist's attire in 7:25, he uses two different words for clothing (*himation* and *himatismos*); in 22:50–51, as he narrates the cutting off and healing of the slave's ear at Jesus' arrest, he uses two words for "ear" (*ous* and *ōtion*).[9]

Among Luke's favorite words in the Gospel are "today" (e.g., 2:11; 4:21); "joy" (e.g., 1:14; 2:10); "rejoice" (e.g., 1:14, 28 [Gk.]; 6:23); "save" (e.g., 6:9; 7:50); "salvation/savior/save" (1:69, 71, 77; 19:9; the word "salvation" is not found in Matthew or Mark and occurs only once in John); "poor" (e.g., 4:18; 6:20); "glory" (e.g., 2:9, 14, 32), "glorify" (e.g., 2:20; 4:15 [Gk.]); "sinner/sinners" (e.g., 5:8, 30, 32).

NARRATIVE TECHNIQUE

Luke's literary artistry is well recognized.[10] He employs (perhaps not always consciously) a range of literary devices, such as *inclusio* (making the Jerusalem temple the location for the opening and closing scenes of the Gospel: 1:5–23; 24:52–53), flash-forward (jumping forward in time at 3:18–20 to describe John's imprisonment), self-fulfilling prophecy (presenting Jesus in 4:18–30 as deliberately bringing about the fulfillment of his saying that no prophet is accepted in his own hometown), understatement (narrating Jesus' sudden deliverance from the lynch mob in Nazareth in 4:30 with the restrained comment "He passed through the midst of them and went on his way"), repetition (relating seven declarations of Jesus' innocence in the passion account: 23:4, 14, 15, 22, 41, 47),[11] and pathos (having Jesus turn to look at Peter after Peter's third denial: 22:61).

The evangelist knows how to build suspense. In the account of Jesus' preaching in the synagogue at Nazareth (4:16–30), Luke carefully narrates each action: "he came . . . went . . . stood up . . . was given . . . unrolled . . . found." Then after Jesus reads Isaiah 61:1–2, the actions are reversed: "rolled up . . . gave back . . . sat down." We read that the eyes of all in the place are fixed on Jesus. All this builds up our expectation until we hear the dramatic words "Today this scripture has been fulfilled in your hearing."[12] Jesus' final trial before Pilate (22:13–25) is similarly marked by mounting tension. Luke narrates a battle of wills between Pilate and the Jewish leaders and crowd. Three times Pilate tries to release Jesus, and each time he meets with stubborn

9. Ibid., 93.
10. Ernest Renan described Luke's Gospel as "the most beautiful book there is" (Christopher Francis Evans, *Saint Luke*, TPINTC [Philadelphia: Trinity Press International, 1990], 42).
11. Cadbury, "Four Features," 88–91.
12. Lieu, *Luke*, 32.

resistance. The resistance grows in intensity, and the tension increases until eventually Pilate gives in and consents to the will of the throng.

Luke tends to concretize the supernatural.[13] This tendency is evident in the birth and resurrection accounts. In contrast to Matthew's brief remark that Mary "was found to be with child from the Holy Spirit" (1:18), Luke tells how the Holy Spirit will come upon Mary, and the power of the Most High will overshadow her (1:35). In his record of Jesus' appearance to the whole company of disciples, Luke emphasizes the physicality of Jesus' resurrection body (24:39–43). Jesus invites his disciples to touch him so that they can be sure he is not a ghost. While they still wonder, he asks for something to eat, and when he is given a piece of broiled fish, he consumes it in their presence.

Luke is also noted for his character pairings.[14] In the birth and infancy narrative, Luke deftly paints a series of similarities and contrasts between John the Baptist and Jesus. The parallelism establishes a close link between the two figures as agents of God's purposes while underlining the superiority of Jesus. Luke frequently pairs male and female characters: Zacharias and Mary (1:5–80), Simeon and Anna (2:25–38), Simon and the sinful women (7:36–50). Particularly revealing is his juxtaposition of characters with contrasting qualities: the self-righteous Simon and the penitent woman, the active Martha and the listening Mary (10:38–42), the prodigal son and the elder brother (15:11–32), the rich man and the poor Lazarus (16:19–31), the proud Pharisee and the humble tax collector (18:9–14), the penitent malefactor and the blaspheming one (23:39–43).

NARRATIVE TIME

Luke claims to offer an "orderly account" of events (1:1), but by "orderly" he means systematic rather than chronological. We gather the general impression of a forward movement through time, but Luke is not obsessed with trying to place episodes into a strict temporal order. An event that is clearly narrated out of sequence is the imprisonment of John the Baptist, which is told before Jesus' baptism! Like Mark and Matthew, Luke arranges some of his material by form and topic (as noted above). Luke's narration of the ministry in Galilee is relatively swift, but time decelerates in the long journey to Jerusalem and slows down even more when Jesus reaches Jerusalem.

Luke dates the birth of Jesus and his public debut in relation to world history to reinforce Jesus' relevance to the entire world, not just Israel: Jesus'

13. Evans, *Saint Luke*, 55–56.
14. Cadbury, *Making of Luke–Acts*, 233–34.

birth takes place in the time of Emperor Augustus, while Quirinius is governor of Syria (2:1–2). John baptizes Jesus in the fifteenth year of the reign of Tiberius, when Pontius Pilate is governor of Judea, Herod is ruler of Galilee, and so forth (3:1–2). In contrast, Luke's account of Jesus' ministry contains few time notes. There are more temporal notes when Jesus gets to Jerusalem, but they are vague: "every day" (19:47; 21:37); "one day" (20:1); "day after day" (22:53). The evangelist provides more precise temporal indicators when narrating the passion and resurrection (22:14, 66; 23:12, 44, 54, 56; 24:1, 13, 33).

NARRATIVE SPACE

Luke's Gospel narrative, from 4:14 onward, exhibits a fairly clear geographical pattern, moving from Galilee to Jerusalem. The section 4:14–9:50 contains mainly Galilean episodes (with events in Judea, 4:44; 7:17; Gerasa, 8:26; Bethsaida, 9:10). The journey to Jerusalem, narrated in 9:51–19:27, seems circuitous: the reference to Samaria in 17:11 suggests that Jesus has not progressed very far since approaching the Samaritan village at the outset of the expedition (9:52). But it would be a mistake to try to read the travel narrative as a travelogue. To a large extent the journey to Jerusalem is a structural device. It gives Luke the space to develop some of his particular themes. Luke 19:28–44 describes Jesus' entry into Jerusalem, and the rest of the narrative unfolds in the capital and its environs. Luke's Gospel both begins and ends in Jerusalem.

Narrative action sometimes takes place at/on the lake (5:1, 2; 8:22, 23, 33; Luke calls it "Lake of Genessaret" rather than "Sea of Galilee") and on mountains (e.g., 6:12; 9:28, 37). Houses, though, are much more frequently mentioned as narrative locations (e.g., 1:23, 40; 4:38).[15] Houses also frequently figure in Jesus' teaching, especially in parables that are distinctive to Luke (15:6, 8, 25; 16:4, 27; 18:14).

The Jerusalem temple features prominently in Luke, especially in the early and later chapters of the Gospel. The announcement of the birth of John the Baptist to Zechariah takes place in the temple (1:5–23). When he is still an infant, Jesus' parents present him in the temple (2:22–40). The holy family makes the annual trip to Jerusalem to celebrate the Passover (2:41). Twelve-year-old Jesus waits behind in the temple, where he amazes the teachers with his understanding (2:46–47). The temple figures only a couple of times in the stretch of narrative from the baptism to his arrival in Jerusalem (4:9; 18:10),

15. On the house as a narrative setting in Luke's Gospel, see David Lertis Matson, *Household Conversion in Acts: Pattern and Interpretation*, JSNT Sup 123 (Sheffield: Sheffield Academic Press, 1996), 53–83.

but it becomes a major setting again when Jesus reaches the capital. Jesus cleanses the temple (19:45–48) and teaches daily there (19:47; cf. 22:53). The temple is the center of Jesus' activity until his arrest. In Luke's Gospel, Jesus' eschatological discourse is delivered within the temple precincts. At the end of the Gospel, the disciples return to Jerusalem and are to be found "continually in the temple" praising and "blessing God" (24:53).

Luke's attitude toward the temple is more positive than Mark's and Matthew's. In Luke the temple incident (19:45–48) is more clearly a "cleansing" rather than a prophetic act signaling coming judgment. Luke records Jesus' prophecy of the temple's destruction (21:5–6) but places more emphasis on the destruction of Jerusalem as a whole (13:34–35; 19:41–44; 23:28–31). In the early chapters of Acts, the temple is a setting for Christian meeting and proclamation (Acts 2:46; 5:42).

THE CHARACTERIZATION OF JESUS

As in all the Gospels, Jesus' identity is made known primarily through the designations that are given to him.

The Titles Used for Jesus

Messiah. This title is given to Jesus in the birth and infancy narrative: the angel announces to the shepherds that "a Savior" has been born, "who is the Messiah, the Lord" (2:11). Simeon recognizes the child Jesus as "the Lord's Messiah" (2:26). The demons know that Jesus is the Messiah (4:41), and Peter confesses him as Christ (9:20). At his trial, the authorities demand that Jesus tell them whether he is the Messiah (22:67), and he refuses to answer directly. Jesus is accused before Pilate of claiming to be the Messiah (23:2). On the cross, the title is applied to him in mockery (23:35, 39). After the resurrection, Jesus implicitly identifies himself as "the Messiah," who had to suffer (24:26, 46).

In the early chapters, Luke emphasizes the Davidic nature of Jesus' messiahship.[16] The angel says of Jesus that the Lord God will give him David's throne and kingship (1:32–33; cf. 1:69). Jesus' birth takes place in "the city of David" (2:4, 11). Jesus' Davidic ancestry is stressed in the genealogy (3:23, 31). Jesus' appropriation of Isaiah 61:1–2 to himself is probably meant to be understood as an indirect claim to Davidic messiahship (4:16–21; cf. 7:18–23). There is evidence that Isaiah 61:1–2 was being applied to the Davidic Messiah

---

16. On the theme of the Davidic Messiah in Luke–Acts, see Mark L. Strauss, *The Davidic Messiah in Luke–Acts: The Promise and Its Fulfillment in Lukan Christology*, JSNTSup 110 (Sheffield: Sheffield Academic Press, 1995).

around the time of Jesus.[17] Only Luke among the evangelists presents suffering as a necessity for "the Messiah" (24:26, 46; cf. Acts 3:18; 17:3; 26:23). There is no conclusive evidence in early Judaism for any expectation that the Messiah would undergo suffering.[18]

Son of God. Jesus' status as "Son of God" is revealed in the annunciation to Mary. The angel tells Mary that the child shall be called "Son of the Most High" and "Son of God" (1:32, 35). The context implies that "Son of God" is more than a messianic designation. Jesus is identified as God's Son by the voice of God at his baptism (3:22), by Satan in the temptation (4:3, 9), by the unclean spirits in exorcisms (4:41; 8:28), and by God again at the transfiguration (9:35). In this Gospel, no human being confesses Jesus as "Son of God." At the return of the seventy, Jesus speaks of himself as "the Son" (10:22). In other passages, Jesus speaks of God as his Father in a close, personal way (2:49; 22:29, 42; 23:34, 46; 24:49).

Lord. The title "Lord" is used for Jesus more often in Luke than in the other Gospels. Indeed, it is Luke's most characteristic christological title, occurring in both the Gospel and Acts. Luke frequently calls Jesus "the Lord" as a narrative designation: "when the Lord saw her" (7:13); "The Lord appointed seventy others" (10:1); "the Lord said" (11:39; 12:42; 18:6); "the Lord answered" (10:41; 13:15); and so forth. This reflects an exalted understanding of Jesus and suggests the transcendent status of Jesus. In many instances *kyrios*, when applied to Jesus by other characters in the narrative, is a polite form of address (= "sir," e.g., 5:12; 7:6; or "master," e.g., 9:54, 61). Jesus is identified as "Christ the Lord" by the angels in 2:11 (cf. 1:43). Given the extent to which "the Lord" is used for God in the birth and infancy narrative (e.g., 1:6, 9, 11, 15, 16), it should probably be understood here as signaling Jesus' divine status. As in Mark and Matthew, Luke seems to identify Jesus with "the Lord" in the citation of Isaiah 40:3 (Luke 3:4; cf. 1:76).[19]

Son of Man. As in Mark and Matthew, Jesus' favorite self-designation in Luke is "Son of Man." The title occurs twenty-five times in the Gospel. Luke's "Son of Man" sayings fall into the three categories of usage we have noticed in Mark and Matthew: earthly mission of the Son of Man (e.g., 5:24; 6:5), suffering and vindication of the Son of Man (9:22, 44, etc.), and future role of the Son of Man (e.g., 9:26; 12:8). Luke's use of the title is not distinctive, but he does have a number of distinctive Son of Man sayings,

17. The Qumran text 4Q521; cf. James D. G. Dunn, *Jesus Remembered*, vol. 1 of *Christianity in the Making* (Grand Rapids: Wm. B. Eerdmans Publishing Co., 2003), 448–49.

18. Cf. Joel Marcus, *Mark: A New Translation with Introduction and Commentary*, vol. 2, *Mark 8–16*, AB 27A (New York: Doubleday, 2009), 1106.

19. On the christological significance of Luke's use of *kyrios* in the Gospel, with reference to both God and Jesus, see C. Kavin Rowe, *Early Narrative Christology: The Lord in the Gospel of Luke*, BZNW 139 (Berlin: de Gruyter, 2006).

including 19:10, "For the Son of Man came to seek out and to save the lost," which highlights the *saving* nature of Jesus' mission, an important Lukan emphasis.

Other titles. Jesus is often addressed as "Teacher" (e.g., 3:12; 7:40; 9:38), always, or almost always, by nondisciples (21:7 is ambiguous). On one occasion, Jesus refers to himself as "the Teacher" (22:11). In Luke, Jesus is especially a teacher of parables (Luke has at least 15 parables unique to him).[20]

More so than the other evangelists, Luke presents Jesus as a prophetic figure. In his sermon at Nazareth, Jesus identifies himself as a prophet and compares his ministry to that of Elijah and Elisha (4:25–27). After raising the widow of Nain's son, Jesus is acclaimed as "a great prophet" (7:16). Simon the Pharisee wonders whether Jesus is a prophet (7:39). The people in general view him as a prophet (9:7–9, 18–19). As he journeys to the capital, Jesus states that "it is impossible for a prophet to be killed outside Jerusalem" (13:33). The two disciples on the road to Emmaus speak of Jesus as "a prophet mighty in word and deed" (24:19). To be sure, the general designation "prophet" does not go far enough in expressing the significance of Jesus: both in Peter's confession (9:20) and in the dialogue between the risen Jesus and the two disciples (24:26), "prophet" is superseded by "Messiah." But the role of a "prophet like Moses," implicitly attributed to Jesus in Luke 9:35, is viewed highly by Luke, and in Acts (3:22–23), Jesus is explicitly identified as this figure.

Despite Luke's early stress on Jesus' Davidic messiahship, the title "Son of David" is given to Jesus only by the blind man at Jericho (18:38–39). Jesus is acclaimed as "king" at the triumphal entry into Jerusalem (19:38). At his trial before Pilate, he is accused of claiming to be a king (23:2–3), and he is mocked and crucified as king (23:37–38).

A title that is wholly confined to Luke's Gospel in the New Testament is the Greek word *epistatēs*, meaning "master."[21] In the Hellenistic world, the title was used of persons in authority. It occurs seven times in the Gospel (5:5; 8:24 [twice], 45; 9:33, 49; 17:13) as an address to Jesus. With the exception of one instance (17:13), *epistatēs* appears on the lips of Jesus' disciples. The title is Luke's equivalent to *Rabbi* ("my teacher"), a term that he does not use, and his alternative to *kyrios* in the sense of "Master."

A christological title distinctive to Luke among the Synoptists (although the Fourth Evangelist uses it in John 4:42) is "Savior," used in the angelic announcement to the shepherds (Luke 2:11; cf. Acts 5:31; 13:23). The title is Hellenistic, and it was applied to various divinities and to the emperor. In the

---

20. Craig L. Blomberg, *Jesus and the Gospels: An Introduction and Survey* (Leicester: Apollos, 1997), 147.

21. Evans, *Saint Luke*, 290.

LXX and in Luke 1:47, it is a title given to God. The application of this title to Jesus at his birth (cf. 1:69; 2:30, "salvation") signals the role he will play as the bringer of God's salvation (see below).

Characterizational Emphases

In Luke's Gospel, perhaps more than in the others, Jesus' humanness comes across.[22] The evangelist includes the only childhood story of Jesus in all the Gospels.[23] Luke emphasizes the child's physical growth and maturation into adulthood (2:40, 52). Only Luke tells us that "Jesus was about thirty years old when he began his work" (3:23). Luke's genealogy takes Jesus back to Adam (3:38), drawing attention to his common human ancestry (and perhaps implying that Jesus is the new Adam and his salvation is for the whole world). Luke has Jesus at prayer at various points in the narrative (see below), indicating a humanly dependence on God;[24] the emphasis on Jesus' Spirit empowerment (see below) similarly underscores his human agency. The evangelist gives prominence to Jesus' sociability (see below). Luke also has Jesus weeping over Jerusalem as he contemplates the fate that awaits the city (19:41).

More so than the other Gospel writers, Luke emphasizes Jesus' humanitarianism (cf. Acts 10:38, "He went about doing good"). First, the evangelist lays emphasis on the healing ministry of Jesus. As well as narrating healings found in Mark and Matthew, Luke includes several healing stories unique to his Gospel (13:11–13; 14:1–4; 17:11–19; 22:50–51) and makes a number of distinctive narrative comments that give prominence to Jesus' role as a healer, such as the remark that "the power of the Lord was with him to heal" (5:17; cf. 6:18; 7:21; 8:2, 47).[25] Second, Luke shows Jesus as having a special concern for the poor and the socially stigmatized. His message of good news is directed especially toward "the poor" (4:18; 7:22). He teaches that the poor are specially blessed (6:20–21) and objects of God's grace (14:21), and he encourages giving to the poor (18:22). He makes a habit of eating and drinking with "tax collectors" (viewed with disdain because of their collaboration with the Romans) and "sinners" (5:29–32; 7:34; 15:1–2; 19:1–10). He shows compassion toward the hated Samaritans (9:52–56; 17:16). Many of those whom Jesus heals likely are

22. Ibid., 65–66. The accent on Jesus' humanity is not polemically motivated. It is unlikely that Luke is opposing docetism (from Gk. *dokeō*, "to seem"), the idea that Jesus only *seemed* to be a human being.

23. The story demonstrates Jesus' extraordinary wisdom but is very different from later childhood stories in the infancy gospels (esp. the *Infancy Gospel of Thomas*), which it inspired.

24. David Michael Crump (*Jesus the Intercessor: Prayer and Christology in Luke–Acts*, WUNT 2/49 [Tübingen: Mohr, 1992]), however, argues that Jesus' prayers in Luke are more christologically significant than this and indicate that Jesus plays an intercessory role.

25. Cf. Robert H. Stein, *The Synoptic Problem: An Introduction* (Grand Rapids: Baker Book House, 1987), 240.

social outcasts. Third, Jesus has many positive dealings with women, more than in any other Gospel. Women figure as beneficiaries of his healing and blessing (e.g., 7:37–50) and as close followers (8:1–3).[26]

All four Gospel writers attribute to Jesus a sense of destiny, but Luke more routinely shows Jesus as acting under divine compulsion.[27] The sense of compulsion underpinning Jesus' activity is expressed by the Greek word *dei* (or *edei*), "it is necessary," or "must," which is especially prominent in Luke (and also in Acts). Jesus "must" be in his Father's house" (2:49); he "must" proclaim the kingdom of God (4:43); he "must" be on his way to Jerusalem (13:33); he "must" stay at Zacchaeus's house (19:5); he "must" suffer (9:22; 17:25); Scripture "must" be fulfilled in him (22:37). Looking back, the risen Jesus asks rhetorically (24:26), "Was it not necessary that the Messiah should suffer these things and then enter into his glory?"

THE CHARACTERIZATION OF THE DISCIPLES

By no means is Luke oblivious to the failings of the disciples (e.g., 8:22–25; 9:12–13), but his portrait of the disciples is more positive than Mark's and even Matthew's.[28] This is evident from a comparison of parallel episodes. Luke does not narrate Jesus' rebuke of Peter at the first passion prediction (9:21–22). Luke makes no reference to the disciples' lack of faith in the story of the epileptic boy (9:41–43). Luke makes allowance for their failure to understand two further passion predications by stating that the meaning of Jesus' words was hidden from them (9:45; 18:34). Jesus indicates that Peter will be restored after his denial (22:31–32). The evangelist makes no mention of the flight of the disciples from the scene of Jesus' betrayal and arrest (22:53–54).

The more positive view of the disciples also is evident in two stories unique to Luke. In 10:17–20, we read of the authority given to the disciples (the seventy) over the power of the enemy. In 22:28–30,[29] one of the sayings following the final meal, Jesus confers on his disciples a kingdom.

Luke calls the disciples "apostles" six times (6:13; 9:10; 11:49; 17:5; 22:14; 24:10), anticipating their role in the book of Acts (they are called apostles in Mark twice and Matthew only once).

26. It remains the case, though, that Jesus' main circle of followers is male. On women in Luke and Acts, see Turid Karlsen Seim, *The Double Message: Patterns of Gender in Luke–Acts* (Edinburgh: T&T Clark International, 1994).

27. Evans, *Saint Luke*, 226.

28. Mark L. Strauss, *Four Portraits, One Jesus: An Introduction to Jesus and the Gospels* (Grand Rapids: Zondervan, 2007), 282–83.

29. Luke 22:30 has a parallel in Matt. 19:28.

THE CHARACTERIZATION
OF THE RELIGIOUS AUTHORITIES

The Pharisees are frequently mentioned in conflict situations (e.g., 5:21, 30, 33; 6:2). They are charged, as in Matthew, with hypocrisy (12:1) and love of honor (11:39–44). To these charges, Luke adds love of money (16:14) and self-righteousness (16:15; 18:9–14). In 7:30, the evangelist, as narrator, issues a strong condemnation of the Pharisees and the scribes, asserting that they "reject God's purpose."

Luke, however, is not uniformly hostile toward the Pharisees. On several occasions, Jesus shares table fellowship with individual Pharisees (7:36; 11:37; 14:1). Some Pharisees warn Jesus of Herod's plot to kill him (13:31). While this may be interpreted as a hostile attempt to scare off Jesus, it more naturally reads as a friendly warning to Jesus, given out of a genuine concern for his life. Luke's account of Jesus' denunciation of the Pharisees in 11:37–54 is less vitriolic than the account in Matthew 23. Matthew has seven woes directed against the Pharisees and the scribes together. Luke separates the scribes (or lawyers) and the Pharisees and targets three woes at each group. The Pharisees are not mentioned in the account of the arrest, trial, and crucifixion of Jesus (both Matthew and John implicate the Pharisees in Jesus' death).

The more sympathetic side of Luke's depiction of the Pharisees is even more pronounced in Acts. Gamaliel, the Pharisee, convinces the ruling council to take no action against the Christians (5:33–42). Pharisees are among the members of the Christian movement (15:5, though they provoke conflict by insisting that it necessary for the Gentiles to keep the law). Paul, the hero of Acts, is himself a Pharisee. He never openly rejects his Pharisaic past; indeed, he exploits his background in Pharisaism when on trial (23:6–9; 26:5).

In Luke, the scribes are also called "lawyers" (*nomikoi*, e.g., 7:30; 10:25) and "teachers of the law" (5:17, cf. Acts 5:34). As in Mark and Matthew, they tend to be linked with either the Pharisees (e.g., 5:21, 30; 7:30) or the chief priests (e.g., 9:22; 19:47). When they appear in the narrative, they are usually antagonistic toward Jesus (e.g., 5:17, 21, 30). They are coconspirators with the chief priests and elders/leaders in the plot to kill Jesus (e.g., 9:22; 19:47; 20:19). Again, Luke is not completely negative about the scribes. Jesus compliments a scribe (10:25–28), and uniquely in Luke, some of the scribes compliment Jesus (20:39).

The chief priests actively figure in the narrative after Jesus' arrival in Jerusalem (20:1, 19; 22:2). They are consistently portrayed as antagonists. The "elders," as a distinct leadership group, are mentioned in association with the chief priests and scribes (9:22; 20:1; 22:52). They are also called "leaders"

(19:47; 23:13, 35; 24:20). Like the chief priests, the elders/leaders are uniformly hostile.[30]

THEMES

Luke has a high number of sayings on the kingdom of God (around 40, on
one estimate).[31] As in the other Synoptic Gospels, the kingdom is the main
theme of Jesus' proclamation (4:43). A saying peculiar to Luke unequivocally
presents the kingdom as present (17:20–21; cf. 11:20). In other sayings, Jesus
refers to the kingdom as near, at hand (10:9, 11).[32] Yet, the kingdom also
belongs to the consummation (22:16, 18).

Salvation

The language of salvation ("save," "salvation," "Savior") is prominent in Luke.
In his ministry, Jesus brings salvation to individuals he encounters (7:50; 8:50;
18:42; 19:9; 23:35). Salvation is expressed in bodily healing (8:36, 48; 17:19),
but it goes beyond physical restoration. It is connected with entrance into
the kingdom (18:25–26) and the forgiveness of sins (1:77; 7:48–50). In Acts,
"salvation" and "forgiveness of sins" appear to be interchangeable concepts
(4:12; 5:31; 10:43; 13:26, 38, 47). In Luke 3:6, the universality of salvation is
indicated. The extension of salvation to the Gentiles is a major theme of Acts
(4:12; 13:47; 16:17; 28:28).

Salvation in Luke is connected with the mission of Jesus generally (19:10)
rather than his death specifically. Luke does not include the "ransom" saying
(Mark 10:45), which attributes saving significance to Jesus' death. The idea
that Jesus dies for others, though, is found in the words of institution at the
Lord's Supper (22:19–20).[33]

---

30. In 22:66, Luke refers to the "the elders of the people," an expression that here designates
the ruling council as a whole; cf. Evans, *Saint Luke*, 834.

31. Caragounis, "Kingdom of God/Kingdom of Heaven," 426.

32. The imminence of the kingdom, though, is less emphasized in Luke than in Mark and
Matthew. Indeed, in 19:11–27, Jesus tells a parable in order to correct any misunderstanding
that the kingdom might dawn immediately (19:11). Hans Conzelmann (*The Theology of Saint
Luke*, trans. Geoffrey Buswell [London: Faber, 1960]) famously argued that Luke has replaced
imminent eschatology with a salvation-historical perspective that propels the consummation
into a far-distant future. However, it is generally accepted that Conzelmann overpressed his
case. While not stressing the imminence of the *parousia*, Luke can still urge readiness for it
(12:40).

33. However, not all ancient manuscripts include 22:19b–20; see Evans, *Saint Luke*,
786–88.

The Holy Spirit

Luke has a profound interest in the work of the Holy Spirit. This comes out in the book of Acts (after Pentecost), but it is also evident in the Gospel. The activity of the Spirit is pronounced in the birth and infancy narrative. The Spirit is imparted to various participants in the opening drama (1:41, 67; 2:25, 27), all of whom deliver Spirit-inspired speech. Jesus is anointed by and filled with the Sprit at baptism (3:22; 4:1); he is led by the Spirit to be tempted (4:1); "filled with the power of the Spirit," he embarks on his ministry (4:14). At the return of the seventy, he rejoices in the Holy Spirit (10:21) and speaks of his exclusive relationship with "the Father," apparently inspired by the Spirit. Jesus promises to share the Holy Spirit with his followers (11:13; 12:12; 24:49); in the book of Acts (1:8; 2:4), this promise is fulfilled.

Praise and Prayer

A notable feature of the Gospel is the praise given to God by recipients of his blessing and by beneficiaries of, or witnesses to, Jesus' healing power. Thus, in the birth and infancy narrative, Mary (1:46–55), Zechariah (1:68–79), and Simeon (2:28–32) offer songs of praise, while the shepherds (2:20) and Anna (2:38) give glory and thanks to God (cf. the angels' praise of 2:14). The paralyzed man, restored to health, glorifies God, as do all those who observe the miracle (5:25–26). Those who see the widow's son raised praise God (7:16). The disabled woman, set free from her illness, extols God (13:13). And so it continues (17:15, 18; 18:43; 19:37–38; 23:47; 24:53).

Related to this emphasis on praise is a particular interest in prayer. Jesus prays more frequently in Luke than in any other Gospel (3:21; 5:16; 6:12; 9:18, 28–29; 11:1; 22:41–45). Jesus is presented as the model of prayerful dependence on God (11:1–2). Prayer is also a subject of three parables exclusive to this Gospel (11:5–8; 18:1–8, 9–14). Acts also contains many references to prayer (e.g., 1:24; 4:24–31; 6:6).

Wealth and Possessions

As noted above, in this Gospel, there is a particular concern for the poor. Correspondingly, there is polemic against and critique of the rich. Mary's song of praise envisions a great reversal in which the poor will be exalted and the rich brought down (1:50–53). Luke's beatitudes announce not only blessings upon the poor but woes upon the rich (6:24–26). The reversal of fortunes of rich and poor is vividly illustrated in the parable of the Rich Man and Lazarus (16:19–31).

There is condemnation of wealth and the accumulation of riches. Wealth threatens spiritual growth (8:15), and it has the character of a god, claiming exclusive loyalty (16:13).[34] Jesus warns against greed (11:39; 12:15) and insists that "one's life does not consist in the abundance of possessions" (12:15). He tells the parable of the Rich Fool to drive home the point (12:16–21).

How, then, should followers of Jesus respond to the dangers of wealth and material possessions? On the one hand, the Gospel seems to indicate that a complete renunciation of possessions is demanded. The first disciples "leave everything" behind to follow Jesus (5:11, 28). Luke alone records the saying, "None of you can become my disciple if you do not give up all your possessions" (14:33). The rich young ruler is told by Jesus, "Sell all that you have and distribute the money to the poor, and . . . come, follow me" (18:22). On the other hand, there are passages that counsel or illustrate sharing, rather than the total abandonment of material goods. Thus the (evidently well-off) women who join Jesus' entourage use their resources to provide material support for Jesus' mission (8:1–3). Jesus urges disciples to use "dishonest wealth" to "make friends" (16:9). Zacchaeus promises to give half of what he owns to the poor (19:8). The parable of the Pounds (19:11–27) encourages wise stewardship of money (and gifts). It is mainly the emphasis on sharing that is carried forward into Acts (2:44–45; 4:32; 6:1–6).[35]

Hospitality

In Luke's Gospel, Jesus is often depicted as enjoying hospitality (4:38; 5:29; 7:36; 10:38; 14:1; 19:5; 22:11–12; 24:28–30). He instructs the seventy to accept the hospitality of those who extend it to them (10:5–7). He himself acts as host at the feeding of the five thousand (9:11, 16; see chap. 8 below), and he assumes the role of host at the Lord's Supper (22:19) and also at the meal at Emmaus, where he is actually guest (24:30). Luke includes teaching on hospitality: Jesus challenges Greco-Roman meal conventions by recommending that people be invited who cannot reciprocate (14:7–14). The interest in hospitality continues in Acts (e.g., 10:24–48), where it is strongly linked to mission.[36]

---

34. Ibid., 100.

35. In recent years a number of treatments of the theme of wealth and possessions in Luke–Acts have appeared; see, e.g., Kyoung-Jin Kim, *Stewardship and Almsgiving in Luke's Theology*, JSNTSup 155 (Sheffield: Sheffield Academic Press, 1998).

36. See further Andrew E. Arterbury, *Entertaining Angels: Early Christian Hospitality in Its Mediterranean Setting*, New Testament Monographs 8 (Sheffield: Sheffield Phoenix Press, 2005).

CONCLUSION

Luke's rendering of the shared gospel story exhibits great literary skill. The evangelist writes in a refined style, and he displays a deft narrative touch. He situates the story in the context of world history and underlines at the outset its global significance. The Gospel joyously celebrates the coming of Jesus and the salvation he brings for all. Luke presents "the Lord" Jesus as the "seeking Savior" and shows him as having compassion for the poor, the oppressed, the vulnerable, and the marginalized, while challenging the rich and self-righteous. Luke's emphasis on the humanness and humanitarianism of Jesus gives his Gospel enormous contemporary appeal.

FOR FURTHER READING

Craddock, Fred B. *Luke*. Interpretation. Louisville, KY: Westminster/John Knox Press, 1990.

Evans, Christopher Francis. *Saint Luke*. New Testament Commentaries. Philadelphia: Trinity Press International, 1990.

Fitzmyer, Joseph A. *The Gospel according to Luke*. 2 vols. Anchor Bible 28–28A. Garden City, NY: Doubleday, 1981–85.

Gonzalez, Justo. *Luke*. Belief: A Theological Commentary. Louisville, KY: Westminster John Knox Press, 2010.

Green, Joel B. *The Theology of Luke*. Cambridge: Cambridge University Press, 1995.

Johnson, Luke Timothy. *The Gospel of Luke*. Sacra pagina 3. Collegeville, MN: Liturgical Press, 1991.

Lieu, Judith M. *The Gospel of Luke*. Peterborough: Epworth Press, 1997.

Marshall, I. Howard. *The Gospel of Luke: A Commentary on the Greek Text*. Exeter: Paternoster Press, 1978.

———. *Luke: Historian and Theologian*. 3rd ed. Exeter: Paternoster Press, 1988.

Ringe, Sharon H. *Luke*. Westminster Bible Companion. Louisville, KY: Westminster John Knox Press, 1995.

Tannehill, Robert C. *Luke*. Abingdon New Testament Commentary. Nashville: Abingdon Press, 1996.

Wright, N. T. *Luke for Everyone*. Louisville, KY: Westminster John Knox Press, 2004.

6

The Gospel according to John

The Fourth Gospel shares features of the genre of ancient biography with the Synoptic Gospels (size, structure, narrative focus on one individual). Like the Synoptics, John's Gospel constitutes an ancient "life" of Jesus. It also has in common with the other canonical Gospels the core gospel story they tell, a story in which Jesus makes his public debut in connection with the ministry of John the Baptist, calls disciples, engages in a mission of miracles and teaching, faces opposition, enters Jerusalem in a procession, and is arrested, tried, executed, and raised from the dead. Like each of the four Gospels, John's Gospel is a distinctive rendition of that mutual story. With John's Gospel, though, the distinctiveness is much more pronounced (as we saw in chap. 1). The Fourth Evangelist has produced a narrative that is quite unique among the four.

John's biography emphasizes the heavenly origins and divine identity of Jesus. Jesus is introduced to us as the preexistent, divine "Word" who has come into the world. John's most important designation for Jesus is "Son of God," or simply "the Son." The Gospel elaborates on Jesus' exclusive filial relationship to God "the Father." Jesus uses the divine name "I am" and can even be called "God." Yet Jesus remains for John a genuine human being: he is the divine Word who "became flesh."

NARRATIVE VOICE

The narrative voice is a much more conspicuous feature of this Gospel than of the other Gospels. The narrator frequently intervenes with narrative asides for various purposes: to translate an Aramaic or Hebrew term (e.g., 1:38; 1:41, 42) or explain a Jewish custom (e.g., 2:6; 4:9); to explain some topographical point (5:2; 6:1; 11:18); to indicate Jesus' supernatural insight or foreknowledge (e.g., 2:24–25; 6:64); to refer to a character, place, or event mentioned earlier in the narrative (e.g., 4:46; 6:23); to indicate the fulfillment of Scripture (e.g., 2:17; 18:9); to mark a failure to understand (e.g., 2:9; 5:13); to clarify the meaning of something that Jesus has just said (e.g., 2:21–22; 5:18) or to provide some other explanatory comment (e.g., 4:2, 8).[1]

The narrative voice sounds very much like that of Jesus: the narrator and Jesus speak in virtually the same idiom. Sometimes this makes it difficult to know where Jesus' speech ends and the narrator's begins. In Jesus' conversation with Nicodemus in John 3, for example, it is not clear whether 3:16–21 is a continuation of Jesus' speech or the commentary of the narrator.

TEXTUAL STRUCTURE

There is relatively little dispute about the general structure of the Gospel. The narrative falls into two main sections, 1:19–12:50 and 13:1–20:31, encompassed by a prologue, 1:1–18, and an epilogue or appendix, 21:1–25.

The two central sections are sometimes designated the "Book of Signs" and the "Book of Glory,"[2] respectively, but these labels are not entirely apposite since 1:19–12:50 contains teaching as well as "signs," and "glory" is a theme that crops up throughout the Gospel, not just in the second half. The headings given below, though basic, give a better reflection of the contents.

1:1–18	Prologue
1:19–12:50	Public Ministry of Signs and Teaching
13:1–20:31	Farewell, Passion, and Resurrection
21:1–25	Epilogue

With regard to the first half of the narrative, many think that chapters 2–4 and 5–10 constitute two major units. Chapters 2–4 begin and end with "signs," or miracles, in Cana. Chapters 5–10 describe ministry conducted at festival times, especially in Jerusalem. Following the last of the signs, the raising of Lazarus (11:1–57), chapter 12 is transitional.

Chapters 13 to 20 divide into two portions: 13–17, covering the last meal, farewell discourses, and Jesus' final prayer; 18–20, dealing with Jesus' arrest, trial, crucifixion, and resurrection.

---

1. Andreas J. Köstenberger, *A Theology of John's Gospel and Letters*, Biblical Theology of the New Testament (Grand Rapids: Zondervan, 2009), 136–41.

2. Raymond E. Brown, *The Gospel According to John I–XII* (Garden City: Doubleday, 1966), cxxxviii.

PLOT

John's Gospel is a rather more selective account of Jesus' ministry than the Synoptic Gospels, with fewer episodes from Jesus' prepassion ministry. Also, the episodes the Fourth Evangelist narrates are more connected than the Synoptic episodes. The Fourth Gospel thus exhibits a tighter storyline than the other Gospels.

Prologue (1:1–18)

John's Gospel opens with a sublime introduction, displaying poetic and even hymnlike qualities (some even have conjectured that an actual hymn, used in early Christian worship, underlies it). The prologue introduces us to "the Word," or *Logos*, who existed before the world began. The Word "was with God" and "was God"; the Word was the agent of creation, the one "through" whom all things came into existence (1:1–3), and is the source of light and life (1:4–5). The divine, preexistent Word, we are told, "became flesh" (1:14). The incarnate Word is then identified as Jesus Christ (1:17).

In addition to making clear the divine identity of Jesus, including his status as the divine Son, which is the main christological emphasis of the Gospel, the prologue also introduces us to themes to be developed in the narrative: the dualism of darkness and light (1:5), witness (1:7), the world (1:10), believing (1:12), new birth (1:13), truth (1:14, 17).

Public Ministry of Signs and Teaching

The narrative proper begins with the ministry of John the Baptist (already introduced in the prologue, 1:6–8, 15) and his public witness to Jesus (1:19–34). When questioned by the Jewish authorities as to his identity, John indicates that he is a messenger, whose role is to announce the coming of a greater one (1:19–28). The next day John sees Jesus and declares that he is the one he was sent to proclaim. He distinguishes Jesus as the "Lamb of God" (1:29) and the "Son of God" (1:34). The evangelist does not narrate Jesus' baptism, but this event is plainly alluded to when John the Baptist speaks of having previously seen the Spirit descend upon Jesus like a dove (1:32; see further chap. 7 below).

Next we read of Jesus' attraction of disciples (1:35–51). Hearing John's testimony regarding Jesus, two of his own disciples leave him and go with Jesus. One of these men is Andrew. He goes to his brother Simon Peter, tells him that they have found "the Messiah," and takes Peter to Jesus. Jesus then calls Philip, who in turn brings Nathanael to him. Though Nathanael is initially skeptical, when Jesus demonstrates to him his supernatural knowledge, Nathanael calls him "Son of God" and "King of Israel" (1:49).

After the call of the first disciples, the evangelist narrates how Jesus turns water into wine during a wedding at Cana (2:1–11). This miracle is designated "the first of his signs." This miraculous deed is followed by the temple-cleansing incident, which takes place during a Passover visit to Jerusalem (2:13–22). While he is in Jerusalem, many believe in him because of his signs (2:23–25).

In an exchange with the Pharisee Nicodemus (3:1–21), Jesus speaks of the need to be "born again" or "born from above" in order to see and enter God's kingdom. The dialogue with Nicodemus gives us the first narrative mention of "eternal life," an important theme of the Gospel (see below). There follows a further testimony of John the Baptist to Jesus (3:22–36).

Discovering that the Pharisees have learned of his success, Jesus leaves Judea and heads for Galilee, passing through Samaria on the way. At the village of Sychar, he meets a woman at a well and engages her in conversation (4:1–42). She responds positively to Jesus' words, and many in her city come to believe in him, through her testimony, and acknowledge him as "Savior of the world." After two days' stay, Jesus goes on into Galilee, where he receives a welcome (4:43–45). At Cana, he heals the dying son of a Roman official (4:46–54); the healing is marked as the "second sign" of the Gospel.

Jesus is back in Jerusalem for an unnamed festival, and at the pool of Bethesda he cures a paralyzed man (5:1–15). The healing takes place on the Sabbath and so generates controversy. Jesus' statement "My Father is still working, and I also am working" (5:17) inflames the situation: the authorities interpret his words as blasphemy and seek to kill him. An extended speech is given in response (5:19–47). Jesus talks about his relationship with the Father (5:19–30), and about the witness borne to him by John the Baptist, his own deeds, the Father, and the Scriptures (5:31–47).

Jesus returns to Galilee, and crowds follow him wherever he goes. He miraculously feeds about five thousand people and walks on the water (6:1–22). Then on the following day, in the synagogue at Capernaum, he delivers his discourse on the "bread of life" (6:22–59). Jesus' teaching proves divisive, and many turn away from following him (6:60–65). Peter, as spokesman for the Twelve, affirms their commitment to him (6:66–70). In the fourth evangelist's equivalent to Peter's confession in the Synoptic Gospels, Peter states, "We have come to believe and know that you are the Holy One of God" (6:69). Jesus knows, though, that one of the disciples will betray him (6:71).

The Feast of Tabernacles (or Booths) is the occasion for the next major plot development. The evangelist tells of the unbelief of Jesus' own brothers

(7:1–7) and narrates Jesus' departure to Jerusalem to attend the festival. His arrival in the capital is inconspicuous, but around the middle of the festival he begins to teach publicly at the temple (7:10–15). Over the course of more than one day (cf. 7:37), a series of exchanges ensues (7:15–8:59).[3] Jesus' identity, especially his messianic identity, is the central issue. The people are divided in their opinion of him. Some think he is the Messiah; others are doubtful because of his Galilean origins. His opponents accuse him of being demon possessed (7:20; 8:48, 52). The opposition hardens, and Jesus' final claim, invoking the divine name ("I am"), is the last straw, inciting an attempt to stone him, but Jesus escapes (8:57–59).

Further controversy issues from Jesus' healing of a man blind from birth (9:1–41). It is the man himself, rather than Jesus, who is subjected to questioning by the Pharisees, in a rare scene when Jesus is offstage. When the healed man is ejected from the synagogue, Jesus finds him, and the man confesses his faith in Jesus and worships him.

The discourse on the good shepherd, which causes further division, comes next (10:1–21). The occasion of the discourse is unclear. It seems to belong to Jesus' visit to Jerusalem for the Feast of Dedication (Hanukkah), mentioned in 10:22. This festival is unambiguously the occasion of the debate in Solomon's colonnade narrated in 10:23–42. The debate again focuses on Jesus' identity. Again Jesus is charged with speaking blasphemy, his opponents try to kill him, and he eludes their grasp (10:39).

The raising of Lazarus (11:1–44) is the seventh and climactic sign of the first half of the Gospel. This incident is extremely significant for the unfolding narrative since it prompts the resolution of the Jewish leadership to get rid of Jesus (11:45–53). Jesus withdraws for a brief time but then returns to Bethany six days before the fateful Passover. He dines at the home of Lazarus, where Mary anoints his feet with costly perfume (12:1–11). The next day, Jesus enters Jerusalem in triumph (12:12–19). The inquiry of some Greeks leads to Jesus' announcement that his "hour has come" (12:23). In a voice from heaven, the Father indicates his approval of Jesus (12:28). In a lengthy aside, the narrator explains why most of the Jewish leaders do not believe in Jesus (12:37–43). He emphasizes, though, that many have come to believe in Jesus, including some of the authorities who secretly believe (12:42). The account of Jesus' public ministry comes to a close with a summative message by Jesus to the crowds, which reiterates some of the themes from the foregoing narrative (12:44–50).

---

3. The pericope on the woman caught in adultery (7:53–8:11), which interrupts this exchange, is a passage that does not appear in the earliest manuscripts of John and was inserted into the Gospel text later. In some manuscripts, it can be found following 7:36 or 21:25. In others, it is included with Luke's Gospel, after 21:38.

Farewell, Passion, and Resurrection (13:1–20:31)

The account of the passion begins with the extended scene of Jesus' final meal with disciples. Jesus washes his disciples' feet (13:1–17), predicts his betrayal (13:18–30), issues "a new commandment" (13:31–35), and predicts Peter's denial (13:36–38). The following chapters are known as the Farewell Discourses, the longest speech by Jesus in the Gospel.

The speech begins with Jesus' impending departure and promise to return (14:1–3) and develops a number of topics: the Father-Son relationship (15:8–14), the Spirit as "Paraclete" (14:16–17, 25–26; 15:26–27; 16:4–15), abiding in Jesus (15:1–11), love (15:12–17), the world's hostility to the disciples (15:18–25). The discourses end with the encouragement that Jesus has overcome the world (16:33). After finishing his speech, Jesus prays to the Father his high-priestly prayer. He prays first for himself, knowing that his hour has come (17:1–5); next for the disciples who must remain in the world after he has departed the scene (17:6–19); and then for those who will come to believe because of the witness of the disciples (17:20–26).

After his final prayer, Jesus takes his disciples across the Kidron valley to a garden, where he is arrested (18:1–11). He is brought before Annas, the father-in-law of Caiaphas the high priest (18:12–14), while Peter and another disciple (perhaps the beloved disciple) enter the courtyard of the high priest (18:15–18). Jesus is questioned about his disciples and his teaching (18:19–23). Annas then sends Jesus to Caiaphas (18:24), and the scene switches to Peter in the courtyard of the high priest (18:25–27). The evangelist glances over the hearing before Caiaphas and moves straight to the trial before Pilate (18:28–19:16), which occupies more narrative space in the Fourth Gospel than in the other Gospels. When Pilate warns Jesus that he has the capacity to release or crucify him, Jesus replies that the governor only has power as given to him by God. Pilate endeavors to free Jesus, but eventually hands him over to be crucified.

The crucifixion scene in this Gospel (19:17–42) has distinctive features, including Jesus' words to his mother and to the beloved disciple. Jesus dies, not with a cry of despair on his lips, but a declaration of triumph (19:30; see further chap. 11 below). The evangelist narrates the piercing of Jesus' side with a spear before recounting the burial of Jesus.

The Fourth Gospel's resurrection account is quite distinctive. On the first day of the week, Mary Magdalene discovers the tomb empty and reports back to Peter and the beloved disciple, who then run to the tomb, see the linen wrappings, and return home (20:1–10, see further chap. 12 below). Jesus appears in the garden to Mary, who announces to the disciples, "I have seen the Lord" (20:11–18). In the evening Jesus appears to all the disciples except Thomas (20:19–23). Thomas refuses to believe (20:24–25); a week later, Thomas is present with the rest of the disciples when Jesus appears to them again (20:26–29). He utters the climactic christological confession of the Gospel, "My Lord and my God!" Having seen the risen Jesus, he believes; yet Jesus tells him that those who believe *without* seeing are blessed. A final statement indicates the purpose of the Gospel (20:30–31).

EPILOGUE

The last two verses of chapter 20 probably constitute the original ending of John's Gospel: chapter 21 seems to have been added later as an appendix. It recounts a further postresurrection appearance by Jesus, in which he miraculously enables the disciples to make an abundant catch of fish (21:1–14). Peter is commissioned to a shepherding role, parallel to that of Jesus himself as the good shepherd. Allusion is also made to Peter's coming martyrdom (21:15–19). Peter asks about the destiny of the one called the "beloved disciple." Jesus replies, "If it is my will that he remain until I come, what is that to you? Follow me!"

The evangelist clarifies that Jesus did not say to Peter that the beloved disciple *would not* die, but that it was not for Peter to know whether the beloved disciple would die or "remain until I come" (21:20–23). This clarification is made to clear up a misunderstanding at the time of writing: that the beloved disciple would live until Jesus returns. The final verses indicate that the testimony of the beloved disciple stands behind the Gospel (21:24–25).

STYLE

John's Greek style is pleasingly simple.[4] He tends to write paratactically, connecting sentences with the conjunctions *kai*, *de*, and *oun*. He uses *oun*, meaning "then/therefore," more often than does any other Gospel writer. Many of his sentences have no conjunction at all. He is fond of syntactic units, especially purpose clauses, introduced by the particle *hina*. When expressing purpose, *hina* means "so that," "in order that." John also makes frequent use of the historic present (he has 164 usages of the historic present, slightly higher than the number found in Mark).[5]

---

4. See Nigel Turner, *Style*, vol. 4 of *A Grammar of New Testament Greek*, by James Hope Moulton, W. F. Howard, and Nigel Turner (Edinburgh: T&T Clark, 1976), 64–79.
5. Ibid., 70.

John's vocabulary is the smallest of the four evangelists (this is why students of NT Greek often begin with John's Gospel). He uses a total of 1,011 different words, of which 112 are hapax legomena.[6] But although in one sense his vocabulary is the "poorest" of the four evangelists,[7] he makes the best use of the words that he employs. For example, the series of short statements that opens the Gospel (1:1–5) makes repeated use of a small number of words, but they express a profound theological message. Certain words occur repeatedly: light, life, truth, world, believe, abide/remain, sign, hour, seek/look for, Father, Son.

Like Mark, John has a number of Aramaic or Hebrew words that he translates for his readers (e.g., 1:38, 41, 42; 4:25; 5:2). His habit of translating such words, along with his explanations of Jewish customs, suggests a predominantly non-Jewish audience, an impression reinforced by talk of "the Jews" in the Gospel (on which see below).

NARRATIVE TECHNIQUE

John utilizes an impressive variety of literary devices.[8] One of his most characteristic techniques is his use of misunderstanding in exchanges between Jesus and others.[9] Jesus makes a metaphorical statement with spiritual nuance, and his meaning is taken literally. For example, Jesus' statement, "Destroy this temple, and in three days I will raise it up" (2:19), is misunderstood by his Jewish critics as a statement about the literal temple, "but he was speaking of the temple of his body" (2:21). When Jesus tells Nicodemus that no one can enter the kingdom of God without being born "from above," Nicodemus wonders how someone can be reborn physically (3:3–4). Jesus speaks to the Samaritan woman about "living water," and she thinks that Jesus is speaking about water to drink (4:10–15). When Jesus tells the disciples that he has food to eat of which they know nothing, they assume that he means physical food (4:31–34). When Jesus speaks about the bread of God that comes down from heaven, the crowd thinks that he is talking about something edible (6:33–34). And so it goes (e.g., 9:39–40; 11:11–13, 23–27).

In the cases of Nicodemus and the Samaritan woman, the misunderstanding is caused by the use of a word or expression with a double meaning.[10]

---

6. Ibid., 76.
7. Ibid., 64.
8. Warren Carter, *John: Storyteller, Interpreter, Evangelist* (Peabody, MA: Hendrickson Publishers, 2006), 107–28; Köstenberger, *Theology*, 135–67.
9. Carter, *John*, 114–16; Köstenberger, *Theology*, 141–45.
10. Carter, *John*, 112–14.

The Greek word *anōthen* can mean either "again" or "from above." When Jesus says he must be born *anōthen*, Nicodemus takes Jesus to literally mean "again," but Jesus means "from above." The phrase "living water" would naturally refer to flowing water, but Jesus means life-giving water in a spiritual sense, with eternal life in view. Another instance of deliberate double entendre is Jesus' talk of being "lifted up" with reference to his crucifixion (3:14; 8:28; 12:32). The Greek word *hypsoō* can mean "lift up" in a basic literal sense or "lift up" in the sense of exalt. Jesus intends both meanings: on one level, his crucifixion is a literal "lifting up"; on another, it is a glorious exaltation.

Like Mark, John frequently employs irony;[11] the Fourth Evangelist is especially fond of dramatic irony. There are numerous occasions in which a character inadvertently speaks the truth without understanding the import of what is said. Philip asks facetiously, "Can anything good come out of Nazareth?" (1:46). The Samaritan woman asks rhetorically (expecting a negative answer), "Are you greater than our ancestor Jacob?" Similarly, the Jewish leaders ask him, "Are you greater than our father Abraham, who died?" (8:53). The most striking instance of dramatic irony is Caiaphas's unwitting prophecy "It is better for you to have one man die for the people" (11:50).[12]

The Fourth Gospel is famous for its symbolism,[13] investing everyday realities (night, birth, water, the wind, etc.) with theological significance. Symbolism is evident in Jesus' "I am" sayings: "I am the bread of life" (6:35); "I am the bread that came down from heaven" (6:41); "I am the light of the world" (8:12; 9:5); "I am the gate for the sheep" (10:7, 9); "I am the good shepherd" (10:11, 14); "I am the resurrection and the life" (11:25); "I am the way, and the truth, and the life" (14:6); "I am the (true) vine" (15:1, 5). These images have an Old Testament background (bread, Exod. 16:4–8; light, Gen. 1:3–5; Ps. 27:1; shepherd, Num. 27:17; Ps. 23:1). The symbolism of darkness and light, with the subsidiary symbols of day and night (9:4), is especially prominent in the Gospel (see below on dualisms).

As mentioned above, the evangelist also deploys repetition,[14] making concentrated use of a key word in a stretch of text, as with "the Son" in 5:19–26; "abide" in 15:1–11; "love" in 15:9–13; "hate" in 15:18–24; "glory" and "glorify" in chapter 17.

11. Ibid., 118–22; Köstenberger, *Theology*, 150–55.
12. For example, see also John 4:12, 25; 7:27; 8:53, 57; 9:40.
13. Carter, *John*, 122–26; Köstenberger, *Theology*, 155–67.
14. Carter, *John*, 110–12.

NARRATIVE TIME

In John's Gospel, narrative time is constructed around Jesus' visits to Jerusalem, especially his three visits for the feast of the Passover (2:13; 6:4; 11:55). The evangelist presents a forward-moving narrative, with snapshots of Jesus' ministry. There is evidence of a schematic arrangement of episodes (the Cana cycle, 2:1–4:54). The overall impression, though, is of consecutive temporal ordering.

At the beginning of the Gospel, John gives us a chronology of seven days (1:19–2:11), which some think alludes to the week of creation in Genesis 1. Time slows down considerably in the second half of the Gospel, with the events of 13:1–19:42 taking place over a twenty-four-hour period, from last meal to burial.

In John's Gospel, the crucifixion takes place on "the day of Preparation for the Passover" (19:14). This timing, which puts Jesus on the cross when the Passover lambs are being slaughtered (19:31), fits nicely with John's emphasis on Jesus as the "Lamb of God" (1:29; 19:29, 31–37; see further chap. 11). It clashes, though, with the Synoptic Gospels, which present the Last Supper as a Passover meal.[15] Nevertheless, John agrees with the Synoptics in having the Last Supper on Thursday evening, the crucifixion on Friday, and the resurrection on Sunday (19:14, 31; 20:1).

NARRATIVE SPACE

Jesus ministers in Galilee (1:43; 2:1–12; 4:43–54; chap. 6; 7:1–9), Samaria (chap. 4), the Judean countryside (3:22), and east of the Jordan (10:40–42; cf. 1:29). The bulk of narrative, though, plays out in Jerusalem and its environs.

Houses are less prominent settings in John's Gospel than in the Synoptics. The house is mentioned in the episode of Jesus' raising of Lazarus (11:20, 31), but the main action in this story takes place at the tomb. Mary's anointing of Jesus, though, occurs in a house (12:3). The sea/seaside is an important narrative location (chaps. 6; 21). The mountain is a place of retreat (6:3, 15) and the scene of the feeding miracle. Gardens are mentioned 18:1, 26; 19:41; cf. 20:15). The temple figures very prominently in the first half of the narrative (e.g., 2:15; 5:14; 7:14). In John's Gospel, Jesus does not predict the temple's

---

15. See, however, Donald Arthur Carson (*The Gospel according to John* [Leicester: Inter-Varsity Press, 1991], 603–4), who argues that the underlying Greek phrase, *paraskeuē tou pascha*, refers to the day of preparation for the Sabbath of Passover week, which would bring John back into the line with the dating of the Synoptics.

destruction. The statement of 2:19, "Destroy this temple, and in three days I will raise it up," is not a literal threat against the temple. But in context (2:21), the implication seems to be that Jesus replaces the temple.

THE CHARACTERIZATION OF JESUS

John's Christology is the richest among the four Gospels. In reviewing his portrayal of Jesus, we may again distinguish between titles given to Jesus and characterizational emphases.

The Titles Used for Jesus

Messiah. The purpose statement of 20:30–31 indicates that the evangelist is concerned to show that Jesus is the Messiah. Interestingly, only John includes the transliterated form of the Hebrew/Aramaic term "Messiah" (1:41; 4:25), though he normally uses the Greek term *Christos* (19 times in all). Jesus is called *Christos* in the prologue (1:17). As the narrative progresses, Jesus is identified as the Messiah by his first followers (1:41), the Samaritan woman (4:25, 29, tentatively), and Martha (11:27). In John, in contrast to the Synoptics, the messiahship of Jesus is a topic of open discussion (7:25–31, 40–44; 12:34). Some in the crowd accept that he is the Messiah (7:41). Yet, as in the Synoptic Gospels, Jesus does not issue a public claim to be the Messiah, and he answers indirectly when asked whether he is the Christ (10:24).

As in the Synoptic Gospels, a Davidic, royal view of the Messiah lies in the background (7:42). The Samaritan woman's talk of "Messiah," though, probably alludes to "a prophet like Moses" of Deuteronomy 18:15 (given the Samaritans' acceptance of the Pentateuch alone as authoritative).[16]

Son of God. This is undoubtedly the most important title given to Jesus in the Gospel. The divine sonship of Jesus is the central feature of John's portrayal of Jesus. The title "Son of God" appears eight times in the Gospel.[17] It is applied to Jesus early in the narrative, first by John the Baptist (1:34) and then by Nathanael (1:49). There is a reference to Jesus as "Son of God" in 3:18, either by Jesus or the evangelist. Jesus refers to himself as "Son of God" during his public ministry in Jerusalem (5:25; 10:36) and in conversation with Martha (11:4). Martha in turn confesses Jesus as God's Son (11:27). The Jewish leaders lay before Pilate their accusation that Jesus' claim to be "Son of

16. See Hugh G. M. Williamson, "Samaritans," in *Dictionary of Jesus and the Gospels,* ed. Joel B. Green, Scot McKnight, and I. Howard Marshall (Leicester: InterVarsity Press, 1992), 724–28.

17. Some manuscripts have "Son of God" instead of "Son of Man" in 9:35.

God" is blasphemous (19:7). Finally, the evangelist states that his purpose is to assure readers that Jesus is "the Son of God" (20:30–31).

Jesus frequently refers to himself in absolute terms as "the Son": the formulation occurs eighteen times in the Gospel.[18] The designation expresses Jesus' *exclusive* filial status. The uniqueness of Jesus' sonship is underlined in talk of Jesus as the "only" or "unique" Son (*monogenēs*, 3:16, 18; cf. 1:14, 18).

Lord. The citation of Isaiah 40:3 in John 1:23 implicitly identifies Jesus as "the Lord" God. Jesus is called *kyrios* by various characters in the narrative, mostly as a respectful form of address (e.g., 4:11, 15, 19, 49), or in the sense of "master" (11:3, 12). But sometimes a more exalted sense is suggested (6:68; 9:38). After the resurrection, from 20:18 onward, the identification of Jesus as "Lord" has a more transcendent significance, especially in Thomas's confession, "My Lord and my God," which clearly signals Jesus' divine status (20:28).

Jesus calls himself "Lord" (of the disciples) in 13:14, but otherwise does not refer to himself as "Lord." The evangelist, as narrator, occasionally refers to Jesus as "the Lord" (6:23; 11:2; 20:20).

Son of Man. Jesus uses "Son of Man" thirteen times as a self-reference, and it appears early in the Gospel, at 1:51, in Jesus' conversation with Nathanael. In the Synoptic Gospels, Jesus' use of the formulation is never questioned, but in John, he is asked by the crowd, "Who is this Son of Man?" (12:34). The Synoptic categories of usage are more or less represented in John. The giving of food that produces eternal life (6:27) relates in the first instance to the earthly mission of the Son of Man. The emphasis on the "lifting up" (3:14; 8:28; 12:34) and "glorifying" (12:23; 13:31) of the Son of Man (3:14; 8:28; 12:23) embraces the Synoptic theme of the suffering, death, and resurrection of the Son of Man. Jesus' talk of the authority given to him, as Son of Man, to execute judgment (5:27) accords to him a future role. More distinctively Johannine, though, are the stress on believing in and partaking of the Son of Man (6:53; 9:35), the statement about angels ascending and descending on the Son of Man (1:51), and especially the idea of the Son of Man as coming down from heaven and returning to it (3:13; 6:62; 8:28).

Other titles. Jesus' role as teacher is featured in the Fourth Gospel (1:38; 3:2): the direct address *Rabbi* occurs more often in John than in any other of the other Gospels (8 times). Jesus is called *Rabbi* by disciples (1:38, 49) and nondisciples (3:2; 6:25). He is presented as a prophet (4:19, 44; 9:17); indeed, he is "the prophet" (6:14), almost certainly the "prophet like Moses" of Deuteronomy 18:15. Jesus is both positively (1:49; 6:15; 12:13, 15) and derisively

18. Köstenberger, *Theology*, 380.

(e.g., 18:33, 37, 39) identified as Israel's "king." The manner in which he fulfills the kingly role is misunderstood (6:15; 18:33, 36–37).

Uniquely among the evangelists, John gives Jesus the title "the Word." The title is confined to the prologue; elsewhere in the Gospel, the Greek word *logos* means "word" in the sense of "speech," "teaching," "message" (e.g., 2:22; 4:37). The term *logos* was used extensively in Greek philosophy. In Stoicism, the *logos* was the rational principle within the cosmos, governing and directing it. In the Old Testament, God's word has a creative function (Gen. 1; Ps. 33:6) and a revelatory force. In the prophetic literature, we often read of "the word of the LORD" coming to the prophet (as in Jer. 1:2; Ezek. 1:3). In Isaiah 55:11, God's word is nearly personified as his emissary. The evangelist is probably exploiting these diverse Greek and Jewish backgrounds.[19] The term "Word," as John utilizes it, epitomizes Jesus' role as divine revealer and communicator.

In a number of statements, Jesus uses the expression "I am" (*egō eimi*) without a predicate. The phrase on its own could simply be a form of self-identification ("It is I"). But in the Old Testament, "I am" is a formula of divine self-revelation: God refers to himself as "I am" in Exodus 3:14 and in passages in Isaiah (43:10, 13, 25). In some passages, Jesus is invoking the divine name, most clearly in debate with his opponents in John 8, where his statement "before Abraham was, I am" (8:58) is treated as blasphemy (8:59). Jesus' utterance of the divine self-revelation formula has a powerful effect at the scene of his arrest. When the soldiers state that they are looking for Jesus of Nazareth, Jesus replies, "I am" (18:5, Gk.). The soldiers immediately draw back and fall to the ground (18:6).

A title exclusive to John's Gospel among the four is "Lamb of God," which appears on the lips of John the Baptist (1:29, 36). The title involves multiple allusions, but primarily it refers to the Passover lamb. The epithet "Lamb of God" points to Jesus' sacrificial role (cf. Rev. 5:6).

John's is the only Gospel to call Jesus "God." The Word is identified as God in the opening verse: "the Word was God" (1:1), though the preceding "was *with* God" preserves a distinction within the divine totality. Jesus' opponents accuse him of making himself God (10:33) and equal to God (5:18). In the climactic confession, Thomas calls Jesus "My Lord and my God" (20:28). As already discussed, John describes Jesus several times by using the divine name for the One God, "I am," and Jesus proclaims, "I and the Father are one" (10:30).

---

19. John's description of "the Word" also has parallels with what is said about divine wisdom (cf. Carter, *John*, 137; drawing on Charles H. Talbert, *Reading John: A Literary and Theological Commentary on the Fourth Gospel and the Johannine Epistles* [New York: Crossroad, 1992], 68–70).

Characterizational Emphases

The Fourth Evangelist lays emphasis on the heavenly character of Jesus. Jesus has come from heaven and will return to it (e.g., 3:13, 31; 6:33). He is "from above"; he is "not of this world" (8:23). Jesus comes across as a more detached and other-worldly figure in John's Gospel than in the Synoptic Gospels, but he is not without human tenderness (see below).

A strong feature of the characterization of Jesus in the Fourth Gospel is the focus on his filial status and his relationship with "the Father." The Father-Son relationship is conditioned by mutuality of love (5:20; 14:31) and knowledge (6:46; 10:15), by reciprocal indwelling (10:38; 14:10–11), and by unity (10:30; 17:22). It is also marked by the Son's subordination to the Father: the Son does the Father's will (8:28; 12:49, 50); he glorifies the Father (14:13; 17:1, 4); he acknowledges that the Father is greater (14:28). Jesus speaks of a relational existence with God as Father "before the world existed" (17:5).

John highlights Jesus' sovereignty and control over events. Jesus' mastery of circumstances is especially evident in the account of the passion narrative. At the final meal, Jesus tells Judas to leave and get on with his act of treachery. At the arrest scene (18:2–13), Jesus takes charge of proceedings. He steps forward and asks the soldiers, "Whom are you looking for?" He identifies himself, leaving the soldiers prostrate. He secures the release of his disciples and then allows himself to be taken and bound. When interviewed by Annas, he remains composed. At his trial before Pilate, it is Pilate, not Jesus, who is afraid (19:8). When the governor asserts that he has power to release or crucify him, Jesus replies, "You would have no power over me unless it had been given you from above" (19:11). On the cross, Jesus exercises control over his death (see further chap. 11 below).

The evangelist emphasizes the glory of Jesus. In the Synoptic Gospels, "glory" is associated with Jesus in his role as the coming Son of Man (though the glory of Jesus is fleetingly glimpsed at the transfiguration). In the Fourth Gospel, it is already evident in his life and mission. We are told that the Son dwelled in glory in the Father's presence before the world began (17:5). In the incarnation, the Son's glory is revealed (1:14). Jesus' glory is made known in the course of his ministry, especially in his signs (2:11; 11:4). He is "glorified" in his death, resurrection, and exaltation (12:16, 23).

Despite the heavy stress on Jesus' divinity in John's Gospel, the humanity of Jesus is reinforced.[20] In the prologue, Jesus is identified as the *incarnate*

---

20. Ernst Käsemann, (*The Testament of Jesus* [London: SCM, 1968], 17) considered John's Gospel to be "naively docetic," picturing Jesus as "God striding over the earth." However, others (e.g., Udo Schnelle, *Antidocetic Christology in the Gospel of John: An Investigation of the Place of the Fourth Gospel in the Johannine School*, trans. Linda M. Maloney [Minneapolis: Fortress Press, 1992]) think that the Gospel is combating docetism.

Word,[21] and his humanness is evident throughout the narrative. Thus he gets tired and thirsty (4:6–7; 19:28); he weeps at the death of a close friend (11:35); his "soul is troubled" (12:27); he bleeds (19:34) and dies (19:30, 33).

THE CHARACTERIZATION
OF THE DISCIPLES

John speaks of a "disciple" or the "disciples" seventy-nine times. The "disciples" as a group are mentioned over sixty times in the Gospel. However, the word "disciples" does not always refer to the Twelve: it can include a larger group (6:60, 61, 66), and often when disciples are mentioned, it is not clear whether the Twelve or the larger band is indicated. The Twelve are referred to explicitly only in 6:67–71 and 20:24.

A particular feature of the Gospel is John's singling out individual disciples for attention (Andrew, Peter, Philip, Nathanael, Thomas, the beloved disciple, and Judas). The two most prominent disciples are Peter and the mysterious "beloved disciple." Andrew brings Peter to Jesus. Peter assumes the role of spokesman for the Twelve, confessing their joint faith in Jesus (6:68–69). At the final meal, he at first refuses to have his feet washed by Jesus and then goes to the other extreme by asking Jesus to wash not only his feet but also his hands and head (13:8–10). At the scene of Jesus' arrest, Peter defends Jesus, striking the high priest's slave and cutting off his ear. He follows the captured Jesus into the house of the high priest, where he denies his master. He witnesses the empty tomb, and in the closing scene, he declares his love for Jesus.

The "beloved disciple" (traditional designation) makes his first narrative appearance at the last meal, where he sits at the side of Jesus (13:23–25). He is present at the crucifixion, where Jesus entrusts his mother to his care (19:26–27). The beloved disciple runs to the empty tomb, and on seeing inside it, he believes (20:4). While fishing with Peter, he recognizes the resurrected Jesus (21:7). He is identified as the one on whose testimony the Gospel rests (21:24). The beloved disciple is portrayed as having an especially close relationship with Jesus. His posture at the meal (13:23, 25), "reclining next to the breast of Jesus" (Gk.), recalls what is said of the Son in 1:18, that he is "close to the Father's bosom" (Gk.). The beloved disciple is presented as the model follower, who exemplifies resurrection faith.

21. See esp. Marianne Meye Thompson, *The Humanity of Jesus in the Fourth Gospel* (Philadelphia: Fortress Press, 1988).

THE CHARACTERIZATION
OF THE RELIGIOUS AUTHORITIES

Of the four main groups of religious authorities appearing in the Synoptic Gospels, the Pharisees and chief priests dominate John's Gospel. (The scribes and elders figure in 7:53–8:11, the story of the woman caught in adultery, but they do not appear again.)[22] The Pharisees and chief priests often appear together, unified in their opposition to Jesus (7:32, 45; 11:47, 57; 18:3). They call the meeting of the council that decides Jesus' fate (11:47–53), and they are present at the scene of Jesus' arrest (18:3). At the trial before Pilate, John has the chief priests swearing their allegiance to Caesar (19:15). However, one Pharisee, Nicodemus, is sympathetic to Jesus (3:1; 7:50–51; 19:39).

While Pharisees and chief priests figure as distinct (but united) oppositional groups, the Jewish religious leaders are more often portrayed as a broad phenomenon and labeled "the Jews." The term "the Jews" appears sixty-three times in the Gospel of John. Sometimes it refers in a neutral way to the Jewish people in general (e.g., 2:6 alt., 13; 4:9, 22), but mostly it is used of the religious leadership, and the usage is predominantly negative. "The Jews," as the ruling authorities, are hostile to Jesus (e.g., 5:18; 7:1; 10:31, 33). And Jesus speaks harshly of them (esp. in 8:39–47). Yet, some of "the Jews" believe in Jesus (8:31; 12:11).

John's pejorative use of the expression "the Jews" raises again the specter of anti-Judaism. However, it must be emphasized that in this Gospel, "the Jews" refers mainly to the religious authorities who are in conflict with Jesus and with other Jews who believe that Jesus is the Messiah. It does not refer to all Jews for all time. John's Gospel reflects a situation (after Jesus' time) when the Jews who believed that Jesus was the Messiah were differentiating themselves from Jews who did not, and when Jewish authorities apparently were expelling the former from synagogues. It is important to recognize that John affirms the Jewishness of Jesus (4:9, 22) and his first followers, and that the Gospel is not condemning "the Jews" as a religious, cultural, or ethnic group.[23]

THEMES

Language of the "kingdom," so prominent in the Synoptic Gospels, is strikingly rare in the Fourth Gospel. The actual phrase "kingdom of God" only

---

22. See n. 3, this chapter for discussion of this passage.

23. For a narrative-critical treatment of John and "the Jews," see Stephen Motyer, *Your Father the Devil? A New Approach to John and "the Jews"* (Carlisle: Paternoster Press, 1997).

occurs twice, in 3:3, 5. In discussion with Pilate, Jesus speaks of his "kingdom" (18:36), emphasizing that it is "not from this world."

John's Gospel is the most thematic of the four Gospels. Space precludes an elaboration of his many themes (love, truth, fulfillment, new birth, the world, witness, etc.). We can only give attention to a selection of them.

Believing

Belief or "believing" must be reckoned the leading theme of the Gospel. The verb "believe" (*pisteuō*) occurs ninety-eight times, making it the most frequently used of John's keywords (strangely, the noun "faith/belief," *pistis* in Greek, never occurs at all in the Gospel). The theme of believing is introduced in the prologue (1:7, 12) and reiterated in the purpose statement: "These are written so that you may believe" (20:31).

John's use of the verb "believe" is very noteworthy. Although he can use it transitively, as in standard Greek, with the dative case to express the object (believing the Scripture, 2:22; believing Moses, 5:46; believing Jesus' works, 10:38), this usage is quite infrequent. The verb is employed in three main ways.[24] First, it is used (in twelve instances) to introduce the content of belief (*pisteuō hoti*, "believe that"). Almost always the content is christological (e.g., "We believe that you came from God"; 16:30).[25] Second, it is used (around thirty-six times) with the preposition *eis* to indicate the object.[26] The construction *pisteuō eis*, taken literally, means "believe into" but is used with the sense "believe in." Nearly always the object is Jesus. Third (around thirty times), the verb is used on its own, without an object. However, the context generally indicates the meaning as faith in Jesus.[27]

The extent to which faith in John's Gospel is directed to Jesus, rather than to the Father alone (cf. 14:1, "Believe in God, believe also in me") is highly significant. Believing is the appropriate response to Jesus; conversely, "not believing" results in condemnation (3:18).

Eternal Life

"Eternal life" figures significantly in Jesus' teaching and is the main soteriological category in the Gospel. It has often been pointed out that "eternal life"

---

24. Richard Thomas France, "Faith," in Green, McKnight, and Marshall, *Dictionary of Jesus and the Gospels*, 223–26, here 225.

25. Ibid., 225.

26. On one occasion (John 3:15), the preposition is *en*, "in."

27. France, "Faith," 225.

assumes the role in this Gospel that the kingdom of God has in the Synoptic Gospels. In John, the actual phrase "kingdom of God" only occurs twice, both occurrences in the dialogue with Nicodemus (3:3, 5), where it does appear to be superseded by "eternal life" (3:15–16).

The underlying Greek phrase, *zōē aiōnios*, says "life of the age" (Gk.). It is shorthand for "life of the age *to come*." As such, the expression reflects belief in a future age of blessedness succeeding the present age (cf. Mark 10:30). In the Synoptic Gospels, "eternal life" is a future prospect (Mark 10:17, 30). In John's Gospel, the life of the age to come is a gift of God to be enjoyed in the present. Eternal life is appropriated through faith in Jesus (3:16; 5:24; 20:31).

The emphasis on eternal life as a present possession reflects John's "realized" eschatology, his stress on the present experience of end-time blessing. The realized dimension, though, does not displace the future hope. Although the Gospel speaks of eternal life now, it also anticipates a future resurrection (6:39–40, 44, 54).

Abiding

The language of mutual "abiding" or "remaining" is used of the relationship between Jesus and the Father (14:10; 15:10). It implies an exceptionally intimate bond. The notion of mutual abiding is applied to the relationship between Jesus and his followers. This theme is developed in 15:1–11. Believers must abide in Jesus, as he abides in them (15:4). The idea is expounded in terms of the analogy of a vine and branches. Only when believers abide in Christ, the vine, can they bear fruit (15:5). Branches that do not abide wither away. Such branches, readers are warned, will be "gathered, thrown into the fire, and burned" (15:6).[28]

The Holy Spirit as Paraclete

The Holy Spirit figures prominently in John's Gospel (e.g., 1:32, 33; 3:5, 6, 8, 34). The most distinctive aspect of John's teaching on the Holy Spirit is his portrait of the Spirit as the "Paraclete." In several passages within the Farewell Discourses, Jesus speaks of the Spirit as a *paraklētos* (14:16–17, 26; 15:26; 16:7–14). The Greek word does not have a precise English counterpart and is translated variously in English Bibles. The NRSV's "Advocate" picks up on the legal dimension of the Spirit's activity in 16:7–12, but the legal role given

---

28. On the relation between divine sovereignty and human responsibility in the Gospel, see Donald Arthur Carson's classic study *Divine Sovereignty and Human Responsibility* (London: Marshall, Morgan & Scott, 1980).

to the Spirit here is actually that of prosecutor rather than advocate. Many interpreters thus prefer to render the term simply as "Paraclete."

The sayings on the Paraclete can be divided into statements about (1) Jesus, (2) the disciples, and (3) the world. With regard to Jesus, the Paraclete functions as a witness, bearing testimony to and glorifying him (15:26; 16:14). With respect to the disciples, the Paraclete functions as teacher, helper, and revealer (14:16–17, 26). With reference to the world, the Paraclete functions as a prosecutor and accuser (16:7–12).

As Paraclete, the Spirit is patterned after Jesus. Jesus also is a "Paraclete," and thus the Paraclete is "another" *like Jesus* (14:16). In the role of Paraclete, the Spirit continues Jesus' ministry, mediates his presence, and brings to remembrance his word (16:7).[29]

Miracles as Signs

In John's Gospel, Jesus' miracles are characteristically called signs (from Gk. *sēmeion*, which occurs seventeen times in the Gospel).[30] The most common Synoptic word for Jesus' miracles, *dynamis*, "deed of power," is not found in John. John records seven miracles performed by Jesus during his ministry (all in the first half of the Gospel): the changing of water into wine, the healing of the official's son, the healing of the paralyzed man; the feeding of the five thousand, the walking on the water, the healing of the man born blind, the raising of Lazarus. Six are directly or indirectly identified as "signs" (the exception is the walking on the water). The resurrection is also implicitly designated a "sign" (2:18–21). As "signs," the miracles point beyond themselves, revealing Jesus' glory (2:11), confirming his identity as Messiah and Son of God (7:31; 20:30–31). Sometimes these signs are misunderstood (6:15) and do not lead to faith (12:37).

Dualisms

It is characteristic of John to employ sharp antitheses: death or life (5:24), perishing or having eternal life (3:16; 10:28), below or above (8:23), "of this world" or "not of this world" (8:23; 17:14–16), flesh or spirit (3:6), and especially darkness or light (1:5; 3:19–21; 8:12; 12:35–36, 46).[31] Scholars often call these contrasts John's "dualisms" (or "dualities"). However, John does not

---

29. On the Holy Spirit in John's Gospel (and the Johannine community), see Gary M. Burge, *The Anointed Community: The Holy Spirit in the Johannine Tradition* (Grand Rapids: Wm. B. Eerdmans Publishing Co., 1987).

30. Köstenberger, *Theology*, 323–35.

31. Carter, *John*, 86–106.

operate with an absolute dualism—two eternal and equivalent sides. God is in ultimate control, and light will triumph over darkness.[32]

John's worldview, with its sharp contrasts and its division of humanity into those who believe and those who do not, has often been labeled "sectarian," meaning the product of an exclusive group, and linked to the social setting of the "Johannine community." John's worldview, though, is more complex than the label "sectarian" would perhaps allow,[33] and the extent to which a distinct community can be reconstructed from the Gospel text is now highly debated (see chap. 1).

CONCLUSION

John tells the same core story as the Synoptists but with a much greater degree of individualism. Such is the distinctiveness of the Gospel that extra effort needs to be made to keep in view the shared story. Emphasis is laid on the heavenly and divine character of Jesus and on his relationship with "the Father," a relationship traced back to before the beginning of the world. Yet for all his stress on Jesus' divinity, John also reinforces Jesus' genuine human- ity: Jesus is the divine Word *made flesh*. John's deeper christological reflection and his development of themes such as believing, eternal life, and abiding give the Gospel a "spiritual" quality that has long been recognized.[34]

FOR FURTHER READING

Ashton, John. *Understanding the Fourth Gospel*. Oxford: Oxford University Press, 1991.

Brown, Raymond E. *The Gospel according to John*. 2 vols. Anchor Yale Bible Commen- taries. New Haven: Yale University Press, 1995.

Carter, Warren. *John: Storyteller, Interpreter, Evangelist*. Peabody, MA: Hendrickson Publishers, 2006.

Köstenberger, Andreas J. *A Theology of John's Gospel and Letters*. Biblical Theology of the New Testament. Grand Rapids: Zondervan, 2009.

Kysar, Robert. *John, the Maverick Gospel*. 3rd ed. Louisville, KY: Westminster John Knox Press, 2007.

32. In older scholarship, the worldview of John tended to be set against a Hellenistic or "gnostic" background; more recently scholars have argued that John's outlook is more reflective of Jewish apocalyptic thought (see, for instance, John Ashton, *Understanding the Fourth Gospel* [Oxford: Clarendon Press, 1991], 383–406).

33. Although "the world" is often viewed negatively in the Gospel, there are some positive references to "the world": cf., e.g., 1:9; 3:16, 17.

34. Less than a century after John was composed, Clement of Alexandria designated it as the "spiritual Gospel" (Eusebius, *Ecclesiastical History* 6.14.7).

Martyn, J. Louis. *History and Theology in the Fourth Gospel*. New Testament Library. Louisville, KY: Westminster John Knox Press, 2003.

O'Day, Gail R., and Susan E. Hylen. *John*. Westminster Bible Companion. Louisville, KY: Westminster John Knox Press, 2006.

Sloyan, Gerard S. *John*. Interpretation. Louisville, KY: Westminster John Knox Press, 2009.

Smith, D. Moody. *John*. Abingdon New Testament Commentary. Nashville: Abingdon Press, 1999.

———. *The Theology of the Gospel of John*. New Testament Theology Series. Cambridge: Cambridge University Press, 1995.

Stibbe, Mark W. G. *John as Storyteller: Narrative Criticism and the Fourth Gospel*. Cambridge: Cambridge University Press, 1994.

Witherington, Ben, III. *John's Wisdom: A Commentary on the Fourth Gospel*. Louisville, KY: Westminster John Knox Press, 1995.

Wright, N. T., *John for Everyone, Part 1*. Louisville, KY: Westminster John Knox Press, 2004.

———. *John for Everyone, Part 2*. Louisville, KY: Westminster John Knox Press, 2004.

PART III

Selected Parallel Episodes

Having considered each Gospel separately, we now bring the "parallel lives" of Jesus into contact with each other as we look at selected common episodes. The exercise will allow us to explore the unity and plurality of the Gospels in a more focused way, with reference to specific passages. We examine six episodes narrated in three or all four Gospels, spanning the beginning, middle, and end of the common gospel story: the baptism of Jesus (chap. 7); the feeding of the five thousand (chap. 8); the walking on the water (chap. 9); the transfiguration (chap. 10); the death of Jesus, which strictly speaking is a scene rather than an episode (chap. 11); the discovery of the empty tomb (chap. 12). In each case, the procedure is to set out the matching passages in parallel columns as in a Gospel synopsis, to identify the shared story, and to investigate the differing narrative renditions of it. The narrative differences are explored by using the categories applied to the Gospels as whole texts in part 2 (but substituting context for structure).

The aim is not to harmonize parallel passages but to bring out their commonality and individuality.

7

The Baptism of Jesus

The story of Jesus' baptism is narrated by all three Synoptic evangelists and alluded to in John's Gospel. In John, the allusion is made by the mention of the Spirit's descent on Jesus, which is the inciting event of the shared story. In the Synoptic Gospels, the baptism is also the occasion of a heavenly announcement of Jesus' divine sonship. Let's look at the Synoptic accounts in parallel:

Matthew 3:13–17	Mark 1:9–11	Luke 3:21–22
13Then Jesus came from Galilee to John at the Jordan, to be baptized by him. 14John would have prevented him, saying, "I need to be baptized by you, and do you come to me?" 15But Jesus answered him, "Let it be so now; for it is proper for us in this way to fulfill all righteousness." Then he consented. 16And when Jesus had been baptized,	9In those days Jesus came from Nazareth of Galilee	21Now when all the people were baptized,
	and was baptized by John in the Jordan.	and when Jesus also had been baptized and was praying,

(continued)

Matthew 3:13–17	Mark 1:9–11	Luke 3:21–22
just as he came up from the water, suddenly <u>the heavens were opened</u> to him and he saw <u>the Spirit of God descending like a dove</u> and alighting on him.	[10]And just as he was coming up out of the water, he saw <u>the heavens torn apart</u> <u>and the Spirit descending like a dove on him.</u>	<u>the heaven was opened,</u> [22]and <u>the Holy Spirit descended upon him</u> in bodily form <u>like a dove.</u>
[17]<u>And a voice from heaven said, "This is my beloved Son,</u>[1] <u>with whom I am well pleased."</u>	[11]<u>And a voice came from heaven, "You are my beloved Son;</u>[1] <u>with you I am well pleased."</u>	<u>And a voice came from heaven, "You are my beloved Son;</u>[1] <u>with you I am well pleased."</u>

THE SHARED STORY

Comparing the three Synoptic versions, we find a common story, with *events*, *characters*, and *setting*. There is a common series of *events* (underlined above):

- Jesus undergoes baptism.
- The heavens open or split apart.
- The Spirit of God descends upon Jesus like a dove, and a voice calls out from heaven, identifying Jesus as God's beloved Son, with whom God is well pleased.

There are common *characters*: Jesus, the Spirit of God, and the heavenly voice (one might expect that John the Baptist would be an essential character in the story, but Luke can narrate the story without reference to him at all). And there is a common *setting*: the river Jordan (in Luke, the Jordan setting is made clear in 4:1). The commonalities are usually explained in source-critical terms as arising from Matthew's and Luke's dependence on Mark (the differences are interpreted as redactional changes made to the source text).

The shared story involves a shared set of Old Testament reminiscences (intertextuality at the story level). The reference to the Spirit as descending "like a dove" recalls Genesis 1:2, where the Hebrew verb used for the Spirit's

1. The wording "my beloved Son" follows the alternative translation given in NRSV notes.

"hovering over" the face of the waters is the word used for the fluttering of a bird. The heavenly declaration alludes to Psalm 2:7 ("You are my son," said of the anointed king) and Isaiah 42:1 ("in whom my soul delights," said of the Lord's Servant).

CONTEXT

In all three Synoptic Gospels, the baptismal episode follows a summary of the ministry of John the Baptist, in which John places himself in the role of forerunner (Mark 1:7–8 par. [and parallel/s]). In Mark and Matthew, the baptism is followed directly by the temptation. In Luke, the genealogy comes between the two incidents (3:23–38).

PLOT

All three evangelists narrate the events that make up the story in their natural sequence. None of the Synoptists dwells on the baptism itself; all three give more attention to the dramatic events accompanying it. Matthew includes an exchange between John the Baptist and Jesus (3:14–15), which is unique to his narrative rendition. Luke does not narrate the involvement of John the Baptist in Jesus' baptism (having just told us about John's imprisonment; 3:18–20). However, the passive clause, "when Jesus also had been baptized" (3:21), makes clear that Jesus does not baptize himself. We are probably meant to infer that it is John who administers the rite. Additionally, Luke does not relate Jesus' emergence from the water after baptism.

STYLE

Each passage betrays typical features of each evangelist's style.

Mark's habit of connecting sentences with *kai* is evident in the Greek: the word *kai* appears at the start of each of Mark's three verses. His favorite word, *euthys*, meaning "immediately" and translated "just as" in the NRSV, occurs in 1:10.

Matthew's account opens with his characteristic "then" (*tote*). His fondness for *de* as a connector appears in the Greek: it occurs at the beginning of three verses: 3:14, 15, and 16.[2] The phrase "to fulfill all righteousness"

---

2. In Greek, *de* is never the first word in a sentence but is placed after the first word.

in 3:15 brings together two items of Matthew's favored vocabulary: "fulfill" and "righteousness." Another typically Matthean expression, *kai idou*, occurs in 3:16 (where it is rendered "suddenly" by the NRSV) and 3:17 (where it is simply translated as "and").

Luke's version of the baptism is the most syntactically complicated, in line with his more elegant Greek: it is one long sentence in the original. Whereas Mark speaks of "the Spirit" (1:10) and Matthew of "the Spirit of God" (3:16), Luke refers to the "*Holy* Spirit." This is Luke's preferred way of speaking of the divine Spirit (cf., e.g., 1:15, 35, 41; the formulation is found over forty times in Acts).

NARRATIVE TECHNIQUE

Mark's violent image of the heavens being "torn apart" (1:10), in contrast to Matthew's and Luke's talk of heaven being "opened," reflects his vivid mode of narration. Mark seems to be referencing Isaiah 64:1, in which the prophet longs for God to "tear open the heavens and come down." Isaiah 64:1 is about God's awesome coming, so by alluding to this verse, Mark gives the baptismal event an "apocalyptic" character.[3] Elsewhere in Mark, the Greek verb *schizō*, "tear apart," is used only in 15:38, with reference to the tearing apart of the temple curtain at the moment of Jesus' death (see chap. 12 below). These two instances of the verb form an *inclusio* and establish a linkage between the baptism and the crucifixion, supported by the twin acclamations of Jesus' divine sonship in 1:11 and 15:39 (note the connection between Jesus' baptism and his death in 10:38–39). Luke has the Spirit descending on Jesus "in bodily form like a dove" (3:22), reflecting his propensity to concretize the supernatural.

In all three Gospels, the heavenly declaration of Jesus' divine sonship is repeated at the transfiguration (see chap. 9 below). In Mark and Luke, one can detect a backward glance at the divine affirmation of Jesus' "beloved" sonship in the parable of the Vineyard, in which Jesus is implicitly the "beloved son" (Mark 12:6; Luke 20:13). Matthew's citation of Isaiah 42:1–2 in Matthew 12:18–21 reiterates Jesus' status as God's "beloved." Luke refers back to the baptism in 4:18 (see below).

---

3. Michael Bird, "Tearing the Heavens and Shaking the Heavenlies: Mark's Cosmology in Its Apocalyptic Context," in *Cosmology and New Testament Theology*, ed. Sean M. McDonough and Jonathan T. Pennington (London: T&T Clark International, 2008), 50.

NARRATIVE TIME AND SPACE

The baptismal episode is narrated briefly in all three Gospels; the actual baptism is related in a clause. Mark's "in those days" reproduces an Old Testament time phrase (e.g., Judg. 17:6; 18:1; 19:1; 21:25; 1 Sam. 4:1);[4] in Mark, the expression may carry eschatological significance (cf. 13:17, 19, 24).[5] Matthew's "then" serves to locate Jesus' baptism during the time of John the Baptist's activity. Luke relates the event to the general time during which all the people were being baptized.

The Jordan River, the scene of the baptism in all three Gospels, has rich Old Testament associations (e.g., Josh. 1–4; 2 Kgs. 5). Mark states that Jesus comes "from Nazareth of Galilee" (1:9). Jesus' Nazarene origins are also stressed in the final scene of Mark's Gospel (16:6). Matthew mentions only Galilee (we already know from 2:23 that Nazareth is Jesus' hometown), in which he has a special interest: Jesus' work begins and ends in Galilee in this Gospel (4:12–16; 28:16–20). Luke makes no reference in the passage to Jesus' point of departure, but we may infer from 2:51 that he comes from Nazareth.

THE CHARACTERIZATION OF JESUS

Jesus is the central character of the shared story, but he is more the recipient and beneficiary of actions than one who makes things happen. Jesus is designated as God's Son. The allusion to Psalm 2:7 indicates that "Son of God" is here in the first instance a messianic concept. The original reference is to the ideal king, equated in early Judaism with the Davidic Messiah.[6] However, the identification of Jesus as God's "beloved" Son strongly suggests that his unique sonship, independent of his messianic status, is in also view. It is possible to take "beloved" as a separate title, "the Beloved" (as in NRSV main text), but "beloved son/daughter" is a standard biblical and postbiblical expression (e.g., Gen. 22:2, 12, 16).[7] The expression "beloved son" carries the nuance of "only son" (as in Gen. 22:2, 12, 16; cf. Mark 12:6; Luke 20:13). With the use of the present tense and the omission of the adoption formula in Psalm

---

4. Morna D. Hooker, *The Gospel according to St. Mark*, BNTC (London: A&C Black, 1991), 45.
5. Joel Marcus, *Mark: A New Translation with Introduction and Commentary*, vol. 1, *Mark 1–8*, AB 27 (New York: Doubleday, 2000), 163.
6. Ibid., 162.
7. Ibid.

2:7 ("Today I have begotten you"),[8] the implication is that divine sonship is a condition already enjoyed by Jesus; he does not become God's Son at the baptism. The words "with whom/you I am well pleased," alluding to Isaiah 42:1, implicitly identify Jesus as the Lord's Servant.

Mark senses no christological difficulty with Jesus' subordinating himself to John, who is Jesus' inferior (1:7–8), and submitting to a "baptism of repentance for the forgiveness of sins" (1:4, which seems to clash with belief in Jesus' sinlessness; cf. 2 Cor. 5:21; 1 Pet. 2:22; 1 John 3:5).[9] This is in keeping with the rawness of Mark's christological portrait. The declaration that Jesus is God's Son is the first clear statement of Jesus' divine sonship in the Gospel (if, as seems likely, the words "Son of God" in Mark 1:1 were not original but added later).

Matthew does more than the other two Synoptic evangelists to portray Jesus as active and willful. He states that Jesus "came . . . to be baptized" (3:13), making him act with purpose (the construction is a purpose clause in Greek). Jesus' resolve is tested when John the Baptist "would have prevented him" (3:14) from being baptized, but Jesus will not be deflected from his aim. The dialogue between John the Baptist and Jesus explicitly treats the issue of why Jesus humbles himself before John: the answer given is that the subordination is temporary and for the fulfillment of God's purposes. The contrast between those who come for baptism while "confessing their sins" (3:6) and Jesus who comes "to fulfill all righteousness" (3:15) may be Matthew's way of safeguarding Jesus' sinless purity. The declaration of 3:17 is not the first statement of Jesus' divine sonship in the Gospel. On his family's return from Egypt, Jesus was identified as God's Son (2:15). The identification of Jesus as the Lord's Servant, implicit in 3:17, is made explicit in 12:18–21, where Matthew quotes Isaiah 42:1–4 (cf. Matt. 8:17; Isa. 53:4).

Luke portrays Jesus as associating himself with "all the people," which may hint at a reason for Jesus' submission to John's baptism of repentance: he undergoes baptism to identify with Jewish people in their expression of contrition.[10] By keeping John the Baptist out of the picture, Luke does not have Jesus explicitly subordinating himself to John. In Luke's version, the dramatic events take place while Jesus prays (3:21), fitting in with his christological emphasis on Jesus' habit of praying. In his account of the preaching at Naza-

8. A variant reading of Luke 3:22 includes the formula, but this reading is unlikely to be original; cf. Judith M. Lieu, *The Gospel of Luke* (Peterborough: Epworth Press, 1997), 26.

9. The problem of Jesus' undergoing baptism for remission of sins is keenly sensed in the *Gospel of the Hebrews* (as cited by Jerome, *Dialogue against Pelagius* 3.2). When his mother and brothers suggest to Jesus that they should all go to be baptized by John, Jesus replies, "In what way have I sinned that I should go and be baptized by him?"

10. Christopher Francis Evans, *Saint Luke*, TPINTC (Philadelphia: Trinity Press International, 1990), 246.

reth, Luke brings out the significance of the Spirit's descent upon Jesus. It marks Jesus' anointing and empowerment for ministry (4:18; cf. Acts 10:38). After his Spirit-anointing at his baptism, Jesus goes "full of Holy Spirit" into the wilderness to face his testing (4:1). In Luke, as in Matthew, the heavenly announcement is not the first narrative signal of Jesus' status as God's Son: we learn of Jesus' divine sonship at the annunciation (1:32, 35).

THEMES

Mark's presentation of the baptism as a more private affair ("he saw," 1:10; "you are," 1:11) fits with the secrecy theme: no other human being knows of Jesus' divine sonship until his death. Matthew's version brings out his emphasis on fulfillment and righteousness. Luke's rendition reveals his particular interest in prayer and the activity of the Holy Spirit.

THE BAPTISM OF JESUS IN JOHN'S GOSPEL

The baptism of Jesus is not narrated in the Fourth Gospel, but it is alluded to in John the Baptist's testimony to Jesus in 1:19–34. John the Baptist sees Jesus approaching and declares, "Here is the Lamb of God who takes away the sin of the world!" The Baptist speaks of a prior encounter with Jesus, in which he saw the Spirit descend upon him like a dove (1:32). This alludes to the occasion of Jesus' baptism, thus presupposing the Gospel's readers' knowledge of it. The Baptist states that he has previously been told (by God) that the one on whom he sees the Spirit descend "and remain is the one who baptizes with the Holy Spirit" (1:33). When he saw the Spirit descend on Jesus, he thus knew Jesus to be the promised one. The Baptist then confesses that Jesus is the "Son of God" (1:34; some manuscripts have "Elect of God," alluding to Isa. 42:1, but "Son of God" is probably the better reading).[11]

Much like the other Gospel writers, John views the descent of the Spirit on Jesus as the inaugural act of Jesus' mission. It is an event that "marks him out as God's unique instrument."[12] The Fourth Evangelist, though, concentrates on its significance for John the Baptist, identifying Jesus *to him* as "the one who is coming" (1:27). He also places emphasis on the Spirit's remaining with Jesus (1:32–33). "Remain/abide" (*menō*) is a key Johannine term and theme. In the present context, it underlines the permanence of the Spirit's rest on Jesus,[13]

11. C. K. Barrett, *The Gospel according to St. John, Second Edition* (London: SPCK, 1978), 178.
12. Raymond E. Brown, *The Gospel According to John I–XII* (Garden City: Doubleday, 1966), 66.
13. Barrett, *St. John*, 178.

in contrast to the passing experiences of the Spirit known by Old Testament figures (such as King Saul, 1 Sam. 16:14).[14] John the Baptist's confession of Jesus as "Son of God" is the Fourth Evangelist's counterpart to the heavenly announcement of Jesus' divine sonship at his baptism in the Synoptics.

CONCLUSION

The Synoptic writers convey the same basic story of Jesus' baptism, culminating in the announcement of his divine sonship, while differing in their narrative renditions. The differences reflect the individual interests and proclivities of the evangelists.

Mark, by means of an *inclusio*, links Jesus' baptism with his death, a linkage in which he is particularly interested. Matthew finds in Jesus' submission to baptism the fulfillment of the divine purpose. Luke emphasizes Jesus' prayerfulness. He objectivizes the Spirit's descent, an example of his tendency to concretize the supernatural. John's Gospel does not contain an account of Jesus' baptism, but it does allude to it, focusing on the Spirit's falling on Jesus, which is the inciting incident of the common gospel story underlying all four Gospel narratives. The Fourth Evangelist emphasizes the Spirit's "remaining" on Jesus, which mirrors his interest in abiding.

FOR FURTHER READING

Beasley-Murray, George Raymond. *Baptism in the New Testament*. Eugene, OR: Wipf & Stock, 2006.

Byars, Ronald P. *The Sacraments in Biblical Perspective*. Interpretation: Resources for the Use of Scripture in the Church. Louisville, KY: Westminster John Knox Press, 2011.

Cullmann, Oscar. *Baptism in the New Testament*. Philadelphia: Westminster Press, 1978.

Ferguson, Everett. *Baptism in the Early Church: History, Theology, and Liturgy in the First Five Centuries*. Grand Rapids: Wm. B. Eerdmans Publishing Co., 2009.

Smith, Ralph Allan. *The Baptism of Jesus Christ*. Wipf & Stock, 2010.

---

14. Donald Arthur Carson, *The Gospel according to John* (Leicester: Inter-Varsity Press, 1991), 152.

8

The Feeding of the Five Thousand

The feeding of the five thousand is one of the most well-known of the miracles performed by Jesus and the only one that is recorded in all four Gospels.[1] It is classed as a "nature miracle," an action by which Jesus demonstrates his authority over the natural world. It has also been called a "gift miracle," in which there is a miraculous and abundant provision of resources.[2] The story of the feeding of the five thousand is remarkably similar in all four Gospels.

Matthew 14:13–21	Mark 6:32–44	Luke 9:10b–17	John 6:1–15
Now when Jesus heard this, he withdrew from there in a boat to a deserted place by himself. But	And they went away in the boat to a deserted place by themselves.	He took them with him and withdrew privately to a city called Bethsaida.	After this Jesus went to the other side of the Sea of Galilee, also called the Sea of Tiberias.

(continued)

---

1. A distinction is usually drawn between miracles performed by Jesus in the context of his ministry and events, such as the virginal conception and the resurrection, in which Jesus is the object of miraculous action: see B. L. Blackburn, "Miracles and Miracle Stories," in *Dictionary of Jesus and the Gospels*, ed. Joel B. Green, Scot McKnight, and I. Howard Marshall (Leicester: InterVarsity Press, 1992), 549–60, here 549.

2. Joel Marcus, *Mark: A New Translation with Introduction and Commentary*, vol. 1, *Mark 1–8*, (New York: Doubleday, 2000), 415.

Matthew 14:13–21	Mark 6:32–44	Luke 9:10b–17	John 6:1–15
when the crowds heard it, they	[33]Now many saw them going and recognized them, and they hurried	[11]When the crowds found out about it, they	[2]A large crowd
followed him	recognized them, and they hurried	followed him;	kept following him, because they saw the signs that he was doing for the sick. [3]Jesus went up the mountain and sat down there with his disciples. [4]Now the Passover, the festival of the Jews, was near. [5]When
on foot from the towns.	there on foot from all the towns and arrived ahead of them.		
[14]When he went ashore, he saw a great crowd; and he had compassion for them	[34]As he went ashore, he saw a great crowd; and he had compassion for them, because they were like sheep without a shepherd; and	and he welcomed them, and spoke to them about the kingdom of God,	he looked up and saw a large crowd coming toward him,
and cured their sick.	he began to teach them many things.	and healed those who needed to be cured.	
[15]When it was evening, the disciples came to him and said, "This is a deserted place, and the hour is now late;	[35]When it grew late, his disciples came to him and said, "This is a deserted place, and the hour is now very late;	[12]The day was drawing to a close, and the twelve came to him and said,	
send the crowds away so that they may go	[36]send them away so that they may go into the surrounding country and villages and	"Send the crowd away, so that they may go into the surrounding villages and countryside, to lodge and	
into the villages and			Jesus said to Philip, "Where are we to buy

(continued)

Matthew 14:13–21	Mark 6:32–44	Luke 9:10b–17	John 6:1–15
buy food for themselves."	buy something for themselves to eat."	get provisions; for we are here in a deserted place."	bread for these people to eat?" [6]He said this to test him, for he himself knew what he was going to do.
[16]Jesus said to them, "They need not go away; you give them something to eat."	[37]But he answered them, "You give them something to eat." They said to him, "Are we to go and buy two hundred denarii worth of bread, and give it to them to eat?" [38]And he said to them, "How many loaves have you? Go and see."	[13]But he said to them, "You give them something to eat."	[7]Philip answered him, "Two hundred denarii[3] would not buy enough bread for each of them to get a little." [8]One of his disciples, Andrew, Simon Peter's brother, said to him,
[17]They replied, "We have nothing here but five loaves and two fish."	When they had found out, they said, "Five, and two fish."	They said, "We have no more than five loaves and two fish— unless we are to go and buy food for all these people." [14]For there were about five thousand men.	[9]"There is a boy here who has five barley loaves and two fish. But what are they among so many people?"
[18]And he said, "Bring them here to me." [19]Then he ordered the crowds to sit down	[39]Then he ordered them to get all the people to sit down in groups	And he said to his disciples, "Make them sit down in	[10]Jesus said, "Make the people sit down." Now there was a

(continued)

3. Here I have changed the NRSV's "six months' wages" to RSV's "two hundred denarii," to bring out the connection with Mark 6:37.

Matthew 14:13–21	Mark 6:32–44	Luke 9:10b–17	John 6:1–15
on the grass.	on the green grass. ⁴⁰So they sat down in groups of hundreds and of fifties.		great deal of grass in the place; so they sat down,
		groups of about fifty each."	about <u>five thousand</u> in all.
		¹⁵They did so and made them all sit down.	
<u>Taking the five loaves</u> and the two fish, he looked up to heaven, and <u>blessed</u> and broke the loaves, and gave them to the disciples, and the disciples <u>gave them to the crowds.</u>	⁴¹<u>Taking the five loaves</u> and the two fish, he looked up to heaven, and <u>blessed</u> and broke the loaves, and gave them to his disciples <u>to set before the people;</u> and he divided the two fish among them all.	¹⁶<u>And taking the five loaves</u> and the two fish, he looked up to heaven, and <u>blessed</u> and broke them, and gave them to the disciples <u>to set before the crowd.</u>	¹¹<u>Then Jesus took the loaves,</u> and when he had <u>given thanks,</u> he <u>distributed them to those who were seated;</u> so also the fish, as much as they wanted.
²⁰And <u>all ate and were filled;</u> and they <u>took up</u> what was left over of the broken pieces,	⁴²And <u>all ate and were filled;</u> ⁴³and they <u>took up</u>	¹⁷And <u>all ate and were filled.</u> What was left over was <u>gathered up,</u>	¹²When <u>they were satisfied,</u> he told his disciples, "Gather up the fragments left over, so that nothing may be lost." ¹³So they <u>gathered them up,</u> and from the fragments of the five barley loaves, left by those who had eaten, they filled
<u>twelve baskets</u> full.	<u>twelve baskets</u> full of broken pieces and of the fish.	<u>twelve baskets</u> of broken pieces.	<u>twelve baskets.</u>

(*continued*)

Matthew 14:13–21	Mark 6:32–44	Luke 9:10b–17	John 6:1–15
[21]And those who ate were about five thousand men, besides women and children.	[44]Those who had eaten the loaves numbered five thousand men.		[14]When the people saw the sign that he had done, they began to say, "This is indeed the prophet who is to come into the world." [15]When Jesus realized that they were about to come and take him by force to make him king, he withdrew again to the mountain by himself.

THE SHARED STORY

Comparison of the four accounts reveals a common story, comprising the following series of *events* (underlined above):

- Jesus goes to a certain place and is met there by a multitude of people.
- The need to feed the throng emerges.
- Only five loaves and two fish are forthcoming.
- A command is issued for the people to sit.
- Jesus takes the bread and offers a blessing / gives thanks.
- The food is given out.
- All the people, who number (at least) five thousand, eat to their satisfaction.
- Twelve baskets of leftovers are collected.

There are common *characters*: Jesus, the disciples, and the multitude. The *setting* of the story, though, varies: in Mark and Matthew, a secluded place; in

Luke, a deserted place near Bethsaida; in John, the other (eastern) side of the Sea of Galilee.

The Synoptic versions are very similar and evidence a literary linkage, normally explained in terms of Matthew's and Luke's use of Mark. There are a number of agreements of Matthew and Luke against Mark (e.g., in both, the crowds "followed" Jesus; both lack Mark's "like sheep without a shepherd"; in both, Jesus heals). These are usually seen as coincidental changes to Mark made independently by Matthew and Luke,[4] though some think they point to Luke's use of Matthew in addition to Mark.[5] John's account dovetails with Mark on several points, especially the mention of two hundred denarii (Mark 6:37; John 6:7). The Mark-John links might indicate the Fourth Evangelist's acquaintance with Mark.

The shared story recalls God's supply of manna in the wilderness through Moses to the Israelites (Exod. 16). It also calls to mind Elisha's feeding of a hundred persons with twenty loaves (2 Kgs. 4:42–44).

CONTEXT

In Mark, the feeding miracle follows the return of the Twelve from their mission (6:30–31). Jesus invites the disciples to come with him to a secluded place where they can "rest a while" and escape the pressure of the crowds, which is now so intense that Jesus' companions cannot even find time to eat (6:31). Only Mark makes the disciples' need for recuperation after their missionary endeavors the motivation for withdrawing to the scene of the miracle.

In Matthew's Gospel, this passage comes directly after the account of Herod's execution of John the Baptist. Unlike Mark and Luke, Matthew does not mention the return of the Twelve from their mission. The withdrawal to a deserted place is not prompted by a wish to get away from the crowds, as in Mark, but by the receipt of some news: "Now when Jesus heard this, he withdrew" (14:13). The information provoking the movement may be either the news that John the Baptist has been executed or news of Herod's belief that Jesus is John the Baptist risen from the dead (14:2; if 14:13 is resuming 14:2, after the excursus of 14:3–12).

Within Luke's larger narrative, the feeding of the five thousand comes after Herod's perplexity about Jesus (9:7–9) and a brief note signaling the disciples' return from their mission (9:10a). The feeding is followed by Peter's confession of Jesus as Messiah (9:18–20).

4. Going by the common two-source hypothesis (see "The Similarity of the Synoptic Gospels" in chap. 1).
5. Going by the Farrer theory (see n. 6 in chap. 1).

In John's Gospel, the feeding miracle follows teaching given in Jerusalem (5:1–47). The walking on the water (6:16–21) comes immediately afterward, as in Mark and Matthew. Then John narrates the discourse on the bread of life (6:22–59), which builds on and interprets the feeding miracle.

PLOT

The Synoptic versions are similar in plot, with relatively minor variations. Only Mark states that Jesus "began to teach them many things" (6:34; cf. 4:2), and only Mark records the sarcastic reply of the disciples (6:37): "Are we to go and buy two hundred denarii worth of bread, and give it to them to eat?" Unique to Matthew is Jesus' command that the bread and fish be brought to him (14:18). Uniquely in Luke, Jesus welcomes the crowds and preaches "about the kingdom of God" (9:11).

John's emplotment of this shared story is characteristically the most distinct. In the Synoptic versions, the disciples raise the issue of how the crowds are to be fed; in John's account, it is Jesus who highlights the problem, drawing it to Philip's attention (6:5). The precise derivation of the loaves and fishes is unclear in the Synoptics; in John, they come from a boy in the crowd. In John's version, Jesus takes the loaves (6:11) but does not break them as he does in Synoptists' renditions. Also, he gives thanks (*eucharistēsas*, 6:11) rather than blesses (*eulogēsen*, Mark 6:41 par.). Jesus gives an instruction for the leftovers to be gathered up "so that nothing may be lost," a concern explicitly expressed only in John (6:12). In the Synoptic accounts, there is no suggestion that the people have any sense of the miraculous nature of the deed, which remains known only to Jesus and the disciples. In the Fourth Gospel, the people see that a miracle has been accomplished, and this leads them to identify Jesus as "the prophet who is to come into the world" (6:14). When Jesus realizes that they want forcibly to make him king, he exits the scene.

STYLE

Mark's penchant for *kai* as a sentence connector is apparent in the Greek. The word *kai* appears at the beginning of ten verses (6:32, 33, 34, 35, 39, 40, 41, 42, 43, 44). The Greek text also displays Mark's liking for the historic present (6:31, 37–38; not evident in translation). The passage gives examples of Markan redundancy: "to a deserted place by themselves" (6:32) repeats "to a deserted place all by yourselves" in 6:31; the disciples' justification for dismissing the multitude, "the hour is now very late" (6:35), restates what the narrator has just said in the same verse. One of Mark's favorite words, "many," is found in 6:31 and 33, and the underlying Greek term *polys* additionally occurs in 6:34 and 35. Another of Mark's favorite words, "all," crops up in 6:33, 39, 41, and 42. In 6:43 (Gk.), Mark speaks of "fullness of baskets," which is a distinctively Markan expression (cf. 8:20 Gk.).

Matthew's tendency to connect sentences with *de* is apparent in the Greek text: the particle appears at the beginnings of six verses (14:13, 15, 16, 17, 18, 21). Recurring Matthean words, *anachoreō* ("withdraw," in 14:13; cf. 2:12, 13, 14) and *ekeithen* ("from there," in 14:13; cf. 4:21; 5:26) also crop up in the passage.

Luke's account is the shortest and neatest of the Synoptic renditions. His wording differs from that of the other two Synoptists at a number of points. Some of the differences reflect his lexical preferences and concern for good Greek. Luke's "drawing to a close" in 9:12 is, literally (in Gk.), "the day began to decline,"[6] a more elevated idiom that the equivalent expressions in Mark and Matthew. Luke uses the idiom again in 24:29. The verb underlying "lodge" (*katalyō*) in 9:12 (also in 19:7) is used exclusively by Luke with this sense in the New Testament.[7] The Greek verb for "sit down" in 9:14 and 15 is *kataklinō*, which is a more technical term for reclining at meals,[8] though it is not certain that Luke is using it with its technical meaning here. The word is distinctive to Luke within the New Testament (cf. 7:36; 14:8; 24:30). Luke's word for "groups" (*klisia*) in 9:14 also occurs only here in the New Testament; it denotes a group that meets for the purpose of a meal.[9] A typically Lukan stylistic feature is the use of "about" when giving numbers: "about five thousand" (9:14 par. Matt. 14:21); "about fifty" (e.g., 6:14; cf. 1:56; 3:23; 8:42). Luke's fondness for lexical variation is evident in his use of "the twelve" (9:12) and "his/the disciples" (9:14, 16) for Jesus' followers, after just previously calling them "the apostles" (9:10a).

John tells the story in his own idiolect, using his preferred word "signs" (*sēmeia*) for Jesus' miracles (6:2, 14), speaking of "the Jews" (6:4), and referring to a Jewish festal occasion as "near" (*engys*, 6:4; cf. 2:13; 7:2; 11:55). The passage exhibits other characteristically Johannine expressions: "looked up" (6:5), which is, literally (in Gk.), "lifted up his eyes" (cf. 4:35; 17:1); "coming toward him" (*erchomai pros auton*, 6:5; cf. 1:29, 47; 3:26); "indeed" (*alēthōs*, 6:14; cf., e.g., 1:47; 4:42); "coming into the world" (6:14, Gk.). The evangelist's fondness for the conjunctions *oun* and *hina* shows up in the Greek text: he uses *oun* six times in the passage (6:5, 10, 11, 13, 14, 15; not used

6. John Nolland, *Luke*, vol. 1, *Luke 1:1–9:20*, WBC 35A (Dallas: Word Books, 1989), 441.
7. Ibid. Elsewhere in the NT, the verb means "destroy."
8. Ibid., 442.
9. Ibid., 442–43.

in the Synoptic renditions) and *hina* four times (6:5, 7, 12, 15; Mark uses it twice in the pericope, Matthew once, and Luke once). The Greek also reveals instances of the historic present (6:5, 8, 12, 15), for which John, like Mark, has a special liking.

NARRATIVE TECHNIQUE

In the Synoptic versions, the actions of Jesus—taking, breaking, blessing, and giving—are reenacted at Jesus' final meal with the disciples, at which he institutes the Eucharist (Mark 14:22–25 par.). The feeding of the five thousand, within each Synoptic Gospel, thus foreshows the Last Supper. The Fourth Evangelist does not narrate the institution of the Lord's Supper. Yet his description of Jesus' taking the bread, giving thanks for it, and distributing it has eucharistic resonances.

Both Mark and Matthew go on to relate a second feeding miracle (Mark 8:1–10 par.), involving four thousand (who are fed with seven loaves and a few small fish). These two miracles are then linked by both evangelists in the story of Jesus' warning about the leaven of the Pharisees (Mark 8:14–21 par.).

The account of the feeding of the five thousand in Mark and Matthew strongly parallels Elisha's feeding miracle in 2 Kings 4:42–44. There are a number of connections: the taking of bread; the command that it be given to the people; the raising of the question as to how so many can be fed by so little; the distribution of the bread; the fact that some food is left over.[10]

Mark's comment, exclusive to him in this passage, that the people are like "sheep without a shepherd," recalls Moses' concern in Numbers 27:17 that the congregation of Israel "may not be like sheep without a shepherd" (Matthew has this comment in an earlier passage: 9:36). Jesus' arrangement of the crowd into groups of hundreds and fifties in Mark's account (6:40) is reminiscent of Moses' arrangement of the congregation of Israel in the wilderness into such numbers in Exodus 18:21, 25. Mark's vivid style of storytelling can be seen in the Greek wording used to describe the seating order: the expression translated "in groups" in 6:39 is, literally (in Gk.), "drinking parties by drinking parties" (*symposia symposia*); the Greek phrase underlying "in groups" in 6:40 is, literally, "garden bed by garden bed" (*prasiai prasiai*). Another vivid detail is the reference to "green" grass in 6:39.

Luke's distinctive focus on preaching the kingdom and healing in 9:11 establishes narrative continuity between the ministry of Jesus and the mission

---

10. W. D. Davies and Dale C. Allison Jr., *The Gospel according to Saint Matthew*, vol. 2, ICC (Edinburgh: T&T Clark, 1991), 482; Marcus, *Mark*, 1:415–16.

of the disciples ("He sent them out to proclaim the kingdom of God and to heal"; 9:2). In Luke, the actions of Jesus in 9:16 anticipate not only his actions at the Lord's Supper but also the meal with the two disciples at Emmaus ("He took bread, blessed and broke it, and gave it to them"; 24:30).

The specification of the loaves as "barley" loaves (barley was customarily food for poor people) in John's version (vv. 9, 13) might be intended as a definite link to 2 Kings 4:42: the loaves multiplied by Elisha are specifically "barley" loaves.[11] The reference to "the prophet" in verse 14 alludes to Deuteronomy 18:15 and Moses' promise of a prophet like himself. The people's attempt to make Jesus a king is a typical Johannine misunderstanding. The people want Jesus to match a worldly, political model of king, but Jesus' kingship is "not from this world" (18:36). In John's narrative, the feeding miracle is connected to the discourse of 6:22–59, delivered in the synagogue at Capernaum. The sermon on the "bread of life," addressed to "you" who "ate your fill of the loaves" (v. 26), is intended as bringing out the significance of the miracle.

NARRATIVE TIME AND SPACE

All three Synoptic evangelists refer to the lateness of the day (Mark 6:35 par.). The late time is part of the rationale for the disciples' request that the crowds be dismissed. In Mark, the observation about the grass being green (6:39) functions as a broad time note: in Palestine, grass would be green in early spring. The story is thus given a setting around the time of Passover. This coheres nicely with John's account, in which the feeding is dated shortly before the Passover festival. The chronological reference in the Fourth Gospel is probably theologically significant, given that Passover is a festival with Mosaic associations.

Mark, Matthew, and John give the event a seaside setting. Mark and Matthew call the location a "deserted place" (Mark 6:31, 32, 35; Matt. 14:13, 15), which is, literally (in Gk.), a "wilderness place"; the expression evokes the wilderness experience of Israel. God provided manna in the wilderness. Luke initially (9:10b) locates the incident at Bethsaida (which in Mark [6:45] is the destination after the feeding miracle), but then (9:12), in line with Mark and Matthew, refers to the setting as a "deserted place." The conflict in locational information in Luke's account is not easy to explain. John locates the miracle "on the other side of the Sea of Galilee" (6:1). The wording indicates the east side (the point of reference being the west side, which was dominantly

11. Donald Arthur Carson, *The Gospel according to John* (Leicester: Inter-Varsity, 1991), 270.

Jewish). John (6:1) indicates that the body of water is also called the Sea of Tiberius, reflecting the nomenclature of the late first century, when that Gospel was written.

THE CHARACTERIZATION OF JESUS

The shared story casts Jesus in the role of a prophet like and yet greater than Elisha. The comparison with Elisha is particularly strong in Mark and Matthew (as a result of the links with 2 Kgs. 4:42–44). The story also shows Jesus acting as the host of a meal.

Mark seems to be drawing a comparison between Jesus and Moses (the allusion to Num. 27:17 in Mark 6:34; to Exod. 18:21, 25 in Mark 6:40). Such a comparison we might have expected in Matthew's version, but surprisingly Matthew shows little concern to depict Jesus in Mosaic terms in this pericope. Characteristically Markan is the mention in 6:34 of Jesus' emotions, here his compassion, and his teaching activity. The discrepancy between what Jesus intends (to escape the crowds, 6:31) and what actually happens (a Markan irony) is in keeping with Mark's rawer Christology.

Matthew, like Mark, mentions Jesus' compassion (14:14), but whereas in Mark, Jesus' compassion leads first to teaching, here it finds initial expression in healing. Elsewhere in Matthew, the compassion of Jesus is linked with his healing ministry (9:35–36; 20:34).

Like Matthew, Luke portrays Jesus as healing (9:11). Characteristically Luke lays emphasis on Jesus' work as a healer. Luke's image of Jesus as welcoming the people (9:11) accentuates his role as host, receiving and entertaining guests. In Luke, this story is followed by Peter's confession of Jesus as Messiah, suggesting that the feeding miracle is an event that brings into focus Jesus' messianic identity[12] (perhaps by anticipating the "messianic banquet"; cf. Isa. 25:6).

John's telling of the story is the most overtly "christological." That Jesus sits down with his disciples (6:3) probably indicates his status as authoritative teacher. Typically in the Fourth Gospel, Jesus exercises control over the situation. Thus it is Jesus who takes the initiative, raising the question as to how the multitude is to be fed. To ensure that the question is not interpreted as ignorance on Jesus' part, the evangelist clarifies that Jesus is testing Philip and that Jesus knows exactly what he intends to do (6:6). In contrast to the Synoptists, John gives the impression that Jesus himself distributes the food (6:11). Jesus orders the disciples to gather up the leftovers. The people think

12. Nolland, *Luke 1:1–9:20*, 434–35.

that Jesus is the expected prophet (of Deut. 18:15), whom they perceive as a royal or messianic figure.[13] Jesus escapes their attempt forcibly to make him king. He is indeed king but not in a this-worldly sense (18:36).

THE CHARACTERIZATION OF THE DISCIPLES

In Mark, the disciples' sarcastic reply to Jesus shows them in a less than favorable light. Nevertheless, they are presented positively as taking an active part in the miracle, distributing the food to the people. However, in the next episode we learn that the significance of the miracle escapes them ("They did not understand about the loaves, but their hearts were hardened"; 6:52; cf. 8:14–21).

In Matthew, the disciples are not mentioned in the passage until 14:15. Their accompaniment of Jesus to the scene, though, is presupposed. The disciples' limited horizons are exposed, but without the disrespectful remark of Mark 6:37, Matthew's portrayal of the disciples comes across as less harsh than Mark's.

In Luke, the disciples respond with bewilderment to Jesus' command to feed the people. To them, Jesus' challenge seems to be totally impractical. Yet as in the other Synoptic versions, they play a role in the miracle by delivering the food to the people.

In the Synoptic accounts, the disciples appear as a collective unit, with group character. John typically focuses on individual followers. In this incident he singles out two disciples: Philip and Andrew. Philip's response to Jesus' test shows that his thinking is limited by the constraints of the situation (6:7). Andrew's action is to introduce the boy (6:9); he continues his role of bringing others to Jesus (1:40–42).

THEMES

Mark's secrecy theme is evident in Jesus' desire to escape the crowds and be alone with his disciples, in the transitional verse (6:31), and in the subsequent movement of Jesus and his disciples to a secluded place, narrated in 6:32. Like other attempts by Jesus in this Gospel to keep something secret, this one "fails." Only Luke has Jesus speaking of the kingdom of God, the central theme of Jesus' proclamation. Luke's reference to Jesus as welcoming the

13. Elsewhere in John's Gospel, "the prophet" and the Messiah seem to be distinct categories (1:20–21; 7:40–42).

people fits with his interest in hospitality. In John, the story exhibits John's characteristic interest in the miracles as signs.

CONCLUSION

The feeding of the five thousand is the only miracle performed by Jesus that is recorded in all four Gospels. It is a clear instance of a single story multiply rendered. In the Synoptic Gospels, the great meal foreshadows the Last Supper. In John's Gospel, the feeding miracle is linked to the discourse of 6:22–59, in which Jesus speaks of his ability to give "food that endures for eternal life" (6:27) and of his role as "the bread of life" (6:35). The Synoptic renditions vary only slightly, but the differences reveal the particular tendencies or interests of the Synoptic evangelists: Mark's tendency to portray the disciples in an unflattering manner; Matthew's link between Jesus' compassion and healing; Luke's interest in hospitality. John's version brings out his emphasis on Jesus' mastery of circumstances and the evangelist's understanding of the miracles as signs.

FOR FURTHER READING

Cotter, Wendy. *Miracles in Greco-Roman Antiquity: A Sourcebook for the Study of New Testament Miracle Stories.* The Context of Early Christianity 1. London: Routledge, 1999.

Fowler, Robert M. *Loaves and Fishes: The Function of the Feeding Stories in the Gospel of Mark.* Chico, CA: Society of Biblical Literature, 1981.

Labahn, Michael, and Bert Jan Lietaert Peerbolte. *Wonders Never Cease: The Purpose of Narrating Miracle Stories in the New Testament and Its Religious Environment.* Library of New Testament Studies. London: T&T Clark, 2006.

Twelftree, Graham H. *Jesus the Miracle Worker: A Historical and Theological Study.* Downers Grove, IL: InterVarsity Press, 1999.

9

The Walking on the Water

The story of Jesus' walking on the water appears in three of the four Gospels: not, as one might expect, in the three Synoptic Gospels, but in Matthew, Mark, and John. Luke does not include this episode; he moves directly from the feeding miracle to the confession of Peter. Like the feeding of the five thousand, the miracle of Jesus' walk on water is a "nature miracle" in that it is a demonstration of Jesus' sovereignty over natural forces. However, it is perhaps more accurately described as an "epiphany," an event in which a heavenly being appears unexpectedly to certain persons, and brings a message or reveals a divine attribute.[1]

Matthew 14:22–34	Mark 6:45–53	John 6:16–21
Immediately <u>he made the disciples get into the boat and go on ahead to the other side,</u> while he dismissed the crowds. [23]And after he had dismissed the crowds, he went up the mountain by himself to pray.	Immediately <u>he made his disciples get into the boat and go on ahead to the other side,</u> to Bethsaida, while he dismissed the crowd. [46]After saying farewell to them, he went up on the mountain to pray.	

(continued)

1. John Paul Heil, *Jesus Walking on the Sea: Meaning and Gospel Function of Matt 14:22–33, Mark 6:45–52 and John 6:15b–20*, AnBib 87 (Rome: Biblical Institute Press, 1981), 8.

Matthew 14:22–34	Mark 6:45–53	John 6:16–21
When evening came,	[47]When evening came,	When evening came, <u>his disciples went down to the sea,</u> [17]<u>got into a boat, and started across the sea to Capernaum.</u> It was now dark, and Jesus had not yet come to them.
	the boat was out on the sea,	
he was there alone,	and he was alone on the land.	
[24]but by this time the boat, battered by the waves, was far from the land,		[18]The sea became rough because
	[48]When he saw that they were straining at the oars against <u>an adverse wind,</u>	
for <u>the wind was against them.</u>		<u>a strong wind was blowing.</u> [19]When they had rowed about three or four miles,
[25]And early in the morning he came walking toward them on the sea.	he came towards them early in the morning, walking on the sea. He intended to pass them by.	
[26]But when <u>the disciples saw him walking on the sea, they were terrified,</u> saying, "It is a ghost!" And they cried out in fear.	[49]But when <u>they saw him walking on the sea,</u> they thought it was a ghost and cried out; [50]for they all saw him <u>and were terrified.</u>	<u>they saw Jesus walking on the sea</u> and coming near the boat, <u>and they were terrified.</u>
[27]But immediately Jesus spoke to them and said, "Take heart, <u>it is I; do not be afraid."</u> [28]Peter answered him, "Lord, if it is you, command me to come to you on the water." [29]He said,	But immediately he spoke to them and said, "Take heart, <u>it is I; do not be afraid."</u>	[20]But he said to them, <u>"It is I; do not be afraid."</u>

(continued)

Matthew 14:22–34	Mark 6:45–53	John 6:16–21
"Come." So Peter got out of the boat, started walking on the water, and came toward Jesus. [30]But when he noticed the strong wind, he became frightened, and beginning to sink, he cried out, "Lord, save me!" [31]Jesus immediately reached out his hand and caught him, saying to him, "You of little faith, why did you doubt?"		
[32]When <u>they got into the boat,</u>	[51]Then <u>he got into the boat with them</u>	[21]Then <u>they wanted to take him into the boat,</u>
the wind ceased.	and the wind ceased.	
[33]And those in the boat worshiped him, saying, "Truly you are the Son of God."	And they were utterly astounded, [52]for they did not understand about the loaves, but their hearts were hardened.	
[34]When they had crossed over, <u>they came to land</u> at Gennesaret.	[53]When they had crossed over, <u>they came to land</u> at Gennesaret and moored the boat.	and immediately <u>the boat reached the land</u> toward which they were going.

The Shared Story

A synoptic comparison of the three passages shows agreement on a basic set of *events*.

- Jesus' disciples get into a boat without Jesus and set off across the sea.
- A storm arises.
- They see Jesus walking on the water, and fear grips them.
- Jesus says, "It is I," and tells them not to be afraid.
- Jesus gets into the boat, or the disciples want Jesus to get into the boat.
- The danger passes and the boat lands.

There are common *characters*: Jesus and the disciples. There is a common spatial *setting*: the Sea of Galilee. And there is a common temporal *setting*: nighttime.

Matthew's version is an abbreviation of Mark's basic story, with the addition of the story of Peter's trying to walk on the water (14:28–32); verses 28–31 have no parallel in Mark. John's version is less elaborate than the Synoptic renditions. Many think that John's account is completely independent of the Synoptics; the similarities are put down to shared oral tradition or to John's use of a different oral version of the same story. But, as with the previous pericope, it is reasonable to assume that John knew Mark's version of the story yet was not literally dependent on it.

The act of walking on water recalls Job 9:8, which praises God "who alone stretched out the heavens, and trampled the waves of the Sea." The LXX translates the verse as: "who alone has stretched out the heavens, and *walks on the sea* as on firm ground." Jesus' self-identification, "It is I," is literally (in Gk.), "I am," *egō eimi*. As noted in chapter 6 (above) on John's Gospel, this is the expression by which God makes himself known in the Old Testament (Exod. 3:14; Isa. 43:10; 51:12 LXX).

CONTEXT

In all three Gospels, the story of Jesus' walking on the water comes directly after the feeding of the five thousand. In Mark and Matthew, it is followed by a summary of healings accomplished by Jesus (Mark 6:54–56; Matt. 14:35–36). Next in John comes the discourse on the "bread of life," in the synagogue at Capernaum (6:22–59). This discourse picks up on the preceding feeding miracle of 6:1–15; no further reference is made explicitly to Jesus' walking on the water, but the crowd's expression of surprise in 6:25 on finding Jesus in Capernaum (knowing that Jesus had not gone into the boat with the disciples, v. 22) indirectly confirms Jesus' miraculous crossing of the sea.[2]

PLOT

Only in Mark do we read that Jesus sees his disciples in trouble (6:48). Also, Mark alone has the curious plot feature that Jesus intends to pass them by (6:48; see below). The disciples are greatly amazed at Jesus' power, but, uniquely in Mark, their hearts are hardened (6:52). Mark's version of the story emphasizes the Markan theme of the disciples' failure to understand who Jesus is.

2. George R. Beasley-Murray, *Word Biblical Commentary*, vol. 36, *John* (Waco, TX: Thomas Nelson, 1987), 90.

The first half of Matthew's narrative rendition is similar to Mark's, but at 14:28 Matthew's narrative takes a distinctive turn. Peter asks Jesus, "Command me to come to you on the water." Jesus does so; Peter leaves the boat and walks toward Jesus. But the disciple wavers, begins to sink, and cries for help. Jesus reaches out, catches him, and rebukes him for his small faith. Peter and Jesus get into the boat, and the wind stops. The disciples worship him and declare him to be God's Son (14:33). The climax given to the story by Matthew, with the disciples uttering a high christological confession, contrasts sharply with the downbeat conclusion in Mark.

John's plot differs from the Synoptic versions in several respects. In Mark and Matthew, Jesus (lit.) "compels" the disciples to get into the boat and cross the lake. In John, the disciples go down to the sea and embark for Capernaum, apparently of their own accord. Probably, though, we are meant to assume that they are acting under Jesus' instruction. When the disciples realize that the figure walking on the water is Jesus, they want to take him into the boat (John 6:21), but we do not know if Jesus actually gets in. In Mark and Matthew, Jesus calms the storm; in John's version, the boat suddenly reaches the land (6:21).

STYLE

The Greek style in which the passage in Mark is written is typically Markan, with the use of *kai* to link sentences (6 of his 9 verses begin with *kai*), the fondness of the historical present, and the employment of explanatory *gar* ("for") clauses (6:48, 50, 52). We have favorite Markan words: "immediately" (vv. 45, 50), "all" (v. 50). And there are characteristic double expressions: "to the other side," "to Bethsaida" (v. 45); "he spoke to them and said" (v. 50); "Take heart; . . . do not be afraid" (v. 50).

Matthew's version in the Greek exhibits his characteristic use of *de* as a sentence connector (9 of his 13 verses have *de* at the beginning) and his partiality to the construction *krazō* + *legōn*, "cry out, saying" (14:30; cf. 8:29; 9:27). His favored vocabulary is evident especially in 14:28–31, the verses entirely distinctive to him: "sink/throw into the sea" (*katapontizomai*, only here and in 18:6 in the whole NT); "Lord, save me"; "reached out his hand" (*ekteinas tēn cheira*, 8:3; 12:13, 49; 26:51); "little faith"; "doubt" (*distazō*, only here and in 28:17 in the whole NT); "worship."

John's account, in the Greek, displays his liking for the conjunction *oun* (6:19, 21). The reference to the "dark" (v. 17; cf. 1:5; 8:12; 12:35, 46; 20:1) and the expression "come to" (*erchomai* + *pros*; v. 17; cf. 1:29, 47; 3:2) are typically Johannine. The divine self-revelation formulation, *egō eimi*, occurs in all three accounts, but it is especially characteristic of John's Gospel.

NARRATIVE TECHNIQUE

Within the Markan narrative, this episode recalls the stilling of the storm narrated in 4:35–41, which has similar features: the evening setting, the boat, the wind, the action of Jesus, the calming of the wind, the fear of the disciples.[3] Mark's comment that the disciples are "straining at the oars"—literally, "tortured in their rowing" (6:48)—is a vivid narrative touch. The expression also has connotations of eschatological suffering (cf. Rev. 9:5; 11:10), which Mark may be intending to evoke (cf. Mark 13).[4] Mark's strange remark that Jesus "intended to pass them by" (6:48) may be a further allusion to Job 9. Job 9:11 explicitly speaks of God's "passing by."[5] The comment may also allude to Exodus 33:22, where God "passes by" Moses, revealing his glory. Jesus' self-identification, "It is I" ("I am"), anticipates his confession before the high priest in 14:62.

Matthew's version likewise recalls the stilling of the storm narrated earlier in his Gospel (8:18–27). The formulation "Lord, save!" (14:30), which is distinctive to Matthew, recalls the disciples' cry for help in that earlier episode (8:25). The incident involving Peter constitutes a "story within a story." We can see in Peter's boldness, sinking, and needing to be rescued a pattern that foreshadows his later declaration of loyalty (26:30–36), denial (26:69–75), and restoration (28:16–17).[6] The disciples' christological affirmation, "Truly you are God's Son" (14:33, Gk.) anticipates the final confession of 27:54.

In John's account of the story, the sudden safe landing of the boat may be deliberately intended to allude to Psalm 107:30 ("He brought them to their desired haven").[7]

NARRATIVE TIME AND SPACE

Mark gives two time notes in the passage. The first, "when evening came" (6:47), is a little difficult since it was already late in the day when the disciples wanted to dismiss the multitude in the preceding episode, but presumably late evening is meant. The second, "early in the morning" (6:48), signaling the time

3. Compare Joel Marcus, *Mark: A New Translation with Introduction and Commentary*, vol. 1, *Mark 1–8*, AB 27 (New York: Doubleday, 2000), 428.

4. Ibid., 423.

5. Sean M. McDonough, *Christ as Creator: Origins of a New Testament Doctrine* (Oxford: Oxford University Press, 2009), 26. I first became aware of the reference to God's "passing by" in Job 9:11 when Richard Hays pointed this out in a lecture given at King's College London.

6. W. D. Davies and Dale C. Allison Jr., *The Gospel according to Saint Matthew*, vol. 2, ICC (Edinburgh: T&T Clark, 1991), 513–14.

7. C. K. Barrett, *The Gospel according to St. John*, 2nd ed. (London: SPCK, 1978), 281.

of Jesus' approach, is, literally (in Gk.), "around the fourth watch of the night." Mark here follows the Roman custom of dividing time from dusk till dawn into four watches (6–9 p.m., 9–12, 12–3 a.m., 3–6). The evangelist also uses this time scheme in 13:35. The period of time indicated here is thus the last one, which ends at dawn. The timing recalls God's rescue of Israel from the Sea of Reeds (which took place "at the morning watch" (Exod. 14:24).[8]

Matthew's time notes are the same as Mark's. As in Mark, the temporal phrase "when evening came" (14:23) causes difficulty because "it was evening" when the five thousand were fed (14:15). We must presume, therefore, that "evening" in 14:23 means late evening. In Matthew, more clearly than in Mark, the disciples struggle in the boat from nightfall till "early in the morning," because, as the Greek text indicates, when evening comes, the boat is already (*ēdē*) a long distance away, being buffeted by the waves (14:24).

The walking on the water takes up little narrative time in John's Gospel. It is the briefest miracle story in the Gospel, and it is not specifically designated a "sign." The time signal, "when evening came," in 6:16, is supported by the note that "it was now dark," in 6:17.

Turning to narrative space, the miracle takes place at sea. In the Old Testament, the raging sea can symbolize chaos (Pss. 65:7; 69:1–2; Dan. 7:2–3); the chaos associations are probably in play in all three narrative renditions.

In Matthew and Mark, the boat lands at Gennesaret, on the western shore of the Sea of Galilee. Mark had specified Bethsaida as the intended destination of the boat journey (6:45). However, Bethsaida is not actually reached till 8:22. Jesus ascends the mountain to pray (6:46), mountains being traditional sites of communion with God. Mark draws attention to the spatial separation of Jesus and the disciples: he is on the land, while they are "in the middle of the sea" (6:47, Gk.). This distance between Jesus and the disciples reinforces the predicament of the latter.

Matthew similarly refers to Jesus' retreat to the mountain (14:23). Matthew speaks of the boat's being (lit.) "many stadia" out at sea (in contrast to Mark's "in the middle of the sea"). In John's account, the boat lands at Capernaum (6:24, 59), which is the scene of the discourse on the "bread of life."

THE CHARACTERIZATION OF JESUS

The shared story shows Jesus as acting in a uniquely godlike way by walking on water. He reveals himself to the disciples by uttering the words of divine identity, "I am." The common story thus strongly conveys a sense of

8. Davies and Allison, *Matthew*, 2:504.

Jesus' "divinity." The impression is reinforced in the two Synoptic versions by Jesus' stilling of the storm: in the Old Testament, calming a storm is a power assigned to God alone (Job 26:11–12; Pss. 65:7; 89:9–10; 107:29).

In Mark and Matthew, Jesus ascends the mountain to pray. The ascent is reminiscent of Moses' going up the mountain (Exod. 24:15, 18).

In Mark's account, Jesus' ability to see the disciples struggling in the boat may be due to supernatural vision.[9] The statement that Jesus "intended to pass them by" is, on the one hand, christologically awkward, since his intent is seemingly thwarted (as happens elsewhere in Mark). On the other hand, the statement is christologically profound since it is suggestive of a theophany, or appearance of God (as in Exod. 33:22).

In Matthew, Jesus not only has the power to walk on the water "but also the ability to share his power and authority with others. . . ."[10] Jesus' divine identity is recognized by the disciples, who worship him and confess him as "Son of God." Here "Son of God" is an epithet indicating Jesus' transcendent status, not a messianic title.

The self-identification "I am" contributes to John's larger emphasis on Jesus as the "I am." John's linkage of the darkness and the absence of Jesus subtly points to the Johannine christological theme of Jesus as the light of the world (8:12), or the light that shines in the darkness (1:5).

THE CHARACTERIZATION OF THE DISCIPLES

In all three accounts, the disciples are terrified at the sight of the figure walking on the water. In Mark and Matthew, they mistakenly think they are seeing a ghost.

In Mark, their terror turns to astonishment (cf. 3:21; 5:42). Yet, they fail to understand because their "heart" (sing. in Gk.) has become hardened (6:52). Mark relates their incomprehension to the previous miracle ("the loaves"). Their inability to understand that miracle in some way affects their capacity to grasp this one. Hard-heartedness in the Bible is usually a characteristic of God's enemies (Exod. 7:3, 13) or unfaithful Israel (Ps. 95:8),[11] so this is an especially strong criticism of the disciples (cf. Mark 8:17).

In Matthew, the disciples are at first afraid, but their fear turns to homage, and they confess Jesus as God's Son. Matthew, as he does elsewhere (16:17–19; 17:24–27), accords Peter a prominent role in the story. Peter shows courage but also an insufficiency of faith, traits that reassert themselves later in the Gospel.

---

9. Marcus, *Mark*, 1:423.
10. Davies and Allison, *Matthew*, 2:507.
11. Marcus, *Mark*, 1:428.

In John's account, Jesus' words seem to calm the disciples' fears. They recognize his voice (cf. 10:4) and are willing to take him into the boat.

THEMES

The reference to Jesus' solitude in Mark 6:47 fits with Mark's secrecy theme. Jesus' criticism of Peter for his "little faith" reflects a minor theme in Matthew's Gospel (6:30; 8:26; 16:8; 17:20). The reference to the "dark" in John 6:17 is probably also symbolic, indicating the absence of Jesus and thus indicative of John's dualism of darkness and light.

CONCLUSION

The shared story is one in which Jesus' divinity shines through. Each evangelist, though, has made the story his own and brings out his own emphases. Mark's reference to Jesus' (seemingly) unsuccessful attempt to "pass by" the disciples fits with the rawness of his christological portrayal; it also reflects his characterizational emphasis on the godlikeness of Jesus since the motif of "passing by" has theophanic connotations. Matthew shows the significance of the event in terms of demonstrating Jesus' divine sonship and worthiness of worship. Matthew's version also illustrates his special interest in Peter. John's version betrays his darkness-light symbolism. The presence of darkness is implicitly linked with the absence of Jesus. The coming of Jesus to the disciples is thus implicitly the coming of light.

FOR FURTHER READING

Heil, John Paul. *Jesus Walking on the Sea: Meaning and Gospel Functions of Matt 14:22–33, Mark 6:45–52 and John 6.15b–21.* Analecta biblica 87. Rome: Biblical Institute Press, 1981.

Labahn, Michael, and Bert Jan Lietaert Peerbolte. *Wonders Never Cease: The Purpose of Narrating Miracle Stories in the New Testament and Its Religious Environment.* Library of New Testament Studies. London: T&T Clark, 2006.

Twelftree, Graham H. *Jesus the Miracle Worker: A Historical and Theological Study.* Downers Grove, IL: InterVarsity Press, 1999.

10

The Transfiguration

The transfiguration is one of the key episodes in the Synoptic Gospels, occurring in all three. Like the baptism with which it connects, the transfiguration is a onetime event in the prepassion ministry of Jesus. It is sometimes classed as an epiphany story, like the walking on the water,[1] but Jesus does not suddenly appear to the chosen disciples; rather he is transformed before them so as to reveal his transcendent glory.

Matthew 17:1–9	Mark 9:2–9	Luke 9:28–36
Six days later,	Six days later,	Now about eight days after these sayings
<u>Jesus took with him Peter and James and his brother John</u>	<u>Jesus took with him Peter and James and John,</u>	<u>Jesus took with him Peter and John and James,</u>
<u>and led them up a high mountain</u>, by themselves.	<u>and led them up a high mountain apart</u>, by themselves.	<u>and went up on the mountain</u> to pray.
		[29]And while he was praying,
[2]And <u>he was transfigured</u> before them, and his face shone like the sun,	And <u>he was transfigured</u> before them,	<u>the appearance of his face changed</u>,
<u>and his clothes became dazzling white.</u>	[3]<u>and his clothes became dazzling white</u>, such as	<u>and his clothes became dazzling white.</u>

(continued)

1. See, e.g., Donald A. Hagner, *Matthew 14–28*, WBC 33B (Dallas: Word Books, 1995), 490.

155

Matthew 17:1–9	Mark 9:2–9	Luke 9:28–36
	no one on earth could bleach them.	
[3]Suddenly there appeared to them Moses and Elijah, talking with him.	[4]And there appeared to them Elijah with Moses, who were talking with Jesus.	[30]Suddenly they saw two men, Moses and Elijah, talking to him. [31]They appeared in glory and were speaking of his departure, which he was about to accomplish at Jerusalem. [32]Now Peter and his companions were weighed down with sleep; but since they had stayed awake, they saw his glory and the two men who stood with him. [33]Just as they were leaving him, Peter said to
[4]Then Peter said to Jesus, "Lord, it is good for us to be here; if you wish, I will make three dwellings here, one for you, one for Moses, and one for Elijah."	[5]Then Peter said to Jesus, "Rabbi, it is good for us to be here; let us make three dwellings, one for you, one for Moses, and one for Elijah." [6]He did not know what to say, for they were terrified.	Jesus, "Master, it is good for us to be here; let us make three dwellings, one for you, one for Moses, and one for Elijah"—not knowing what he said.
[5]While he was still speaking, suddenly a bright cloud overshadowed them,	[7]Then a cloud overshadowed them,	[34]While he was saying this, a cloud came and overshadowed them; and they were terrified as they entered the cloud.
and from the cloud a voice said, "This is my beloved Son;[2] with him I am well pleased; listen to him!" [6]When the disciples heard this, they fell to the ground and were overcome by fear. [7]But Jesus came and touched them, saying, "Get up and do not be afraid."	and from the cloud there came a voice, "This is my beloved Son;[2] listen to him!"	[35]Then from the cloud came a voice that said, "This is my Son, my Chosen; listen to him!"

(continued)

2 . Here "my beloved Son" is from RSV, replacing NRSV's "my Son, the Beloved."

Matthew 17:1–9	Mark 9:2–9	Luke 9:28–36
⁸And when they looked up, <u>they saw no one except</u> <u>Jesus himself alone.</u> ⁹As they were coming down the mountain, <u>Jesus ordered them,</u> <u>"Tell no one</u> about the vision until after the Son of Man has been raised from the dead."	⁸Suddenly when they looked around, <u>they saw</u> <u>no one with them any</u> <u>more, but only Jesus</u>. ⁹As they were coming down the mountain, <u>he</u> <u>ordered them to tell no</u> <u>one</u> about what they had seen, until after the Son of Man had risen from the dead. ¹⁰So they kept the matter to themselves, questioning what this rising from the dead could mean.	³⁶When the voice had spoken, <u>Jesus was found alone.</u> And <u>they kept silent and</u> <u>in those days told no</u> <u>one</u> any of the things they had seen.

THE SHARED STORY

Across the Synoptics, the transfiguration story shows a common series of *events*. The sequence runs as follows:

- Jesus takes Peter, James, and John to a mountain.
- He is transfigured before their eyes.
- His garment becomes brilliantly white.
- Moses and Elijah appear and talk with him.
- Peter offers to make three booths, one for Jesus, one for Moses, and one for Elijah.
- A cloud overshadows them.
- A voice from the clouds identifies Jesus as God's Son and tells those present, "Listen to him."
- Jesus then appears alone.

There are common *characters*: Jesus, Peter, James, John, Moses, Elijah, and the divine voice. And there is a common *setting*: the mountain.

The similarities of the three passages are credited to Matthew's and Luke's dependence on Mark. There are some minor agreements between Matthew and Luke against Mark, which most scholars explain in terms of coincidental editing of Mark, but some see as indicating Luke's use of Matthew as a source alongside Mark.

The shared story exhibits a number of parallels with the account of Moses' ascent to Mount Sinai to meet with God in Exodus 24:[3] the three companions (24:1), the mountain (24:12, 15–18), the cloud (24:15–18), the voice from the cloud (24:16). The overshadowing of the cloud recalls the settling of the cloud over the tabernacle, indicating that the glorious presence of God filled the place (Exod. 40:35).

Like the heavenly declaration at Jesus' baptism, the words uttered by the voice from the cloud allude to Psalm 2:7. The phrase "Listen to him" recalls Deuteronomy 18:15, referring to the "prophet like Moses."

John does not record the transfiguration, probably because for him Jesus' glory is evident throughout his earthly ministry (1:14) and revealed especially in his death (7:39; 12:16). Yet John has a partial parallel to the story in 12:27–33, where in response to Jesus' prayer, "Father, glorify your name," a voice calls out from heaven, "I have glorified it, and I will glorify it again."

CONTEXT

The transfiguration occurs at the same place in the larger narrative development in all three Synoptics. It comes directly after the sequence of Peter's confession, first passion prediction, teaching on the conditions of discipleship. In Mark and Matthew, the transfiguration is followed by discussion about the coming of Elijah.

In all three Gospels the transfiguration is preceded by an enigmatic statement by Jesus that some standing with him would see the kingdom of God (the wording differs across the Gospels) within their own lifetime (Matt. 16:28; Mark 9:1; Luke 9:27). The fact that the transfiguration immediately follows suggests that the event is a partial fulfillment of Jesus' promise. Matthew's version of that saying makes Jesus speak more clearly of his *parousia* (a theme in which Matthew is particularly interested): "There are some standing here who will not taste death before they see *the Son of Man coming in his kingdom*" (16:28). Matthew's addition of the coming "Son of Man" seems to make the transfiguration more precisely an anticipation of Jesus' future *parousia*.[4]

---

3. Compare Joel Marcus, *Mark: A New Translation with Introduction and Commentary*, vol. 2, *Mark 8–16*, AB 27A (New York: Doubleday, 2009), 1114.

4. In 2 Pet. 1:16–18 the transfiguration is interpreted as a dramatic foreshadowing of Jesus' eschatological advent.

PLOT

The story is told in all three accounts with relatively little variation. Mark and Matthew are particularly close in their narrative renditions. When narrating the appearance of the two heavenly visitors, Moses and Elijah, Mark mentions Elijah first (9:4);[5] both Matthew and Luke refer to Moses first, in the chronological order in which they appear in the Old Testament,[6] though their placement of Moses first probably has as much to do with their theological interests (both, as we will see, accentuate the Jesus-Moses parallel in this pericope) as a concern for correct historical order.

Mark alone recounts the disciples' confusion as to what Jesus means by talk of rising from the dead at the end of the pericope (9:10). Distinctive to Matthew is the prostration of the disciples before Jesus, and Jesus' comforting of them (17:6–7). Luke has the highest number of distinctive plot elements. Only Luke indicates that Jesus and the three go to the mountain specifically to pray (9:28). Luke alone mentions the subject of the conversation between Jesus and the patriarchs: the "departure," which Jesus is soon to accomplish at Jerusalem (9:31). Luke alone tells of the sleepiness of the disciples (9:32). Only Luke indicates that it is just as Moses and Elijah are leaving that Peter makes his proposal about the three dwellings (9:33). And only Luke states that the disciples enter into the cloud (9:34).

STYLE

The trademark features of Mark's style can be discerned in the Greek: the use of *kai* to link sentences, his preference for the historic present, and the explanatory *gar* ("for," 9:6). Mark 9:2 betrays Mark's fondness of dual expressions ("apart, by themselves").

One of Matthew's favorite expressions, *kai idou*, occurs in 17:3, 5 (and *idou* on its own also occurs in 17:5). Luke's ability to utilize a rich Greek vocabulary is evident in his rendition. When referring to the whiteness of Jesus' clothes in 9:27, he uses a rare Greek word, *exastraptō*, meaning white "as a flash of lightning."[7] Another very rare Greek word occurs in Luke 9:32: the verb *diagrēgoreō*, underlying "stayed awake," is found here for the very first

---

5. Peter's suggestion, as recorded by all three evangelists, places Moses first.

6. According to Marcus (*Mark*, 2:637), the precedence of Elijah in Mark's narrative probably has to do with the greater prominence of Elijah in Jewish eschatological expectation (cf. Mal. 4:5–6).

7. Christopher Francis Evans, *Saint Luke*, TPINTC (Philadelphia: Trinity Press International, 1990), 416.

time in extant Greek literature.[8] Favorite Lukan words occur, such as "glory" (9:31, 32) and *epistatēs*, "Master" (9:33). The typically Lukan use of "about" with numbers appears in 9:28.

NARRATIVE TECHNIQUE

In all three versions, the voice announcing that Jesus is God's Son recalls the voice at Jesus' baptism. The back reference to the baptism is especially pronounced in Matthew's rendition. In (the Gk. of) Matthew, the statement of the voice from the cloud ("This is my Son, the Beloved; with him I am well pleased") agrees precisely with the words of the heavenly voice at the baptism (Matt. 3:17), with the exception of the final "Listen to him!"

In Mark and Matthew, the temporal reference, "six days later," is another echo of Exodus 24. According to 24:16, six days passed before God called to Moses out of the cloud.

Mark's comment that Jesus' clothes became "dazzling white, such as no one on earth could bleach them" (9:3) is a vivid detail typical of this Gospel writer.

Matthew's remark that Jesus' face "shone like the sun" (17:2) recalls Exodus 34:29, which says that Moses' "face shone because he had been talking with God." A Jewish tradition, already evident in the first century, compares Moses' glowing face to the sun.[9] Matthew's reference to the shining face of Jesus also recalls the statement earlier in the narrative that "the righteous will shine like the sun in the kingdom of their Father," an eschatological saying found only in Matthew (13:43).[10] "Jesus came" in Matthew 17:7 is, literally, "Jesus approached." Matthew uses this Greek verb *proserchomai* with Jesus as its subject here and in 28:18, in the resurrection narrative.[11] Jesus' coming to his disciples on the mount of transfiguration thus foreshadows his coming to them at the resurrection.

Whereas the other evangelists speak of Jesus' being transfigured, Luke says that "the appearance of his face changed" (9:29). The formulation fits with Luke's pattern of objectifying the supernatural. Luke's word for "departure" in 9:31 is *exodos*, which plainly calls to mind the exodus from Egypt yet was also a euphemism for death (cf. Wis. 3:2).[12] Luke thus seems to draw a parallel between the key redemptive event in Israel's history and Jesus' death,

    8. Ibid., 418.
    9. W. D. Davies and Dale C. Allison Jr., *The Gospel according to Saint Matthew*, vol. 2, ICC (Edinburgh: T&T Clark, 1991), 696.
    10. Ibid.
    11. Ibid., 703.
    12. Evans, *Saint Luke*, 418.

resurrection, and ascension (all three are probably in view). Luke's reference to the sleepiness of the disciples (9:32) is a possible foreshadowing of their falling asleep at Gethsemane just before Jesus' arrest (22:45). In his version of the statement of the voice from the cloud, instead of using the term "beloved," as do Mark and Matthew, Luke has "Chosen" (9:35), which alludes to Isaiah 42:1 ("Here is my servant, . . . my chosen").

NARRATIVE TIME AND SPACE

Mark and Matthew give a precise temporal reference, "six days later" (Mark 9:2; Matt. 17:1), which is unique in both Gospels outside of the passion and resurrection narrative. The point from which time is being reckoned is not clear; presumably in both cases it is the confession of Peter. As noted above, the temporal reference may be partly intended to bring to mind Exodus 24:16. Luke has "about eight days after" (9:28). Luke's time reference could perhaps be a gesture toward the Roman nundinal cycle of eight-day weeks.[13]

The mountain setting, as indicated above, is one of several links with Exodus 24. In Mark and Matthew, the mountain is said to be "a high mountain," which may be an allusion to Isaiah 40:9 LXX ("You who brings good tidings to Zion, go up on a high mountain"). In Matthew, the mention of a high mountain echoes the "high mountain" to which Jesus was brought during his temptation (4:8).

THE CHARACTERIZATION OF JESUS

The echoes of Exodus 24 at the level of the shared story show that Jesus is being paralleled with Moses. The transformed appearance of Jesus alludes to Moses, whose face radiated because he had been in the presence of God. Both Matthew and Luke speak of the change of Jesus' face, clearly recalling Moses' experience. The Jesus-Moses parallel is further enhanced in Luke's account by the reference to Jesus' *exodos*, his "departure." The allusion to Deuteronomy 18:15 in all three accounts identifies Jesus as the "prophet like [Moses]," whom "you shall heed."

The reference to the bright whiteness of Jesus' garments in all three versions gives him a transcendent quality. Angels and other heavenly figures are often described as being clothed in white (cf. 2 Macc. 11:8; *1 Enoch* 71:1; Matt. 28:3; Mark 16:5; Luke 24:4; Acts 1:10; Rev. 1:14). The heavenly significance

---

13. Ibid., 415. Though Luke otherwise reflects the Jewish seven-day week (cf. 24.1).

of Jesus' bright white clothing is brought out by Mark: "such as no one *on earth* could bleach them" (Mark 9:3, emphasis added).

The divine voice singles out Jesus as God's Son, a designation that supersedes Peter's calling Jesus "Master" (conveyed by Mark's use of "Rabbi," Matthew's "Lord," and Luke's *epistatēs*, which all have this meaning). As in the divine announcement of Jesus' filial status at the baptism, the primary thought is of his messianic role, but the reference probably goes further and points to Jesus' intrinsic divine sonship, especially in Mark and Matthew. Both these evangelists use the qualifier "beloved," which carries the nuance of "only."

Matthew's fuller version of the heavenly declaration, with the words, "with him I am well pleased" (alluding to Isa. 42:1), identifies Jesus as the Lord's Servant, perhaps reflecting his special interest in this christological theme. The eschatological resonances of the motif of Jesus' face shining like the sun add to the sense of this event as a foretaste of Jesus' revelation as the coming Son of Man (16:27–28).

Characteristically in Luke, a major christological event happens as Jesus prays (9:28). Luke states that the disciples behold Jesus' "glory." The transfiguration is essentially a demonstration of Jesus' glory, but only Luke makes this explicit. In Luke's Gospel, as in the other Synoptic Gospels, glory is primarily associated with Jesus in his role as coming Son of Man (9:26), yet Luke makes Jesus' ascension his entry "into his glory" (24:26). For Luke, the transfiguration thus gives a brief glimpse into Jesus' eschatological and exaltation glory. The word "Chosen" in 9:35, alluding (as noted above) to Isaiah 42:1, serves to identify Jesus as the Lord's Servant.

In Mark and Matthew, after the transfiguration, as they descend the mountain, Jesus warns the disciples against telling anyone about what they have seen until after he has been raised (Mark 9:9; Matt. 17:9), referring to himself as "Son of Man," his characteristic self-designation in the Synoptic Gospels.

THE CHARACTERIZATION OF THE DISCIPLES

In all three accounts, the three disciples who are chosen to witness the transfiguration are plainly viewed as privileged. In all three, the disciples are characterized as fearful, though the evangelists differ on the point at which their fear emerges (in Mark, they become afraid when they see Jesus transfigured and Moses and Elijah appear; in Matthew, when they hear from the voice from the cloud; in Luke, when they enter the cloud).[14]

14. Walter L. Liefeld, "Transfiguration," in *Dictionary of Jesus and the Gospels*, ed. Joel B. Green, Scot McKnight, and I. Howard Marshall (Leicester: InterVarsity Press, 1992), 834–41, here 838.

In all three versions, Peter's proposal to build three dwellings is regarded as foolish. Indeed, the statement of the voice from the cloud is partly a censure of Peter's suggestion. Mark attributes Peter's foolish proposal to the collective fear of the disciple; as typical in Mark, the disciples are uncomprehending when Jesus speaks about rising from the dead (9:10).

In Matthew, Peter prefaces his suggestion with the deferential "if you wish," which somewhat offsets the folly of his proposition.[15] Also, Peter speaks for himself—"I will make"; he does not presume to speak for the others. This fits with Matthew's heightening of Peter's prominence. The disciples fall on their faces, which in Matthew is an act of worship (cf. 2:11; 4:9; 18:26) as well as fear.[16]

Luke suggests that Peter's reckless proposal is partly due to his sleepiness. Peter makes his proposal just as the heavenly visitors "were leaving," which suggests that his motive is to prolong the event.[17]

THEMES

Mark's interest in secrecy is evident in his version of the story. The story itself is one in which Jesus withdraws with an inner group of disciples. Mark's double expression "apart, by themselves" emphasizes the seclusion. On coming down from the mountain, Jesus issues a command to silence. In Mark, the silence injunction is followed by a reference to the disciples' lack of understanding. Luke's telling of the story brings out his characteristic focus on prayer.

CONCLUSION

In the Synoptic accounts of Jesus' transfiguration, commonality is evident not only in the shared story but also, to a significant extent, in the narrative renditions. Yet each evangelist makes a distinct christological contribution. Mark lays emphasis on the otherworldliness of Jesus at the moment of transfiguration. Matthew makes the transfiguration an anticipation of Jesus' *parousia*. Luke makes explicit that the transfiguration is a revelation of Jesus' glory. The passages also reveal characteristic tendencies and interests of the Synoptists: Mark's interest in secrecy and his tendency to cast the disciples in a more negative light; Matthew's special interest in Jesus as a new Moses; Luke's interest in prayer.

15. Davies and Allison, *Matthew*, 2:699.
16. Hagner, *Matthew 14–28*, 494.
17. Evans, *Saint Luke*, 418.

FOR FURTHER READING

Heil, John Paul. *The Transfiguration of Jesus: Narrative Meaning and Function of Mark 9:2–8, Matt 17:1–8 and Luke 9:28–36*. Analecta biblica 144. Rome: Biblical Institute Press, 2001.

Lee, Dorothy. *Transfiguration*. New Century Theology. London: Continuum, 2005.

McGuckin, John Anthony. *The Transfiguration of Christ in Scripture and Tradition*. Lewiston, NY: Edwin Mellen Press, 1986.

Perry, John Michael. *Exploring the Transfiguration Story*. Exploring Scriptures Series. Kansas City, MO: Sheed & Ward, 1993.

Wilson, Andrew P. *Transfigured: A Derridean Rereading of the Markan Transfiguration*. Library of New Testament Studies 319. London: T&T Clark, 2007.

11

The Death of Jesus

The crucifixion and death of Jesus is the "crucial" event of the shared gospel story, the climactic occurrence to which the whole course of events has been leading. Crucifixion was an excessively cruel and drawn-out mode of execution, designed to shock and intimidate those viewing it.[1] Descriptions of it are rare in ancient literature. Literary writers evidently found the practice too distasteful and shameful to record in detail. The Gospel writers themselves avoid graphic depiction. The act of crucifixion itself (the affixing of Jesus to the cross) is conveyed in a short statement, given in all four accounts: "they crucified him/Jesus" (Matt. 27:35; Mark 15:24; Luke 23:33; John 19:18).

THE SHARED STORY

There are common *events* in the four Gospel narratives of the crucifixion (Matt. 27:33–56; Mark 15:22–41; Luke 23:33–49; John 19:17–37), with some variation in the sequence in which these events are narrated.

- Jesus is crucified.
- Two others are crucified with him.
- His garments are divided.
- The titulus (inscription) reads: "King of the Jews."
- Jesus is offered sour wine to drink.
- He speaks his last words from the cross.
- Jesus dies.

---

1. See Martin Hengel, *Crucifixion in the Ancient World and the Folly of the Message of the Cross*, trans. John Bowden (London: SCM Press, 1977).

There is a common *setting*: "Golgotha," or "Skull place." There are common *characters*: Jesus, the two men crucified alongside him, the Roman execution squad, and a number of women. The Roman execution squad is the implicit subject of the third-person plural: "They crucified him." The presence of Roman soldiers, though, is more explicitly indicated in Matthew (27:54), Luke (23:36), and John (19:23). The attendance of women is signaled in all four Gospels (Matt. 27:55–56; Mark 15:40–41; Luke 23:49; John 19:25–27). In the Synoptic Gospels, they watch from a distance; in John, they stand near the cross (19:25). Mary Magdalene is explicitly named as one of the women witnesses by Matthew, Mark, and John. Luke all but names her by referring back to 8:1–3 (where she is mentioned). The Synoptic evangelists place the Jewish religious authorities at the execution scene; they mock Jesus as he hangs on the cross (Matt. 27:41–43; Mark 15:31–32; Luke 23:35). In John, the presence of the Jewish leaders seems to be suggested in 19:21, 31. The centurion, the Roman official in overall charge of the execution, is a character common to all three Synoptic accounts.

Here we focus on the death of Jesus, the climactic point of the crucifixion. Each of the four Gospel writers narrates Jesus' death in a distinctive way.

Matthew 27:45–54	Mark 15:33–39	Luke 23:44–48	John 19:28–30
From noon on, darkness came over the whole land until three in the afternoon.	When it was noon, darkness came over the whole land until three in the afternoon.	It was now about noon, and darkness came over the whole land until three in the afternoon, [45]while the sun's light failed; and the curtain of the temple was torn in two.	After this, when Jesus knew that all was now finished, he said (in order to fulfill the scripture), "I am thirsty."
[46]And about three o'clock Jesus cried with a loud voice, "Eli, Eli, lema sabachthani?" that is, <u>"My God, my God, why have you forsaken me?"</u>	[34]At three o'clock Jesus cried out with a loud voice, "Eloi, Eloi, lema sabachthani?" which means, <u>"My God, my God, why have you forsaken me?"</u>		
[47]When some of the bystanders	[35]When some of the bystanders		

(continued)

Matthew 27:45–54	Mark 15:33–39	Luke 23:44–48	John 19:28–30
heard it, they said, "This man is calling for Elijah."	heard it, they said, "Listen, he is calling for Elijah."		
			[29]A jar full of sour wine was standing there. So they put a sponge full of the wine on a branch of hyssop and held it to his mouth.
[48]At once one of them ran and got a sponge, filled it with sour wine, put it on a stick, and gave it to him to drink.	[36]And someone ran, filled a sponge with sour wine, put it on a stick, and gave it to him to drink, saying,		
[49]But the others said, "Wait, let us see whether Elijah will come to save him."	"Wait, let us see whether Elijah will come to take him down."		
[50]Then Jesus cried again with a loud voice	[37]Then Jesus gave a loud cry	[46]Then Jesus, crying with a loud voice, said, "Father, into your hands I commend my spirit." Having said this, he breathed his last.	[30]When Jesus had received the wine, he said, "It is finished." Then he bowed his head and gave up his spirit.
and breathed his last. [51]At that moment the curtain of the temple was torn in two, from top to bottom. The earth shook, and the rocks were split. [52]The tombs also were opened, and many bodies of the saints who had fallen asleep were raised. [53]After his resurrection they came out of the tombs	and breathed his last. [38]And the curtain of the temple was torn in two, from top to bottom.		

(continued)

Matthew 27:45–54	Mark 15:33–39	Luke 23:44–48	John 19:28–30
and entered the holy city and appeared to many. [54]Now when the centurion and those with him, who were keeping watch over Jesus, saw the earthquake and what took place, they were terrified and said, "Truly this man was God's Son!"	[39]Now when the centurion, who stood facing him, saw that in this way he breathed his last, he said, "Truly this man was God's Son!"	[47]When the centurion saw what had taken place, he praised God and said, "Certainly this man was innocent." [48]And when all the crowds who had gathered there for this spectacle saw what had taken place, they returned home, beating their breasts.	

CONTEXT

In Mark and Matthew, Jesus' death follows his derision by the religious leaders. In Luke, it comes after Jesus' dialogue with the penitent criminal (23:39–43), which is exclusive to this Gospel. In John, it follows Jesus' words to his mother and to the beloved disciple (19:26–27), which are particular to John's account. The Fourth Evangelist goes on to narrate the piercing of Jesus' side (19:31–37). In the Synoptic accounts, next comes the notice about the attendance of women (Matt. 27:55–56; Mark 15:40–41; Luke 23:49).

PLOT

Mark narrates a sequence of events as follows: Darkness descends at midday. Three hours later, Jesus utters a cry of desolation. Some of the bystanders misunderstand his words and think that he is calling for Elijah (there was a Jewish tradition that Elijah would come to the aid of the righteous in trouble[2]). One of them offers Jesus sour wine (a malicious act aimed at prolonging Jesus' suffering, not an act of compassion) and mocks Jesus: "Let us see whether Elijah will come." Jesus gives a loud cry and then dies, and at that very moment the temple curtain is torn in two. The Roman centurion, witnessing Jesus' death, confesses him as God's Son.

Matthew's plot more or less parallels Mark's (Matthew attributes the mockery not to the individual who gives Jesus the sour wine, as in Mark, but to "others") up until the mention of the tearing of the temple curtain. At this point, Matthew speaks of spectacular events: an earthquake, the splitting of rocks, the opening of tombs, the raising of saints, and their appearance to many (27:51b–53).[3] In describing these events, Matthew compresses an extended time sequence, which goes beyond the crucifixion. It is "after his [Jesus'] resurrection" that the raising and appearing of the saints take place. The confession that Jesus is "God's Son" is made by the centurion "and those with him" (27:54).

Luke moves straight from the persistence of darkness to the tearing of the temple curtain, which he places before the death of Jesus. He narrates Jesus' final words, which are either spoken in a loud voice or preceded by a loud cry (the Greek can mean both). Jesus' last words express trust in God, not a sense of abandonment, as in Mark and Matthew. In Luke's account, the centurion does not proclaim Jesus' divine sonship but praises God and declares Jesus "innocent" or "righteous" (see below).

John's version is the most distinct and also the most succinct of the four. Jesus states, "I am thirsty." A sponge soaked in "vinegar" (RSV) is put on a branch of hyssop and held up to him. When he receives the drink, he declares, "It is finished," and dies.

STYLE

Mark's love of *kai* as a sentence connector shows up in the Greek (four of seven verses begin with *kai*). The word that Mark uses for "centurion" in 15:39 is the loanword *kentyriōn* from Latin (rather than the more usual Gk. *hekatontarchos/ēs*, used by Matthew and Luke). His choice of this term shows his fondness for Latinisms. Matthew's preference for *de* as a sentence connector

---

2. See Marcus, *Mark 2*, 1064.

3. These verses, as N.T. Wright notes (*The Resurrection of the Son of God: Christian Origins and the Question of God*, vol. 3 [London: SPCK, 2003], 633) present "all kinds of puzzles." Wright thinks that they reflect a tradition about strange happenings at the time of the crucifixion, which Matthew retells in such a way as to bring out the eschatological significance of Jesus' death (635).

is evident in Greek (six of his ten verses begin with *de*). "At that moment" in Matthew 27:51 is *kai idou*, a favorite Matthean expression. In describing the failure of the sun in 23:45, Luke uses the Greek word *ekleipō*, the technical term for an eclipse and in line with his more elevated vocabulary.[4] Luke tells us that it is "about noon" ("the sixth hour," RSV) when the darkness falls and that it lasts till three o'clock (Luke's use of "about" with numbers is typical). John's favorite conjunctions *hina* and *oun* both occur (*hina* in 19:28; *oun* in 19:29, 30). His word for "fulfill" in 19:28 is *teleioō*, a term characteristically Johannine (cf. 4:34; 5:36; 17:4, 23).

LITERARY TECHNIQUE

The fall of the darkness at noon, common to all three Synoptic accounts, recalls Amos 8:9 ("On that day, says the Lord God, I will make the sun go down at noon, and darken the earth in broad daylight"). In Mark and Matthew the cry of dereliction echoes Psalm 22:1 ("My God, my God, why have you forsaken me?"). The sour wine offered to Jesus to drink (Matt. 27:48; Mark 15:36; John 19:29; cf. Luke 23:36) probably alludes to Psalm 69:21 ("For my thirst they gave me vinegar to drink"). The Greek word underlying "sour wine" in the Gospel account is *oxos*, "wine vinegar," the word used in the septuagintal version of Psalm 69:21.[5]

In chapter 7 (above) we noticed the *inclusio* in Mark's Gospel involving the verb "tear" (*schizō*). In Mark 1:10, the sky is "torn" open at Jesus' baptism. At 15:38, the curtain of the temple is "torn." The twin references to tearing, coupled with the two declarations of Jesus' divine sonship in 1:11 and 15:39, link the beginning and end of Mark's narrative. That it is a Gentile solider, rather than one of Jesus' close followers, who is the first human (other than Jesus himself) in Mark's Gospel to confess Jesus as God's Son may be one of the evangelist's ironies.

Matthew gives the opening words of Jesus' cry of dereliction as *ēli, ēli,* in contrast to *Elōi, Elōi* in Mark. Both mean "My God." But Matthew's more Hebraic-sounding "*eli, eli*" makes more appreciable the bystanders' confusion with the name "Elijah."[6] In Matthew the spectacular events following Jesus' death match those on Easter morning (28:2; see chap. 12 below). The

---

4. Christopher Francis Evans, *Saint Luke*, TPINTC (Philadelphia: Trinity Press International, 1990), 876.

5. W. D. Davies and Dale C. Allison Jr., *The Gospel according to Saint Matthew*, vol. 3, ICC (Edinburgh: T&T Clark, 1997), 626.

6. Ibid., 624.

acknowledgment of Jesus by Gentiles from the West (the centurion and those with him) at Jesus' death mirrors his acknowledgment by the Magi, Gentiles "from the East," shortly after his birth (2:1, 11), forming a subtle *inclusio*.

Luke's presentation of darkness falling at midday as an eclipse fits with his tendency to objectify the supernatural. The dying words of Jesus in 23:46 recall Psalm 31:5 ("Into your hand I commit my spirit"). Luke's reference to the crowds "beating their breasts" (a sign of mourning) in 23:48 after Jesus dies echoes the earlier mention of the people "beating their breasts" as Jesus is led to crucifixion in 23:27. The two references to breast-beating thus frame the crucifixion scene.

In the Greek, the Fourth Evangelist uses three *tel-* words in quick succession (repetition): the verb *teleioō* in 19:28 ("fulfill") and the cognate verb *teleō* ("finished") in 19:28 and 30. The "scripture" that is fulfilled in 19:28 when Jesus says, "I am thirsty," is probably Psalm 69:21, which is alluded to in John 19:29 (as noted above). John's reference to the branch of hyssop in 19:29 is probably an allusion to the Passover.[7] Exodus 12:22 stipulates the use of hyssop for daubing the blood of the lamb on the lintel and doorposts of a house on Passover night. To further enhance his allusion to the Passover lamb and Jesus' fulfillment of that role, John comments that Jesus' bones were not broken (19:36), because Exodus 12:46 specifies that no bone of the Passover lamb shall be broken.[8]

NARRATIVE TIME AND SPACE

All three Synoptists speak of darkness as descending at "noon" ("the sixth hour," RSV, Gk.) and lasting until "three in the afternoon" ("the ninth hour," RSV, Gk.). Mark and Matthew put Jesus' cry of despair, with his death following quickly afterward, at three o'clock. On the Synoptic timescale, Jesus hangs on the cross from morning (according to Mark 15:25, "It was nine o'clock in the morning when they crucified him") till midafternoon. John apparently projects an even shorter period of execution (19:14). Compared to most victims of crucifixion, Jesus dies relatively quickly. Those enduring the torturous execution could take up to several days to die. The unusually short length of time before Jesus' death surprises Pilate in Mark 15:44. A sense of surprise at the quickness of Jesus' death is also evident in John's narrative (19:33).

The Synoptic evangelists speak of "the whole land" being covered with darkness. The underlying Greek could mean "whole earth," but it seems

---

7. C. K. Barrett, *The Gospel according to St. John*, 2nd ed. (London: SPCK, 1978), 553.
8. Donald Arthur Carson, *The Gospel according to John* (Leicester: Inter-Varsity Press, 1991), 627.

more likely that the land of Palestine is in view. The reference to the tearing of the curtain in the temple clearly has symbolic significance. The curtain in view is most likely the veil separating the holy place from the most holy place, where traditionally the presence of God dwelled. Its rending probably symbolizes for the evangelists the opening of access into God's presence through Jesus' death (cf. Heb, 9:8; 10:19–20). Matthew refers to Jerusalem as the "holy city" (27:53; cf. 4:5), a designation that encodes a positive religious estimation of the city (cf. 5:35).

THE CHARACTERIZATION OF JESUS

Mark portrays Jesus as experiencing abandonment by God. This is the culmination of a progressive desertion of Jesus. He has been abandoned by his disciples, condemned by human authorities, and rejected by the people. Now he is forsaken even by God.[9] It is upon witnessing the manner of Jesus' death that the centurion confesses him as "God's Son" (whether or not with full christological understanding; 15:39). Mark thus makes a direct connection between Jesus' death and his divine sonship; it is in dying that the true nature of Jesus' sonship is revealed.

Matthew similarly presents Jesus as alone and forsaken by God. Matthew relates Jesus' death in a more dignified fashion than does Mark: Jesus "yields up his spirit" (cf. RSV; but NRSV does not catch the Gk. idiom). The formulation also suggests the voluntary nature of Jesus' death.[10] The disturbances following Jesus' death give it an "apocalyptic" character (cf. 24:29). It is in reaction to these events that Jesus is declared to be God's Son (27:54). The confession of Jesus' divine sonship is not the great moment of recognition that it is in Mark, but it is still a peak point in Matthew's unfolding Christology.

In Luke's account of the crucifixion, as in John's, Jesus speaks three times from the cross (23:34, though its saying is not textually certain; 23:43); in Mark and Matthew, he speaks only once (overlooking the "loud voice/cry" of Mark 15:37; Matt. 27:50). Jesus' final words in Luke 23:46 are drawn from the first line of Psalm 31:5, to which he prefaces the direct address "Father," as characteristic of his prayer language in Luke (e.g., 10:21; 11:2).[11] Given Luke's interest in Jesus at prayer, it is fitting that Jesus' last words on the cross should be an audible prayer. The short prayer expresses surrender to God, in the certainty of vindication. Like Matthew, Luke presents Jesus as deliberately

---

9. Morna D. Hooker, *The Gospel according to St. Mark*, BNTC (London: A&C Black, 1991), 375.

10. Davies and Allison, *Matthew*, 3:628.

11. Judith M. Lieu, *The Gospel of Luke* (Peterborough: Epworth Press, 1997), 196.

handing over his spirit (or perhaps his own "self") to God rather than simply expiring, though like Mark, Luke has Jesus "breathe his last." The watching centurion praises God and calls Jesus *dikaios*, which probably has a double significance for Luke. On one level, the centurion's statement witnesses to Jesus' judicial status: he is an innocent man. The political innocence of Jesus is an important Lukan theme in the passion narrative (e.g., 23:22). On a higher level, perhaps beyond the centurion's own understanding (dramatic irony), it witnesses to Jesus' status as a "righteous" man (cf. 1:6; 2:25; 14:14; 23:50), whom God will vindicate (14:14).[12]

In the Fourth Gospel the death scene shows Jesus in control. Jesus deliberately brings about the fulfillment of Scripture by asking for a drink (though the words "I am thirsty" are undoubtedly also meant to express real thirst, underlying the reality of Jesus' human experience, a characterizational emphasis in John). Jesus' last word, a single word in the Greek text, *tetelestai*, focuses on completion, i.e., the completion of the work that the Father gave him to do (19:30; cf. 17:4). In this Gospel his final word before death is thus a cry of triumph and accomplishment. Jesus deliberately "hands over" (a literal translation of *paredōken*) his spirit (19:30). He has already indicated that no one takes his life from him; he has authority to lay it down of his own volition (10:17–18).[13] As noted above, the reference to hyssop in 19:29 and the subsequent remark in 19:36 about Jesus' bones being unbroken probably allude to the Passover lamb and thus Jesus' role as "the Lamb of God" (1:29, 36).

THEMES

The witness of the Roman soldiers to Jesus' divine sonship accords with the Matthean theme of the inclusion of the Gentiles. The centurion's praise to God in Luke's account exhibits a characteristically Lukan motif. John's portrait of Jesus' death gives prominence to completion (e.g., 4:34; 5:36), a Johannine theme.

CONCLUSION

The four Gospel accounts of Jesus' death diverge significantly. The divergences have long proved to be troublesome. Early pagan critics seized upon them as an illustration of the contradictory nature of the Gospels. Apologetic

---

12. Ibid., 197.
13. Carson, *John*, 621.

attempts to reconcile the differences have their place, but it is important to take each narrative rendition on its own terms.

Each evangelist brings out a particular aspect of Jesus' death. Mark highlights the connection between Jesus' death and his divine sonship. Matthew portrays Jesus' death as an apocalyptic event, accompanied by signs and portents in the heavens and on earth. Luke shows Jesus dying as a righteous sufferer. John emphasizes Jesus' completion of the task that the Father sent him to do. Each rendition also reflects a wider narrative interest of the evangelist: to set in parallel Jesus' baptism and his death (Mark); to connect Jesus' death and his resurrection (Matthew); to show Jesus as the model of prayerful dependence on God (Luke); to show his sovereignty over events (John).

FOR FURTHER READING

Brown, Raymond E. *The Death of the Messiah: From Gethsemane to the Grave; A Commentary on the Passion Narratives in the Four Gospels.* 2 vols. New York: Doubleday, 1994.

Chapman, David W. *Ancient Jewish and Christian Perceptions of Crucifixion.* Grand Rapids: Baker Academic, 2010.

Evans, Craig A., and N. T. Wright. *Jesus, the Final Days.* Louisville, KY: Westminster John Knox Press, 2009.

Green, Joel B. *The Death of Jesus: Tradition and Interpretation in the Passion Narrative.* Tübingen: J. C. B. Mohr, 1988.

Hengel, Martin. *Crucifixion in the Ancient World and the Folly of the Message of the Cross.* London: SCM Press, 1977.

Senior, Donald. *The Passion of Jesus in the Gospel of John.* Collegeville, MN: Liturgical Press, 1991.

———. *The Passion of Jesus in the Gospel of Luke.* Wilmington, DE: Michael Glazier, 1989.

———. *The Passion of Jesus in the Gospel of Mark.* Wilmington, DE: Michael Glazier, 1984.

———. *The Passion of Jesus in the Gospel of Matthew.* Wilmington, DE: Michael Glazier, 1985.

12

The Empty Tomb

None of the four evangelists describes Jesus' actual resurrection, but they all report the discovery of the empty tomb, and all except Mark recount appearances of the risen Jesus to his followers. The resurrection accounts of the four Gospels are notoriously difficult to harmonize,[1] a fact that has often been cited as evidence of the basic historicity of the events underlying them.[2] The Synoptic accounts of the empty-tomb story converge sufficiently for parallel analysis. John's version differs considerably from the others and so will be treated separately.

Matthew 28:1–8	Mark 16:1–8	Luke 24:1–12
After the sabbath, as the first day of the week was dawning, Mary Magdalene and the other Mary	When the sabbath was over, Mary Magdalene, and Mary the mother of James, and Salome bought spices, so that they might go and anoint him. [2]And very early on the first day of	But on the first day of the week, at early dawn,

(continued)

1. For an attempt to reconcile the accounts and offer an integrated sequence of events, see Craig L. Blomberg, *Jesus and the Gospels: An Introduction and Survey* (Leicester: Apollos, 1997), 354–55. For a more detailed harmonization, see John Wenham, *The Easter Enigma* (Exeter: Paternoster Press, 1984).

2. If they were the fabrications of a group of Jesus' followers, so it is argued, one might expect the details of the story to be more consistent.

Matthew 28:1–8	Mark 16:1–8	Luke 24:1–12
went to see the tomb.	the week, when the sun had risen, they went to the tomb.	they came to the tomb, taking the spices that they had prepared.
	³They had been saying to one another, "Who will roll away the stone for us from the entrance to the tomb?" ⁴When they looked up, they saw that the stone, which was very large,	
²And suddenly there was a great earthquake; for an angel of the Lord, descending from heaven, came and rolled back the stone and sat on it.	had already been rolled back.	²They found the stone rolled away from the tomb,
	⁵As they entered the tomb,	³but when they went in, they did not find the body. ⁴While they were perplexed about this,
³His appearance was like lightning, and his clothing white as snow.	they saw a young man, dressed in a white robe, sitting on the right side; and they were alarmed.	suddenly two men in dazzling clothes stood beside them. ⁵The women were terrified and bowed their faces to the ground,
⁴For fear of him the guards shook and became like dead men. ⁵But the angel said to the women, "Do not be afraid; I know that you are looking for Jesus who was crucified. ⁶He is not here; for he has been raised, as he said.	⁶But he said to them, "Do not be alarmed; you are looking for Jesus of Nazareth, who was crucified. He has been raised; he is not here.	but the men said to them, "Why do you look for the living among the dead? He is not here, but has risen.

(continued)

Matthew 28:1–8	Mark 16:1–8	Luke 24:1–12
Come, see the place where he lay.	Look, there is the place they laid him.	
		[6]Remember how he told you, while he was still in Galilee, [7]that the Son of Man must be handed over to sinners, and be crucified, and on the third day rise again." [8]Then they remembered his words,
[7]Then go quickly and tell his disciples, 'He has been raised from the dead, and indeed he is going ahead of you to Galilee; there you will see him.' This is my message for you."	[7]But go, tell his disciples and Peter that he is going ahead of you to Galilee; there you will see him, just as he told you."	
[8]So they left the tomb quickly with fear and great joy, and ran to tell his disciples.	[8]So they went out and fled from the tomb, for terror and amazement had seized them; and they said nothing to anyone, for they were afraid.	[9]and returning from the tomb, they told all this to the eleven and to all the rest. [10]Now it was Mary Magdalene, Joanna, Mary the mother of James, and the other women with them who told this to the apostles. [11]But these words seemed to them an idle tale, and they did not believe them. [12]But Peter got up and ran to the tomb; stooping and looking in, he saw the linen cloths by themselves; then he went home, amazed at what had happened.

The Synoptic renditions evince a shared core story. Across the three narratives, there is a shared sequence of *events*:

- Early on the day after the Sabbath, women go to the tomb in which Jesus
  was buried.
- The stone is found rolled away.
- They meet (an) angelic personage(s).
- The women are told that Jesus "is not here" but has risen.
- The women leave the scene.

There are shared *characters*. Mary Magdalene and Mary the mother of
James are indicated in all three (the latter is "the other Mary" of Matthew's
account; cf. 27:56, and see below). In all three accounts, the women encounter
(an) angelic figure(s). Moreover, there is a common *setting*: the spatial setting
is the tomb of Jesus; the temporal setting is early morning on the first day of
the week.

Matthew 28:5–8 exhibits verbal agreements with Mark 16:6–8, but the first
half of Matthew's account shows little literary dependence on Mark. Luke
does not follow Mark very closely. The three evangelists were probably drawing on different circulating traditions reporting the discovery of the empty
tomb.[3] The common elements that constitute the shared story thus probably
represent commonalities across the varying underlying traditions.

CONTEXT

The empty-tomb episode follows the burial of Jesus in all three Synoptic
Gospels (Matt. 27:57–61; Mark 15:42–47; Luke 23:50–56), which takes place
on the Friday immediately after the crucifixion. In recounting Jesus' entomb-
ment, the three Synoptists tell how Joseph of Arimathea, after Jesus' death,
goes to Pilate to ask for Jesus' body, wraps it in a linen cloth, and lays it in a
(new) tomb hewn out of rock. Both Mark and Matthew narrate how a stone
is rolled against the entrance to the sepulchre, but Luke makes no mention of
this. His empty-tomb account, however, clearly presupposes the prior placement of a stone at the tomb's opening (24:2). In all three versions of Jesus'
burial, the women see where the body of Jesus is laid, which prepares for their
coming to the tomb on Sunday morning.

Matthew, in a unique passage, inserts between the burial and empty-tomb
stories the account of a guard being posted at the sepulchre (27:62–66). This

---

3. James D. G. Dunn, *Jesus Remembered*, vol. 1 of *Christianity in the Making* (Grand Rapids:
Wm. B. Eerdmans Publishing Co., 2003), 831.

episode in Matthew prepares for another pericope also found only in this Gospel, in which the Jewish leaders bribe the guards to tell people that the disciples stole the body of Jesus (28:11–15). Matthew's inclusion of both episodes is clearly apologetically motivated (which is not to deny that he may also be drawing on tradition[4]).

Mark's Gospel, in the best manuscripts, ends abruptly at 16:8, with the women fleeing from the empty tomb. In Matthew, the empty-tomb narrative is immediately followed by a brief account of an appearance by Jesus to the women en route to the disciples (28:9–10). Luke follows his empty-tomb account with the story of Jesus' appearance to the two disciples on the way to Emmaus (24:13–35).

PLOT

Although the three Synoptists convey the same basic story, their plots differ quite significantly. In Mark, the women buy spices to anoint Jesus' body and then come to the tomb. Approaching the tomb, they wonder how they will move the stone; then they look up and see that the stone has already been rolled back. Going inside, they see a young man, who tells him that Jesus has risen. He invites them to see the place where Jesus had lain and instructs them to tell the disciples to go to Galilee, where they will meet Jesus. The women exit the tomb and flee in terror, saying nothing to anyone. The episode thus concludes, somewhat typically for Mark, with the failure of Jesus' followers. Even so, we are surely meant to infer that their silence is temporary and that the promise of Jesus' reunion with his disciples in Galilee is eventually fulfilled. The promise reiterates a prediction made by Jesus earlier in Mark's narrative (14:28), and as readers, we know that Jesus' word is reliable (cf. 13:31).

In Matthew, the women go directly to the tomb. A violent earthquake accompanies the descent of an angel from heaven, who moves away the stone and sits on it. Matthew does not clearly indicate whether the women witness the quake and the rolling away of the stone or simply arrive at the scene after these dramatic events to find the angel sitting on the rolled-away stone. The guards certainly witness the whole process and tremble with fear. The angel speaks to the women, first calming their fears and then telling them that Jesus is no longer inside the tomb but has been raised. The angel bids them to come and see the spot where Jesus had lain. The women are commissioned to tell

---

4. See the discussion in N. T. Wright, *The Resurrection of the Son of God: Christian Origins and the Question of God*, vol. 3 (London: SPCK, 2003), 636–40.

the disciples about Jesus' resurrection and that he will see them in Galilee. They leave quickly and run to tell the disciples.

In Luke, the women arrive at the tomb, bringing the spices they have prepared in advance (cf. 23:56). They find the stone rolled away. Entering, they are mystified by the absence of Jesus' body. Two men appear and announce Jesus' resurrection. The women are reminded of Jesus' own predictions of his passion and resurrection. Unlike in Mark and Matthew, the women are not explicitly commissioned to "go and tell." They do, though, go and report everything to the eleven and to others. The disciples, however, are incredulous. In 24:12 we read that Peter, evidently stirred by the words of the women, runs to the tomb. Looking inside, he sees the linen cloths in which Jesus' body was wrapped. He goes home amazed. This verse, however, is omitted by some manuscripts and so may not be original.

STYLE

Regular features of Mark's style are evident: the use of *kai* to connect sentences, historic presents, double expressions ("very early on the first day of the week, when the sun had risen"), the explanatory *gar* (16:8).

Matthew's version contains some favorite Matthean words and expressions: *kai idou* (28:2); *idou* (28:7); "earthquake" (in 28:2 the full Gk. construction, "and behold there was a great earthquake," repeats the statement of 8:24 verbatim); the verb *seiō*, "shake" (28:4; among the four Gospels, this verb is found only in Matthew; cf. 21:10; 27:51).

Luke's refined writing style is evident in the Greek of 24:2–3. These verses form a single smooth Greek sentence, with balancing clauses: "They found the stone rolled away, . . . but . . . they did not find the body."[5] The Greek word underlying "dazzling" (*astraptō*) in 24:4 is found only in Luke in the New Testament (cf. 17:24). Similarly, the word underlying "stood beside" (*ephistēmi*) is used only by Luke among the evangelists (24:4).[6]

NARRATIVE TECHNIQUE

In all three versions, the description of the angelic figure(s) resonates with the earlier description of the transfigured Jesus: the white clothing in Mark

---

5. Christopher Francis Evans, *Saint Luke*, TPINTC (Philadelphia: Trinity Press International, 1990), 893.
6. Ibid., 894.

and Matthew (cf. Mark 9:3; Matt. 17:2), and the "dazzling" clothes in Luke (cf. 9:29, where Luke uses a cognate Greek word, *exastraptō*, for "dazzling").

In Mark the young man's message to the women—that Jesus is going before the disciples to Galilee, where they will see him—echoes the prediction of Jesus in 14:28 ("But after I am raised up, I will go before you to Galilee"). Matthew also records that prediction (26:32), but in Mark, Jesus' promise is explicitly recalled by the angelic messenger. The women's retreat into silence when commissioned to tell the disciples is a Markan irony, the last one of the Gospel.

In Matthew the earthquake links the empty tomb and the crucifixion (27:54). An "angel of the Lord" makes an appearance at the beginning and end of Matthew's Gospel. On both occasions, the angel says, "Do not be afraid" (cf. 1:20).[7] The repetition of "quickly" in 28:8 (from 28:7) makes the response of the women correspond to the command of the angel.[8]

Luke uses repetition to match the response of the women to the instruction of the angels: "'Remember how he told you.' . . . Then they remembered his words" (24:6–8). The angels' recapitulation of Jesus' prophetic words ("The Son of Man must be handed over to sinners, and be crucified, and on the third day rise again"; 24:7) neatly reuses elements of earlier passion predictions (9:22, 44; 18:32–33) in such a way as to recall them all.[9]

NARRATIVE TIME AND SPACE

Mark has three time notes. The first, "when the Sabbath was over" (16:1), signals when the spices are bought. The reference is to after sundown, when trade recommences after the Sabbath rest. The other two temporal markers, "very early on the first day of the week" and "when the sun had risen" (16:2), indicate the time of arrival at the tomb, the latter clarifying "very early." Early morning, in the Old Testament, is the time of divine deliverance (cf. Ps. 30:5; Isa. 37:36). It is possible that the rising of the sun is meant to offset the darkness at the crucifixion (15:33).[10] Matthew provides two time notes (28:1). The first, "after the sabbath," is a little difficult. The underlying Greek strictly means "late on the Sabbath."[11] This would put the events described on the

7. W. D. Davies and Dale C. Allison Jr., *The Gospel according to Saint Matthew*, vol. 3, ICC (Edinburgh: T&T Clark, 1997), 665.

8. Ibid., 668.

9. John Nolland, *Luke*, vol. 3, *Luke 18:35–24:53*, WBC 35C (Dallas: Word Books, 1993), 1190.

10. Joel Marcus, *Mark: A New Translation with Introduction and Commentary*, vol. 2, *Mark 8–16*, AB 27A (New York: Doubleday, 2009), 1083.

11. Davies and Allison, *Matthew*, 3:663.

Saturday evening. It does not seem plausible, however, that the women would go to "see the tomb" at nightfall. Also, the second time note, "as the first day of the week was dawning," clearly indicates first light. It thus seems proper to take the first time note in the sense of "after the Sabbath," as in the NRSV.[12] Luke's temporal reference, "on the first day of the week, at early dawn" (24:1), is unambiguous and succinct.

The main events take place at the tomb of Jesus, previously described in all three Gospels as hewn out of rock. Probably we are to imagine a cave-tomb, many ancient examples of which have been discovered in and around Jerusalem.[13] In Mark's and Luke's accounts, the women enter the tomb, but in Matthew, we are not explicitly told that they go in.

In Mark and Matthew, the angelic announcement contains the message that Jesus is going ahead of his disciples to Galilee, where he will meet them (repeated in Matt. 28:10 by the risen Jesus). Matthew goes on to narrate the Galilean rendezvous in 28:16–20. Luke's version also mentions Galilee, but as the place where Jesus prophesied his passion.

THE CHARACTERIZATION OF JESUS

Jesus does not directly figure in this story, but in all three accounts, he is the subject of the message of the angelic personage/s to the women. Jesus is proclaimed as "risen." Given the absence of Jesus' body at the tomb, it is clear that a bodily resurrection is in view.

In Mark (16:6) and Matthew (28:5), Jesus is described (lit. in Gk.) as "the crucified one." Luke also refers to Jesus' crucifixion (24:7). In Mark (16:6), Jesus is also called (lit.) "the Nazarene." This way of identifying Jesus underlines the continuity between the one who appears at the beginning of the narrative for baptism (1:9) and the one who is raised at the end. Many manuscripts have the words "of the Lord Jesus" after "the body" at the end of Luke 24:3.[14] Identifying Jesus as "the Lord" is typically Lukan (though the expression "the Lord Jesus" is not otherwise found in the Gospel; even so, it is quite common in Acts: e.g., 1:21; 4:33; 8:16). In Luke's account, the angels' rhetorical question identifies Jesus as "living" (in the sense of alive beyond death).[15] Elsewhere Luke emphasizes that the risen Jesus is "alive" (e.g., Luke 24:23; Acts 1:3; 3:15). The continuation of the angels' speech highlights Jesus' role as the suffering and indeed crucified yet vindicated Son of Man. The angels'

12. Ibid.
13. Marcus, *Mark*, 2:1072.
14. Evans, *Saint Luke*, 894.
15. Ibid., 895.

message that the Son of Man "must" (*dei*) suffer and be raised fits with Luke's stress on the sense of divine compulsion that dominates Jesus' life.

THE CHARACTERIZATION OF THE WOMEN

Women are the main characters in this story. Given the widespread tendency in antiquity to disregard the testimony of females, it is extraordinary that women should be presented as the first witnesses of the resurrection. The unexpected prominence of women in such a key episode, many would argue, supports the basic historicity of the story.

There is variation on the identity and number of women involved. Mark mentions three women: Mary Magdalene, Mary the mother of James, and Salome (16:1). Matthew refers to two women: Mary Magdalene and "the other Mary" (28:1). These two were present at Jesus' burial (Matt. 27:61). By "the other Mary," Matthew almost certainly means Mary the mother of James and Joseph, mentioned in 27:56 along with Mary Magdalene. Luke names the women as Mary Magdalene, Joanna, and Mary the mother of James (24:10). Mary Magdalene and Joanna are mentioned in Luke 8:2–3 as two of the women who accompanied Jesus in his mission. Luke also speaks in 24:10 of "the other women with them," implying the presence of at least two more women beyond the three named.

In all three accounts, the women are portrayed are devoted to Jesus. Their devotion is expressed in the very act of visiting his tomb. In all three accounts, the women exhibit fear.

Mark's portrayal of the women is the least flattering, in keeping with his more critical presentation of Jesus' followers generally. In Mark, the women appear somewhat foolish: they set off to anoint the body of Jesus but do not anticipate the problem of the stone until they approach the tomb.[16] The sight of the young man, evidently an angelic figure, makes them afraid. Their reaction to his words is to flee in terror and keep silent. We must assume that their silence is short-lived and they do eventually deliver the message so that Jesus' promise of a Galilean reunion gets fulfilled, but Mark chooses to end his story emphasizing their failure and fear, an implicit exhortation to the reader to avoid their example, to have faith, and to go and tell without delay.

In Matthew, the women only go to see the tomb, an achievable objective. They are not explicitly described as fearful at the sight of the angel; it is the guards who tremble with fear. The opening words of the angelic utterance,

---

16. However, Marcus (*Mark*, 2:1079–80) argues that the question, "Who will roll away the stone for us from the entrance to the tomb?" is a lament rather than a real question.

though, imply their fearful response. The women leave the scene with both fear "and great joy." In obedience they make their way to tell the disciples. As the narrative continues, they meet Jesus and respond in worship (28:9).

In Luke, as in Mark, the women go to the tomb to anoint Jesus' body. Since they have not seen the tomb sealed with a stone, they are ignorant of that problem. The women are perplexed when they do not find the body. They are terrified at the appearance of the two men, and uniquely in Luke bow their faces to the ground, a typical act of obeisance. The women remember Jesus' words, as they are called to do. They go and report their experience to the apostles. Their report, however, is discounted by the apostles. Here Luke reflects the ancient prejudice against women's testimony.[17] It should be clear, though, that Luke himself does not share this prejudice. The women are presented as faithful followers of Jesus, in contrast to the male disciples, reflecting a pattern found elsewhere in the Gospel (1:5–80; 7:36–50).

THE CHARACTERIZATION OF THE YOUNG MAN/ ANGEL/TWO MEN

Mark refers to a "young man" (*neaniskos*). Mark also mentions a "young man" at the scene of Jesus' arrest (14:51), and the two figures have sometimes been equated. However, the "young man" here is almost certainly an angel. In Jewish literature (Tob. 5:5, 7; 2 Macc. 3:26, 33; Josephus, *Antiquities*, 5.213, 277), the form of an angel is often described as that of a young man. His garb, "a white robe," is typical of an angel (cf. 2 Macc. 11:8; Acts 1:10). The women's fearful reaction and his reassurance fit the pattern of biblical angelophanies,[18] The young man/angel announces Jesus' resurrection and commissions the women to take the news to the disciples.

Matthew speaks explicitly of "an angel of the Lord" (cf. 1:20, 24; 2:13, 19). The being is portrayed in supernatural terms: descending from heaven; exercising extraordinary power in rolling away the stone. He causes the guards to tremble with fear and become "like dead men." The angel's words are more or less repeated by the risen Jesus when he appears to the women in 28:9–10.

Luke mentions "two men in dazzling clothes," but again there can be little doubt that the evangelist is referring to angels (cf. 24:22–23: "Some women of our group . . . came back and told us that they had indeed seen a vision of angels who said that he was alive"). In Acts 10:30, Luke uses the same language ("a man in dazzling clothes") with reference to a figure explicitly identified as an angel (Acts 10:3, 22; 11:13).

17. Nolland, *Luke*, 3:1191.
18. See Judg. 6:22–23; Dan. 8:17; Luke 2:9–10; cf. Marcus, *Mark*, 2:1085.

THEMES

The silence of the women at the end of the pericope (16:8) in Mark fits with that Gospel's secrecy theme, but in an ironic way. Matthew's mention of the earthquake is indicative of this evangelist's fondness of seismic occurrences (8:24; 24:7; 27:51, 54). The use of the verb "remember" in 24:6, 8 reflects a minor Lukan theme (1:54, 72; 16:25; 23:42; Acts 10:31; 11:16).

THE EMPTY-TOMB EPISODE IN JOHN'S GOSPEL (JOHN 20:1–10)

As in the Synoptics, the discovery of the empty tomb in the Fourth Gospel follows the burial of Jesus (19:38–42). In John's version, Nicodemus (introduced in John 3) joins Joseph of Arimathea in wrapping Jesus' body in linen cloths. Jesus is buried in a garden tomb located "in the place where he was crucified." The tomb is said to be a new one, in which no one had been laid. Unlike in the Synoptics, there is no explicit mention of the presence of women at the scene, though presumably Mary Magdalene witnesses the burial since she knows the whereabouts of Jesus' tomb).

While the Synoptists narrate a number of women visiting the tomb, the Fourth Evangelist mentions only Mary Magdalene (though the plural "*we* do not know" of 20:2 might suggest that others are with her). She discovers the stone (as in Luke, hitherto unmentioned) rolled away and runs to tell Peter and the beloved disciple that Jesus' body has been removed. The two men run to the tomb. The beloved disciple arrives first but delays entering; Peter goes in, and the beloved disciple follows. They see Jesus' grave clothes, and the beloved disciple believes. Both then return to their homes.

John goes on to narrate an appearance of the risen Jesus to Mary, who is at the tomb again (her return is not narrated, and it is not clear whether she comes back to the tomb with the two disciples at 20:3, or after their departure). Weeping, she looks inside the tomb and sees two angels and then, turning round, she sees Jesus, whom she takes to be the gardener. When Jesus speaks her name, she recognizes him (as expected in this Gospel, she recognizes the shepherd's voice calling her by name; 10:3). Jesus tells her not to hold on to him since he will shortly ascend to the Father. He commissions her to tell the disciples of his resurrection, and she carries out her task.

It is clear that John's account of the discovery of the empty tomb is not merely a different form of the shared story of the Synoptics: it is a different story. John's version may begin similarly, but at 20:2, a different sequence of events follows. The continuation in 20:3–10 has an affinity with Luke 24:12, but as noted above, this verse may have been added to Luke later (perhaps under the influence of John 20:3–10). The resurrection appearance to Mary in John 20:11–18 has certain points in common with the shared empty-tomb story of the Synoptics (the angelic personage/s, the reference to seeking), but again, the sequence of events is different. Whether or not John knew one or more of the Synoptic Gospels (and we think it likely that he did), his resurrection account is almost certainly independent of them.

John's narration of the empty-tomb episode (20:1–10) is, though, in keeping with his own wider narrative. The story is told in John's typical Greek style, with use of the historic present and instances of *oun*. The description of the grave clothes links back to the raising of Lazarus (11:44).[19] Lazarus came out from the tomb, at Jesus' command, with the wrappings still binding him, "and his face wrapped in a cloth." Jesus, by contrast, leaves the linen wrappings and head cloth behind. The parallel thus emphasizes the superiority of Jesus' state of having been raised, with the accompanying implication that Jesus will not die again, as Lazarus surely must. The temporal reference, "while it was still dark" (20:1), might reflect John's light-darkness dualism, with the darkness signifying misunderstanding (to be replaced by resurrection faith; 20:8).[20] The pairing of Peter and the beloved disciple reflects other Gospel scenes where the two appear together (13:23–25; 21:7–8, 20–23). The beloved disciple, who has been closer to Jesus, demonstrates greater spiritual insight. The passage brings out John's emphasis on believing (20:8) and makes the beloved disciple the exemplar of resurrection faith.

CONCLUSION

The Gospel accounts of the discovery of the empty tomb vary considerably, but the Synoptic renditions evince a basic core story. The Synoptists' different tellings of that story reflect wider individual interests and tendencies. Mark typically portrays Jesus' followers in an unflattering light. The ending he gives to the story combines his interest in secrecy and his sense of irony. Matthew's version reveals a concern to establish continuity between Jesus' death and his resurrection and to characterize both as apocalyptic occurrences. Matthew's references to the guard at the tomb manifest a distinctive apologetic concern evident in the burial and resurrection sections of his narrative. The mention of Galilee, while not distinctive to Matthew, reflects his geographical interest.

19. George R. Beasley-Murray, *John*, WBC 36 (Waco: Word Books, 1987), 372.
20. Grant R. Osborne, "Resurrection," in *Dictionary of Jesus and the Gospels*, ed. Joel B. Green, Scot McKnight, and I. Howard Marshall (Leicester: InterVarsity Press, 1992), 673–88, here 684.

In Luke's account, we find the theme of remembrance. As elsewhere in the Gospel, he highlights the responsiveness of women over against the failings of men. John's story of the empty tomb is different from that of the Synoptic Gospels, though it fulfills the same narrative function. John's story brings out his interest in the figure of the beloved disciple, his darkness-light symbolism, and his emphasis on believing.

FOR FURTHER READING

Jansen, John Frederick. *The Resurrection of Jesus Christ in New Testament Theology.* Louisville, KY: Westminster John Knox Press, 1990.

Osborne, Grant R. *The Resurrection Narratives: A Redactional Study.* Grand Rapids: Baker Academic, 1984.

Perkins, Pheme. *Resurrection: New Testament Witness and Contemporary Reflection.* Garden City, NY: Doubleday, 1984.

Wenham, John. *The Easter Enigma.* Exeter: Paternoster Press, 1984.

Wright, N. T. *The Resurrection of the Son of God.* London: SPCK, 2003.

Conclusion

This book set out to provide an introduction to the four Gospels that respects the unity and individuality claimed for them in the Christian canon. Appropriating a distinction made in narratology, and drawing a comparison with multiple-narrative films and novels, I showed that the four Gospels can be read as a single story in four distinct narrative forms. The core story, with events, characters, and setting, was identified and related to what was perhaps a well-used pattern of proclamation in the early church. The four narrative presentations were then discussed at length under the headings of structure, plot, style, narrative technique, and so forth. By treating each of the four Gospels in terms of its narrative components, the aim was both to give an overview of its contents and to highlight individualizing features. The story/narrative scheme of analysis was subsequently applied to particular Gospel episodes found in three or all four Gospels. In each case, we sought to uncover the elements of a unifying story across the parallels and to use our narrative classifications to bring out the more distinctive aspects of each account. We saw how differences between parallel passages often reflect and exemplify wider patterns of individuation evident in the four narratives at large.

Taking on board the new consensus that the Gospels belong to the ancient biographical genre, this book has suggested that the four Gospels can be viewed as "parallel lives" of Jesus, on account of their close correspondence to each other. However, the question remains: Do these "lives" bear witness to the same Jesus, or do they effectively narrate four different Jesuses?

The four Gospels deal with a common biographical subject: Jesus of Nazareth, a first-century Galilean Jew, with natural family ties. He is the hero (protagonist) of the shared story, a story that follows a unique trajectory (even though it conforms to a common story structure), beginning with the ministry of John the Baptist and the Spirit's descent on Jesus, and ending with his death and resurrection, with specific incidents in between. Not only do all four Gospels agree on the basic "character" of Jesus and the course of his mission; to a significant extent they also agree in their "characterizations" of Jesus, exhibiting a shared understanding of his identity. He is prophet, teacher, and doer of mighty deeds. More significantly, he is the Son of Man, Davidic Messiah, Lord, and Son of God. All four evangelists attribute "divine" qualities to Jesus, and all four testify to the uniqueness of his divine sonship (in all four, on at least one occasion, Jesus speaks of himself in exclusive and absolute terms as "the Son"). One can therefore speak of the *singular* Jesus of the Fourfold Gospel witness.

At the same time, as this book has shown, the four Gospels, or "parallel lives," display a rich diversity in characterization as they elaborate in different ways on the person and significance of Jesus. The four Gospels thus present us with a singular Jesus *multiply* rendered. The singularity of Jesus is not compromised by the multiple characterizations but is enhanced by them.

Bibliography

Alexander, Loveday. "What Is a Gospel?" In *The Cambridge Companion to the Gospels*, edited by Stephen C. Barton, 13–33. Cambridge: Cambridge University Press, 2006.

Allison, Dale C., Jr. *The New Moses: A Matthean Typology*. Minneapolis: Fortress, 1993.

Arterbury, Andrew E. *Entertaining Angels: Early Christian Hospitality in Its Mediterranean Setting*. New Testament Monographs 8. Sheffield: Sheffield Phoenix Press, 2005.

Ashton, John. *Understanding the Fourth Gospel*. Oxford: Clarendon Press, 1991.

Bacon, Benjamin W. *Studies in Matthew*. London: Constable, 1930.

Barrett, C. K. *The Gospel according to St. John*, 2nd ed. London: SPCK, 1978.

Bauckham, Richard. "For Whom Were Gospels Written?" In *The Gospels for All Christians: Rethinking the Gospel Audiences*, edited by Richard Bauckham, 9–48. Grand Rapids: Wm. B. Eerdmans Publishing Co., 1998.

———. *Jesus and the Eyewitnesses: The Gospels as Eyewitness Testimony*. Grand Rapids: Wm. B. Eerdmans Publishing Co., 2006.

———. "John for Readers of Mark." In *The Gospels for All Christians: Rethinking the Gospel Audiences*, edited by Richard Bauckham, 147–71. Grand Rapids: Wm. B. Eerdmans Publishing Co., 1998.

Bauer, David R. "Son of David." In *Dictionary of Jesus and the Gospels*, edited by Joel B. Green, Scot McKnight, and I. Howard Marshall, 776–69. Leicester: InterVarsity Press, 1992.

Beasley-Murray, George R. *John*. Word Biblical Commentary 36. Waco: TX, 1987.

Beaton, Richard. *Isaiah's Christ in Matthew's Gospel*. Cambridge: Cambridge University Press, 2002.

Best, Ernest. *Following Jesus: Discipleship in the Gospel of Mark*. JSNTSup 4. Sheffield: JSOT Press, 1988.

Bird, Michael. "Tearing the Heavens and Shaking the Heavenlies: Mark's Cosmology in Its Apocalyptic Context." In *Cosmology and New Testament Theology*, edited by Sean M. McDonough and Jonathan T. Pennington, 45–59. Library of New Testament Studies. London: T&T Clark International, 2008.

Blackburn, B. L. "Miracles and Miracle Stories." In *Dictionary of Jesus and the Gospels*, edit by Joel B. Green, Scot McKnight, and I. Howard Marshall, 549–60, Leicester: InterVarsity Press, 1992.

Blomberg, Craig L. *Jesus and the Gospels: An Introduction and Survey*. Leicester: Apollos, 1997.

Bockmuehl, Marcus, and Donald A. Hagner, eds. *The Written Gospel*. Cambridge: Cambridge University Press, 2005.

Boxall, Ian. *New Testament Interpretation*. Norwich: SCM Press, 2007.

Brown, Jeannine K. *The Disciples in Narrative Perspective: The Portrayal and Function of the Matthean Disciples*. Atlanta: Society of Biblical Literature, 2002.

Brown, Raymond E. *The Gospel According to John I–XII: Translated with an Introduction and Notes*. Garden City: Doubleday, 1966.

———. *The Community of the Beloved Disciple*. New York: Paulist Press, 1979.

Burge, Gary M. *The Anointed Community: The Holy Spirit in the Johannine Tradition*. Grand Rapids: Wm. B. Eerdmans Publishing Co., 1987.

Burkett, Delbert Royce. *Rethinking the Gospel Sources: From Proto-Mark to Mark*. New York & London: T&T Clark International, 2004.

Burnett, Fred W. *The Testament of Jesus-Sophia: A Redaction-Critical Study of the Eschatological Discourse in Matthew*. Washington, DC: University Press of America, 1981.

Burridge, Richard A. *Four Gospels, One Jesus?* London: SPCK, 1994.

———. *What Are the Gospels? A Comparison with Graeco-Roman Biography*. Cambridge: Cambridge University Press, 1992.

Cadbury, Henry J. "Four Features of Lucan Style." In *Studies in Luke–Acts: Essays Presented in Honor of Paul Schubert*, edited by Leander E. Keck and J. Louis Martyn, 87–102. London: SPCK, 1968.

———. *The Making of Luke–Acts*. London: MacMillan, 1927.

———. *The Style and Literary Method of Luke*. Part 1, *The Diction of Luke and Acts*. Part 2, *The Treatment of Sources in the Gospel*. Cambridge, MA: Harvard University Press, 1919–20.

Camery-Hoggatt, Jerry. *Irony in Mark's Gospel: Text and Subtext*. Society for New Testament Studies Monograph Series 72. Cambridge: Cambridge University Press, 1992.

Caragounis, Chrys C. "Kingdom of God/Kingdom of Heaven." In *Dictionary of Jesus and the Gospels*, edited by Joel B. Green, Scot McKnight, and I. Howard Marshall, 417–30. Leicester: InterVarsity Press, 1992.

Carson, Donald Arthur. *Divine Sovereignty and Human Responsibility*. London: Marshall, Morgan & Scott, 1980.

———. *The Gospel according to John*. Leicester: Inter-Varsity Press, 1991.

Carter, Warren. *John: Storyteller, Interpreter, Evangelist*. Peabody, MA: Hendrickson Publishers, 2006.

Chatman, Seymour B. *Story and Discourse: Narrative Structure in Fiction and Film*. Ithaca, NY, and London: Cornell University Press, 1978.

Conzelmann, Hans. *The Theology of Saint Luke*, trans. Geoffrey Buswell. London: Faber, 1960.

Crossley, James G. *The Date of Mark's Gospel: Insight from the Law in Earliest Christianity*. Journal for the Study of the New Testament: Supplement Series 266. London: T&T Clark International, 2005.

Crump, David Michael. *Jesus the Intercessor: Prayer and Christology in Luke–Acts*. WUNT 2/49. Tübingen: Mohr, 1992.

Davies, W. D., and Dale C. Allison Jr. *The Gospel according to Saint Matthew*. 3 vols. International Critical Commentary. Edinburgh: T&T Clark, 1988, 1991, 1997.

Deutsch, Celia M. *Lady Wisdom, Jesus, and the Sages: Metaphor and Social Context in Matthew's Gospel*. Valley Forge, PA: Trinity Press International, 1996.

Dodd, C. H. "The Framework of the Gospel Narrative." *Expository Times* 43 (1932): 396–400.

Dunn, James D. G. *Jesus Remembered*. Vol. 1 of *Christianity in the Making*. Grand Rapids: Wm. B. Eerdmans Publishing Co., 2003.

————, and John W. Rogerson, eds. *Eerdmans Commentary on the Bible*. Grand Rapids: Wm. B. Eerdmans Publishing Co., 2003.

Evans, Christopher Francis. *Saint Luke*. TPI New Testament Commentaries. Philadelphia: Trinity Press International, 1990.

Fitzmyer, Joseph A. *The Gospel according to Luke*. 2 vols. Anchor Bible 28–28A. Garden City, NY: Doubleday, 1981–85.

Fowler, Roger, ed. *A Dictionary of Modern Critical Terms*. Revised Edition. London: Routledge & Kegan Paul, 1987,

France, Richard Thomas. "Faith." In *Dictionary of Jesus and the Gospels*, edited by Joel B. Green, Scot McKnight, and I. Howard Marshall, 223–26. Leicester: InterVarsity Press, 1992.

Gardner-Smith, Percival. *Saint John and the Synoptic Gospels*. Cambridge: Cambridge University Press, 1938.

Gathercole, Simon J. *The Pre-Existent Son: Recovering the Christologies of Matthew, Mark, and Luke*. Grand Rapids: Wm. B. Eerdmans Publishing Co., 2006.

Geddert, Timothy J. *Watchwords: Mark 13 in Markan Eschatology*. JSNTSup 26. Sheffield: JSOT Press, 1989.

Goodacre, Mark. *The Synoptic Problem: A Way through the Maze*. London: T&T Clark International, 2001.

Goodspeed, Edgar J. "The Vocabulary of Luke and Acts." *Journal of Biblical Literature* 31 (1912): 92–94.

Green, Joel B. "Hermeneutical Approaches to the New Testament Tradition." In *Eerdmans Commentary on the Bible*, edited by James D. G. Dunn and John W. Rogerson, 972–88. Grand Rapids & Cambridge: Wm. B. Eerdmans Publishing Co., 2003.

Green, Joel B., Scot McKnight, and I. Howard Marshall, eds. *Dictionary of Jesus and the Gospels*. Leicester: InterVarsity Press, 1992.

Hagner, Donald A. *Matthew 14–28*. Word Biblical Commentary 33B. Dallas: Word Books, 1995.

Heil, John Paul. *Jesus Walking on the Sea: Meaning and Gospel Functions of Matt 14:22–33, Mark 6:45–52 and John 6:15b–21*. Analecta biblica 87. Rome: Biblical Institute Press, 1981.

Hengel, Martin. *Crucifixion in the Ancient World and the Folly of the Message of the Cross*. Trans. John Bowden. London: SCM Press, 1977.

————. *The Four Gospels and the One Gospel of Jesus Christ*. Harrisburg, PA: Trinity Press International, 2000.

Hoehner, Harold W. "Herodian Dynasty." In *Dictionary of Jesus and the Gospels*, edited by Joel B. Green, Scot McKnight, and I. Howard Marshall, 317–26. Leicester: InterVarsity Press, 1992.

Hooker, Morna D. *The Gospel according to St. Mark*. Black's New Testament Commentaries. London: A&C Black, 1991.

Hurtado, Larry W. "God." In *Dictionary of Jesus and the Gospels*, edited by Joel B. Green, Scot McKnight, and I. Howard Marshall, 270–76. Leicester: InterVarsity Press, 1992.

————. *Lord Jesus Christ: Devotion to Jesus in Earliest Christianity*. Grand Rapids: Wm. B. Eerdmans Publishing Co., 2003.

Käsemann, Ernst. *The Testament of Jesus*. London: SCM, 1968.

Kernen, Robert. *Building Better Plots*. Cincinnati: Writers Digest Books, 1999.

Kim, Kyoung-Jin. *Stewardship and Almsgiving in Luke's Theology*. JSNTSup 155. Sheffield: Sheffield Academic Press, 1998.

Kingsbury, Jack Dean. *Matthew: Structure, Christology, Kingdom.* Philadelphia: Fortress Press, 1975.

Köstenberger, Andreas J. *A Theology of John's Gospel and Letters.* Biblical Theology of the New Testament. Grand Rapids: Zondervan, 2009.

Liefeld, Walter L. "Transfiguration." In *Dictionary of Jesus and the Gospels,* edited by Joel B. Green, Scot McKnight, and I. Howard Marshall, 834–41. Leicester: InterVarsity Press, 1992.

Lieu, Judith M. *The Gospel of Luke.* Peterborough: Epworth Press, 1997.

———. "How John Writes." In *The Written Gospel,* edited by Marcus Bockmuehl and Donald A. Hagner, 171–83. Cambridge: Cambridge University Press, 2005.

Marcus, Joel. *Mark: A New Translation with Introduction and Commentary.* Vol. 1, *Mark 1–8.* Vol. 2, *Mark 8–16.* Anchor Bible 27–27A. New York: Doubleday, 2000–2009.

Marshall, I. Howard. *New Testament Theology: Many Witnesses, One Gospel.* Downers Grove, IL: InterVarsity Press, 2004.

Matera, Frank J. *New Testament Christology.* Louisville, KY: Westminster John Knox Press, 1999.

Matson, David Lertis. *Household Conversion in Acts: Pattern and Interpretation.* JSNT Sup 123. Sheffield: Sheffield Academic Press, 1996.

McDonough, Sean M. *Christ as Creator: Origins of a New Testament Doctrine.* Oxford: Oxford University Press, 2009.

McKnight, Scot. "Justice, Righteousness." In *Dictionary of Jesus and the Gospels,* edited by Joel B. Green, Scot McKnight, and I. Howard Marshall, 413–15. Leicester: InterVarsity Press, 1992.

Mitchell, Margaret M. "Patristic Counter-Evidence to the Claim That 'The Gospels Were Written for All Christians.'" *New Testament Studies* 51 (2005): 36–79.

Morgenthaler, Robert. *Statistik des neutestamentlichen Wortschatzes.* Zurich and Frankfurt: Gotthelf-Verlag, 1958.

Motyer, Stephen. *Your Father the Devil? A New Approach to John and "the Jews."* Carlisle: Paternoster Press, 1997.

Nolland, John. *Luke.* Vol. 1, *Luke 1:1–9:20.* Vol. 2, *Luke 9:21–18:34.* Vol. 3, *Luke 18:35–24:53.* Word Biblical Commentary 35A–C. Dallas: Word Books, 1989–93.

Osborne, Grant R. "Resurrection." In *Dictionary of Jesus and the Gospels,* edited by Joel B. Green, Scot McKnight, and I. Howard Marshall, 673–88. Leicester: InterVarsity Press, 1992.

Patzia, Arthur G. *The Making of the New Testament: Origin, Collection, Text and Canon.* Leicester: Apollos, 1995.

Riches, John. "Matthew for the Church's Year." *Expository Times* 122, no. 2 (November 2010): 73–81.

Rhoads, David, and Donald Michie. *Mark as Story: An Introduction to the Narrative of a Gospel.* Philadelphia: Fortress Press, 1982.

Rowe, C. Kavin. *Early Narrative Christology: The Lord in the Gospel of Luke.* BZNW 139. Berlin: de Gruyter, 2006.

Saldarini, Anthony J. *Matthew's Christian-Jewish Community.* Chicago and London: University of Chicago Press, 1994.

Schnelle, Udo. *Antidocetic Christology in the Gospel of John: An Investigation of the Place of the Fourth Gospel in the Johannine School,* trans. Linda M. Maloney. Minneapolis: Fortress Press, 1992.

Seim, Turid Karlsen. *The Double Message: Patterns of Gender in Luke–Acts.* Edinburgh: T&T Clark International, 1994.

Sim, David C. "The Rise and Fall of the Gospel of Matthew." *Expository Times* 120 (July 2009): 478–85.

Stanton, Graham N. *The Gospels and Jesus*. Oxford: Oxford University Press, 1989.

———. *Jesus and Gospel*. Cambridge: Cambridge University Press, 2004.

Stein, Robert H. *The Synoptic Problem: An Introduction*. Grand Rapids: Baker Book House, 1987.

Strauss, Mark L. *The Davidic Messiah in Luke–Acts: The Promise and Its Fulfillment in Lukan Christology*. JSNTSup 110. Sheffield: Sheffield Academic Press, 1995.

———. *Four Portraits, One Jesus: An Introduction to Jesus and the Gospels*. Grand Rapids: Zondervan, 2007.

Swain, Simon. "Biography and Biographic in the Literature of the Roman Empire." In *Portraits: Biographical Representation in the Greek and Latin Literature of the Roman Empire*, edited by Mark J. Edwards and Simon Swain, 1–38. Oxford: Clarendon Press, 1997.

Talbert, Charles H. *Reading John: A Literary and Theological Commentary on the Fourth Gospel and the Johannine Epistles*. New York: Crossroad, 1992.

Temple, William. *Readings in St. John's Gospel*, First Series, *Chapters I–XII*. London: Macmillan, 1940.

Thompson, Marianne Meye. *The Humanity of Jesus in the Fourth Gospel*. Philadelphia: Fortress Press, 1988.

Toolan, Michael J. *Narrative: A Critical Linguistic Introduction*. London: Routledge, 1988.

Turner, Nigel. *Style*. Vol. 4 of *A Grammar of New Testament Greek*, by James Hope Moulton, W. F. Howard, and Nigel Turner. Edinburgh: T&T Clark, 1976.

Tuckett, Christopher M. *Christology and the New Testament: Jesus and His Earliest Followers*. Edinburgh: Edinburgh University Press, 2000.

Twelftree, Graham H. "Scribes." In *Dictionary of Jesus and the Gospels*, edited by Joel B. Green, Scot McKnight, and I. Howard Marshall, 732–35. Leicester: InterVarsity Press, 1992.

Watson, Francis. "The Fourfold Gospel." In *The Cambridge Companion to the Gospels*, edited by Stephen C. Barton, 34–52. Cambridge: Cambridge University Press, 2006.

Weeden, Theodore J. *Mark: Traditions in Conflict*. Philadelphia: Fortress Press, 1971.

Wenham, John. *The Easter Enigma*. Exeter: Paternoster Press, 1984.

Williamson, Hugh G.M. "Samaritans." In *Dictionary of Jesus and the Gospels*, edited by Joel B. Green, Scot McKnight, and I. Howard Marshall, 724–28. Leicester: InterVarsity Press, 1992.

Winn, Adam. *The Purpose of Mark's Gospel: An Early Christian Response to Roman Imperial Propaganda*. WUNT 2/245. Tübingen: Mohr Siebeck, 2008.

CPSIA information can be obtained at www.ICGtesting.com
Printed in the USA
LVOW120951280413

331257LV00017B/528/P